C0-CEU-426

R00824 44303

REFERENCE
THE CHICAGO PUBLIC LIBRARY

Music Section
Fine Arts Division
Chicago Public Library

FORM 19

THE MONOPHONIC LAUDA

and the Lay Religious Confraternities
of Tuscany and Umbria
in the Late Middle Ages

The Monophonic Lauda
and the Lay Religious Confraternities
of Tuscany and Umbria
in the Late Middle Ages

by
Cyrilla Barr

Early Drama, Art, and Music
Monograph Series, 10

Medieval Institute Publications
Western Michigan University
Kalamazoo, Michigan
1988

REF
PQ
4219
.R5
B37
1988

© Copyright 1988 by the Board of the Medieval Institute

Printed in the United States of America

ISBN 0-918720-89-3
ISBN 0-918720-90-7 (paperback)

In memoriam

Dorothy

Contents

List of Illustrations

1. *Disciplinato* in the Habit, Florence.

2. The *Mandato* and *Disciplinato* in the Habit, Bologna.

3. *Signore scribe*, with marginal stage directions, Perugia.

4. List of costumes and properties, Perugia.

5. List of properties and costumes on loan to the Compagnia di San Domenico, Perugia.

6. Damaged opening page of the *Laudario di Cortona*.

7. *Lauda* No. 51, *Allegramente e de buon core con fede*, to Margaret of Cortona. Cortona *Laudario*.

8. Entrance to the Church of San Francesco, Cortona, with remains of entrance to Oratory of *Laudesi*.

9. Illumination showing Descent of the Holy Spirit upon the Apostles, with SS. Augustine and Benedict.

10. Illumination showing the Three Living and the Three Dead, above, and opening section of the *Lauda* on Death.

11. Illumination showing Christ in Majesty.

12. Fourteenth-century illumination of Christ enthroned in mandorla and surrounded by twelve Apostles.

Preface

The discovery of the Cortona *laudario* in 1876 was auspicious since it came only a few years after the unification of Italy. Nationalism undoubtedly contributed to the rash of articles about the *lauda* repertoire which appeared in Italian literary and philological journals of the late nineteenth century. That the *laude*, which include some of the earliest poetry in the Italian vernacular, should have engaged the attention of the literary scholars of the time is not surprising. However, as the present study shows, the *lauda* as a musical genre was slow to gain respectability--a situation due at least in part to the nascent state of musicological scholarship at that time. The fact that the entire corpus of surviving monophonic *lauda* repertoire in the vernacular is contained in only two manuscripts, one of which was lost for an indeterminate period of time, may also help to explain the lack of attention to the *lauda* when medieval monophony of the transalpine and insular schools was being studied seriously. The music of the *lauda* was, however, apparently known in the eighteenth century, since Charles Burney spoke of examining at least one manuscript (now lost) of *laude* with music during his travels to Italy. Nevertheless, as recently as 1917 Edward J. Dent could say of the monophonic *lauda*: "About it hardly anyone knows anything."

Literary scholars of the last century had been quick to point out the need for a comprehensive study of the music of the *lauda*, for they recognized that knowledge of the melodies would be invaluable for their understanding of the texts. The earliest notice of this repertoire came from German scholars, Friedrich Ludwig and Friedrich Gennrich, whose studies, though significant, are flawed by insistence upon a rhythmic interpretation now considered untenable. Only in 1935 did there appear a complete musical study of the two surviving manuscripts of the monophonic period. In that year Fernando Liuzzi published his sumptuous two-volume edition entitled *La lauda e i primordi della melodia italiana*, a work hailed by Higinio Anglès as "an epoch-making event in modern musicology." In spite of its many flaws the study remains a landmark which soon elicited reactions from other musicologists, most notably Jacques Handschin and Yvonne Rokseth. The most significant scholarship to follow Liuzzi's contribution was that of Higinio Anglès, whose interest emerges in a segment of his monumental study of the *cantigas* attributed to Alfonso el Sabio. Yet these works manifest an almost total preoccupation with the rhythmic interpretation of the music and hence fail to address the important issue of the association of the *laude* with the religious confraternities, the provenance of the manuscripts, and the dissemination of the repertoire. I shall be discussing both the early studies and Liuzzi's work in the present book in an attempt to place the historical development of the scholarship on the *lauda* in perspective, though my main goal must be to provide an English language study of the *lauda* since such a work has not previously been available.

Some mention of the current state of research nevertheless requires attention at the beginning of this study. Just as research on the early drama in England is being presently enhanced by the concerted work on records by the Records of Early Drama project and by the systematic study of the iconography and the visual arts being sponsored by the Early Drama, Art, and Music project, so too the *laude* are now better understood by attention being given to documents such as confraternity ordos, offices, and other non-musical sources and to the illuminations associated with *lauda* manuscripts. These documents in particular are found to be highly valuable as a source of information about the paraliturgical context of the *lauda* and about its role in late medieval spirituality. The study of archival materials relating to the confraternities has received renewed interest among historians, who have built on the pioneering research of Gennaro Maria Monti, whose well-known *Le confraternite medievali dell'alta e media Italia* (1927), despite its nearly exclusive reliance on statutes alone, remains a classic work on the subject. Among the more recent scholars who have worked with this archival material are Gilles Meersseman, O.P. (perhaps the *doyen*, though his writings are characterized by a predictable Dominican bent), John S. Henderson, Ronald Weissman, and Angela Maria Terrugia. Among musicologists, Frank D'Accone has made a significant contribution in his sorting out the musical references in the documents of four of the major *laudesi* companies of Florence in the fourteenth and fifteenth centuries. A recent and corporate undertaking is the multi-volume work entitled *Laude cortonesi dal secolo XIII al XV*, which is Part V of the *Biblioteca Rivista di storia e letteratura religiosa studi e testi*, a collaborative effort of Giorgi Varanini, Luigi Banfi, Anna Ceruti Burgio, and Giulio Cattin, who bring together expertise in philology, literary criticism, and musicology.

I am, of course, indebted to the work of Federico Ghisi and Nino Pirrotta on the *ars nova* as well as also to many additional scholars who have produced important *lauda*-related studies--e.g., Agostino Ziino, Giulio Cattin, F. Alberto Gallo, Piero Damilano. I can only express my gratitude to these distinguished scholars and to others whose work is acknowledged in the notes and the Select Bibliography.

In quoting from Italian sources, all translations, unless otherwise noted, are my own. Translations from manuscript sources are accompanied by the original texts given in the notes without comment and without the addition of modern punctuation or diacritical markings, though I have made exceptions for those long passages that lack punctuation in the original, in which cases I have silently added capitalization and periods for the convenience of the reader. In each instance

I have indicated such emendations in the notes. I have also used the preferred modern spelling of *lauda* (singular) and *laude* (plural), except in titles and quotations in which earlier spellings (e.g., *lode, lalde, laude* [sing.], *laudi* [pl.]) are retained. The terms *compagnia* and *confraternita* are used reciprocally, while *disciplinati, battuti,* and *flagellanti* all refer specifically to those companies which practiced self-flagellation. All dates from Florentine references are modernized. The library sigla used, mainly in the notes, are in conformity with RISM usage, though additional abbreviations are provided to identify specific sources not included in RISM. While my research was done primarily from manuscript, the texts of the *laude* from Cortona 91 are quoted in accordance with Varanini, while those from the Magliabechiano manuscript (Mgl1) are in agreement with Liuzzi and therefore reflect the editorial procedure of these scholars.

Finally, this book should properly be viewed as a collection of essays on various aspects of the monophonic *lauda* and its history. An earlier draft of one chapter (on the service of *tenebrae*) has been published previously, and I am grateful to the editors of *L'Ars nova italiana del Trecento* for allowing me to present a revision as Chapter V of this book. Due to the very nature of the material presented here--and to the vast number of sources which lack music--my work is necessarily selective. For this reason I have avoided using the term 'history' in my title since to do so would in this instance be presumptuous.

The reader who is familiar with the *lauda* will also at once notice that I am not proposing any new theories concerning the problematic notation of the music, nor do I address certain local traditions, most notably the Roman *lauda* which has an important history of its own especially as it relates to the activities of the Oratorian Society. I have thus not attempted to discuss all the many and varied local developments, intriguing though they may be, but have kept my scholarly focus directed toward a treatment of the early monophonic *lauda* as it relates to the confraternities that played such an important role in its dissemination. Following the classic lines of demarcation provided by Monti, the major manuscript sources chosen for more detailed discussion are, with one exception, from Tuscany and Umbria--i.e., *media Italia* rather than *alta Italia*. The exception is the manuscript from Bologna which is one of the two major documents chosen for study in Chapter V. However, in those sections which are devoted to general discussion of the *laudesi* and *disciplinati*, some passing references are of necessity made to sources from *alta Italia*.

It is a pleasure to acknowledge those who have in some manner contributed to this work. First of all these thanks must go to the Davidsons, Audrey and Clifford, whose enthusiasm for the *lauda*-related papers that I have read over the years at the various meetings of the International Congress on Medieval Studies at Western Michigan University has resulted in the invitation to prepare this volume for publication in the Early Drama, Art, and Music series by Medieval Institute Publications. Their encouragement and support throughout the work is deeply appreciated.

I owe a profound debt to the late Federico Ghisi, my mentor during the earliest stages of my research which initially resulted in a doctoral dissertation on the subject. His enthusiasm for the work and generous advice continued to the end of his life, when as late as one month before his death he generously read early drafts of the manuscript of this book. Among others who have kindly read portions of my work in progress are John Henderson and Jørgen Meyer. For the benefit of their scholarship in certain specialized areas and their kind criticisms I am most grateful. Dr. Henderson in particular provided many helpful insights into the more purely historical aspects of the study. I am also grateful for the interest and advice of Agostino Ziino, who served as coordinator of the conference at Certaldo in July of 1975 at which my paper on the service of *tenebrae* was read and who edited the *Acts* of that meeting.

Numerous staff members of various libraries and archives whose sigla are listed elsewhere have been generous in their assistance in locating materials and obtaining permissions to publish. Of these special thanks must go to Don Aldo Brunacci, Archivist of the Cathedral of San Rufino in Assisi, and his associate, Don Elmo Antonini, for their generosity in allowing me unrestricted access to the materials housed there during my repeated visits to Assisi, some of which necessarily occurred during periods when the archive was officially closed. Also, to Maria Adalaida Bacherini Bartoli of the Music Division of the Biblioteca Nazionale Centrale in Florence and to her assistants, Antonietta Spini and Ernesto degli Innocenti, go my thanks for their consistently generous assistance to me during my sojourns in that city. Likewise, similar help was graciously given by Luigi Pancrazi of the Biblioteca Comunale e dell'Accademia Etrusca during the early stages of my work in Cortona.

Although the translations of the archival materials are my own, I was assisted with certain problems in editing the early Italian texts by Gino Corti. I am indebted to Kathleen Falvey for her valuable perception of textual variants, especially as they relate to the dramatic *laude*. She and Dr. Henderson have also generously allowed me to quote from various of their works which are as yet unpublished. Similarly, I am grateful to Henry J. Grossi for permission to quote from his unpublished doctoral dissertation on the Florentine *laudario*.

Research for this monograph would not have been possible without the assistance of various grants which I gratefully acknowledge. At the inception of my work when I was still writing my dissertation on the subject, I was aided by a Fulbright Scholarship to the University of Florence. I am also indebted to the American Council of Learned Societies for Grants-in-Aid that enabled me to spend two consecutive summers in Italy collecting further material. But the greater part of the research was done while I was a Fellow at Villa i

Tatti, the Harvard University Center for Italian Renaissance Studies in Florence. In addition, I am indebted to the Catholic University of America not only for a sabbatical leave which made possible the writing of the monograph but also for a grant from the research fund of the university which helped to defray expenses of preparing the final copy and obtaining the necessary photographs for the plates.

To the following libraries and archives which have graciously permitted me to publish photographs of items in their collections I wish to express my appreciation: the Biblioteca dell'Archiginnasio, Bologna; the Biblioteca Comunale e dell'Accademia Etrusca, Cortona; the Biblioteca Nazionale Centrale, Florence; the Archivio di Stato, Florence; the Pierpont Morgan Library, New York; the Biblioteca Comunale Augusta, Perugia; the Archivio Sodalizio Braccio Fortebracci, Perugia; the British Library; and the National Gallery of Art, Washington, D.C.

And finally, thanks of a more personal nature must go to my typist, Mary Di Quinzio, my proofreader, Henriette Lund, and above all to my editor, Clifford Davidson, for his keen perception and dedicated attention to detail. Lastly I wish to acknowledge my sincere gratitude to my many friends and colleagues whose encouragement and support helped to make this book a reality.

Cyrilla Barr
The Benjamin T. Rome School of Music
The Catholic University of America

Introduction

The phenomenon of popular hymnody may in many ways seem remote from present-day experience, and the investigation of its manifestations in medieval Italy is necessarily complicated by the ambiguity of the origins of this important genre, which deserves to be of interest to a broad range of scholars. Popular religious forms of the thirteenth, fourteenth, and fifteenth centuries are now at last becoming the focus of the scholarly attention which they deserve, and the current study is designed to provide insight into one such form. Nevertheless, the popular religious music of Italy, despite various theories and considerable speculation concerning its antecedents, remains in some respects as obscure today as the unrecorded names of those men who cut and carried stones for the cathedrals and churches or who lost their lives in the crusades--men whose immortality in stone and poetry is real, albeit anonymous. This problem is caused in some measure by the tendency of medieval persons toward the anonymity of a communitarian life.

In the realm of the spiritual, medieval communitarianism expressed itself in part in the formation of numerous lay confraternities, which were known by various terms such as 'guilds,' 'societies,' 'companies,' 'brotherhoods,' and 'schools.' In spite of the differing terms used to describe them, they were alike in their pursuit of personal piety through prayer and charitable works, and each followed a rule which required the members to gather at regular intervals for their devotions. They have been characterized by John Henderson as "'lay' inasmuch as the vast majority of their members were laymen, and 'religious' because their practices were loosely adapted from a monastic rule."[1]

The singing of popular hymns in the vernacular became an important part of the confraternities' way of life, and in time many of these groups were instrumental in disseminating a vast literature of religious lyric poetry and song known as the *lauda*. There is evidence that singing had already been incorporated into religious societies as early as the tenth century in Italy; however, nothing is known of the manner in which this occurred.[2] But by the thirteenth century Florentine chronicles in particular began to mention groups of lay people, *popolo bordone*, who gathered before the figure of the Madonna at the end of the day's work and addressed to her their prayers and songs. Because of the nature of the "praise songs" which they sang, the groups came to be called *laudesi* and their songs *laude*.[3]

The earliest *laude* were simple lyrical hymns in the vernacular. Unfortunately, their music was seldom notated since the *lauda* represents an oral tradition of singing--a tradition which may be one of the longest in the history of Western music. Nevertheless, there are two surviving manuscripts containing *laude* from the Middle Ages which do contain musical notation. The sumptuous fourteenth-century Magliabechiano manuscript (Mgl[1]) seems very likely to have been a votive work rather than a performance score, in contrast to the plain and unpretentious Cortona *laudario* of the previous century. With the exception of clerics, few of those who sang the *laude* contained in the latter were likely able to read, and especially few would be able to read either the newly emerging vernacular in which the manuscript is written or its musical notation. Hence it may be argued that, in spite of the existence of these two collections of *laude* with notation, oral transmission must necessarily have remained the principal practical mode of dissemination.

It has been suggested that the *lauda* was the invention of St. Francis of Assisi whose *Cantico delle creature*, written in

1225,[4] marked the beginning of a long tradition of Italian lyric poetry.[5] Though such speculation must be regarded with suspicion, it is not therefore surprising that the mendicants, especially Franciscans and Dominicans, should recognize this genre as a practical tool for their apostolate, to be used to teach, edify, exhort, and perhaps also to entertain in a language comprehensible even to the illiterate. The Franciscan chronicler Salimbene in fact speaks of several friars in his acquaintance who were gifted in singing and composition.[6] An old pedagogical principle was at work here: large doses of religious dogma could more easily be administered in simple rhymes and sweet tunes which possibly also, like a kind of spiritual nostrum, helped to mitigate the austerities of medieval life. Perhaps more importantly, the form helped to induce a devotional mood which was very important in the life of the confraternity. Further, in much the same way that folk music chronicles the existence of a people--their living, working, loving, and dying--so too the *lauda* reflects certain changes taking place in the confraternities themselves as well as in the larger world outside the brotherhood.

Although the first half of the thirteenth century saw the multiplication of various religious groups, both canonical and lay, the third quarter of that century was marked by a curious phenomenon which to the modern mind might be characterized as religious aberration, a manifestation of "psychic disorientation."[7] This phenomenon was the flagellant mania of 1260 which was initiated in Perugia at the instigation of Raniero Fasani. In its wake there followed the numerous penitential processions that soon spread over nearly all of northern Italy.[8]

The foundation of flagellant confraternities known as *disciplinati* or *battuti* has often been linked to the events of 1260, but in fact the phenomenon should be considered within the broader context of contemporary piety that placed great emphasis upon the incarnate life of Christ. This theme was characteristic of the preaching of the mendicants, who stressed imitation of the God-man from the cradle to the cross.[9] Thus the Mass became a visual re-enactment of the Passion, and the admonition to penance in the form of flagellation was viewed as the ultimate imitation of Christ. Because these outbursts of fervor were frequently precipitated by disasters, either real or prophesied, they appear to have been motivated by fear of an angry God whose wrath could only be appeased by the expiation of Christ's sufferings through the physical act of self-flagellation.[10]

Reports of these penitential activities around 1260 are found in the accounts of the processions contained in various medieval chronicles, which, to be sure, tend to repeat each other in many details. The story grows to a climax with the statement that the hermit's cry of *penitenza* was sufficient to incite the populace to such extremes of self-inflicted scourging that "in those days Italian blood flowed like water."[11] Medieval fondness for hyperbole notwithstanding, the occurrence was an important factor in the development of the confraternities after 1260. Hence it is appropriate to consider how certain of the political events of mid-thirteenth-century Italy may have contributed to the success of the flagellant movement.

Historians have indeed demonstrated that the events leading up to 1260 provided the proper setting for the outbreak of penitential fervor. Italy had suffered under the scourge of Frederick II, who was regarded by some as the Antichrist, and of his son-in-law Ezzelino da Romano. The already baleful political climate was exacerbated by the preaching of various heretical sects--the Waldenses, Cathari, and other assorted evangelizers. To these must be added the Joachites, who styled themselves the spiritual progeny of Joachim of Fiore (1135-1202).[12] Although the enigmatic figure of Joachim properly belongs to the twelfth century, his influence reached far beyond his own time and his native province of Calabria. His life as a Cistercian, and later as founder of his own order, was exemplary. Apparently even in his own lifetime he was thought to possess prophetic powers, for Pope Lucius III engaged him to interpret sibylline prophecies and subsequently commissioned him to write the *Liber Concordiae Novi et Veteris Testamenti*.[13] Dante, who placed him in the company of Hugh of St.-Victor, Rabanus Maurus, and Anselm, claimed for him a prophetic spirit (*Paradiso,* Canto 13). Likewise, the Bollandists found fit to include his life in the *Acta Sanctorum*.[14] In justice to Joachim it must be emphasized that the extent of his influence was mainly due to those, most notably the Spiritual Franciscans, who enlarged upon his theses.[15] These followers eagerly seized upon the notion of an evangelical band of barefoot scholars as prefiguring their mission and justifying their attitude toward the rigid observance of the rule of St. Francis.

Joachim believed in an organically developing Church as opposed to what he considered a static foundation. His concept of history was symbolically trinitarian, and, according to his concordance of events in the Old and New Testaments, the Age of the Father had been enlightened by the Old Testament with Adam as the herald of Abraham. Similarly John the Baptist was the precursor of Christ and as such ushered in the era of the New Testament. He devised a system of apocalyptic calculations whereby he determined that the second age was to consist of forty-two generations of thirty years each, or 1,260 years. Thus the year 1260 was to mark the beginning of the Age of the Spirit.[16] According to the interpretation of Gerard of San Donnino, the herald of this new era was Benedict, and the coming of the hero was to be preceded by troubled times in which war, famine, and ecclesiastical corruption would abound. The era would be announced by a new religious order which would cleanse the Church of its impurities and restore it to its pristine state. The Spiritual Franciscans were certain that they were the chosen ones to announce this gospel. Gerard then proclaimed that the third period, the Age of the Spirit, was to be enlightened by the *Eternal Evangel*, a book containing three of Joachim's works with an introduction and gloss written by himself. This book was to supersede the Old and New Testaments which had been viable during the first two ages in succession. Scholars at the University of Paris were quick to alert the pope, Alexander IV, whereupon the matter was examined by Vatican theologians. Ultimately Gerard was censured (in 1256), and from that time until his death eighteen years later he was kept in detention by the Franciscan Order.[17] Furthermore, the reputation which Joachim's works had accrued eventually resulted in their condemnation at the Provincial Council of Arles.

It would, however, be simplistic to interpret the events summarized above as a *mise en scène* for the drama enacted in Perugia when the hermit Raniero emerged from solitude and began to preach the message of penitence which according to legend had been revealed to him in a vision of the Blessed Virgin Mary. Modern historians have pointed out that, while many chroniclers relate the story of the penitential processions instigated by Raniero, there is a curious silence about the question of Joachim's possible association with the origin of the movement.[18] As Henderson indicates in his study of the flagellants of 1260, the only contemporary chronicler to mention Joachim in this context was Salimbene, whose writings are the chief source for our knowledge of the spread of Joachimism among the Franciscans.[19] But even Salimbene seems to suggest that it was merely coincidental that the occurrence should have taken place in 1260. Perhaps it is typical of the medieval mind to interpret natural phenomena and disasters as signs of an irate God meting out justice and punishment. Thus, according to Henderson, Joachimism probably "helped to generate a mood rather than provide any specific influences to lead to the outbreak of fervor."[20]

Several accounts of Raniero's preaching exist, and there are various theories concerning his identity though these are of little significance to the present study.[21] Far more important is the fact that he was responsible at least indirectly for the formation of the first *disciplinati* society, that of Gesù Cristo in Perugia which was to be the model for many others, some of which would also even assume its name.

6

Response to the example of the zealous penitents was not, however, universally positive, though their effect on the Italian confraternities was widespread. Some individuals were re-pelled by their fanaticism, and rulers in certain regions denied the flagellants entrance into their towns.22 In the face of opposition and censure, the more fanatic element fled from Italy to the North, and soon they were found along with their followers in the Midi and as far north as Poland. Within Italy, the influence of the flagellant movement on the character of the confraternities and consequently also upon the *lauda* is of the greatest significance for our study. Groups of *laudesi* already existed, of course, and now penitential confraternities calling themselves *disciplinati* came into being and espoused the custom of singing *laude* along with their practice of flagellation. Both the earlier type of confraternity and the *disciplinati* continued to exist side-by-side, and at times these two types are difficult to distinguish from each other.23

In view of the continued association of *lauda*-singing with the brotherhoods, it is not surprising that the changes which occurred in the structure and practice of the confraternities should have been reflected in the *laude* themselves. The *laude* of the pre-flagellant period had been lyrical in character, and in subject matter leaned heavily upon Marian themes as well as upon laments of the Passion. The suddenness of the outbreak in 1260 would have precluded the composition of an entirely new repertoire for the use of penitents, however. Furthermore, the penitential processions which developed are described by the chroniclers in a manner that seems to indicate only a very simple kind of chanting, perhaps in litany fashion, repeating invocations over and over.24 Later manuscripts of *laude* belonging to *disciplinati* societies contain considerable evidence of their penitential devotion and manifest a preoc-cupation with death, judgment, and punishment. The later *laude* are indeed markedly realistic at times in their descrip-tions of dying or the decomposition of the body and bear comparison with such pictorial representations as the *Trionfo*

7

della morte at the Campo santo in Pisa.[25]

Documentation of the activities, particularly the musical practices, of the confraternities depends upon examination of two kinds of manuscript sources: (1) manuscripts containing texts of *laude* with musical notation, and (2) the official writings and records of the brotherhoods--in other words, documents not primarily of a musical nature. The former category, as noted above, is unfortunately very limited, whereas the confraternity records are very extensive indeed, though these will have only scattered references of interest to the musicologist among the notations of items relating primarily to life within the organization. Such sources, however, are vital in providing the necessary context within which the musical activities of the confraternities may be understood, and hence they will receive consideration in this study before we turn to the musical sources themselves.

1

Non-Musical Documents: *Laudesi*

Between the extant monophonic *laude* of the late thirteenth and early fourteenth centuries and Petrucci's first printed collections of polyphonic *laude* in 1507-08, no major collections with musical notation have survived.[1] However, though some decline in popular *lauda*-singing is documented during this period, the lack of extant *laude* with notation may not in itself be interpreted as a sign of decay in the established practice of singing this music, for such an assumption would need to discount the records and non-musical documents of the confraternities which demonstrate that *laude* were very much alive and often thriving throughout the intervening years of the late fourteenth century as well as the entire fifteenth century. The existence of such an abundance of records and documents reflects the growing stability achieved when the companies settled into a more sedentary existence, attaching themselves to monasteries and friaries where they could be under the watchful supervision of an appointed cleric as spiritual director.

These lay confraternities generally did not yet possess their own oratories but were granted the use of the crypt, cloister, or some other part of an existing structure for their meetings. Records of some companies reveal that the place of assembly occasionally resulted in a change of affiliation. For example, the company of San Benedetto Bianco in Florence was established in the Camaldolese monastery in 1357, but it transferred first in 1371 to the chapel of San Jacopo Corsini in

San Zenobi and then in 1383 to Santa Maria Novella.[2] Whether compensation was normally required from the confraternities for such use of facilities is not entirely clear, but the records suggest some kind of arrangement with the church or monastery must have existed. In the case of one Florentine company, the Compania della laude which met in Santa Maria del Carmine, there was an agreement that the confraternity "will provide for us three banquets in perpetuity . . . one for the feast of the Conception, another for the feast of St. Nicholas, and the other for the Annunciation. They must spend for these three, 34 lire."[3]

Because the present study is confined to the music and ritual of the confraternities from the thirteenth through the fifteenth centuries, no effort will be made here to survey the entire range of records from these organizations, but rather the focus will be on those documents which illuminate the basic structure and function of the organizations and their practice of *lauda*-singing. The numerous records of the Companie Religiose Soppresse in the Archivio di Stato, Florence, testify to the widespread activity of groups which engaged in such singing and in the related rituals. Though sources of this kind do not directly provide examples of the music of the *laude*, they verify the context in which *lauda*-singing existed so that we are able to reconstruct in some measure the function and practice of music and ritual as a part of the daily devotions of the members of such pious lay confraternities.

The documents and records to be examined in this chapter are of two types: (1) those documents (e.g., rules, statutes, letters of indulgence) which relate to and regulate life within the confraternity and thereby have some bearing on ritual and music; and (2) records (e.g., *laudari*, ordines, inventories, fiscal records) which reflect directly upon performance practice.

Problems in Differentiating Types of Confraternities. The statutes of the confraternities reveal that in their origin, organization, and structure the early companies had much in common. Their statutes generally spell out their governance, including their electoral processes and terms of office. Apparently many confraternities assumed some charitable works such as lodging travelers along pilgrimage routes or accompanying the priest as he took the Eucharist to the sick of his parish.[4] Furthermore, though the companies were under ecclesiastical jurisdiction, they nonetheless were governed by a layman, elected from among the ranks, who was designated by a title such as *governatore* or *priore.* He was usually assisted by counselors, a treasurer, an infirmarian, a master of novices, and sometimes a physician.[5] As the increasing stability of the confraternities enabled them to acquire material goods, the maintenance of such property and the keeping of accounts necessitated the election of sacristans and scribes.[6] Some statutes also make note of singers (*cantori*) whose duty it was to intone the singing of psalms and *laude.*[7] Unfortunately, the statutes do not always record changes which occurred in the companies and in their paraliturgical practices, since these documents were revised and brought up to date only periodically.[8] A more detailed picture of confraternal life, including its musical dimension, can be established only when the statutes are supplemented by account books, ordos, inventories, and other related documents.

In spite of apparent similarities, the two types of confraternity--the *laudesi* and the *disciplinati*--were actually quite different in many respects. Weissman, in his demographic study of Florentine companies in the Renaissance, illustrates distinctly divergent patterns in the makeup of the membership of the *laudesi* and *disciplinati.* Although his comparison is based primarily on his study of only two companies, the *laudesi* of San Zenobi and the *disciplinati* of San Paolo, he nevertheless establishes that the *laudesi* in question were mostly shopkeepers and artisans, while the *disciplinati* were wealthier and younger.[9] Weissman's research gives evidence that the *disciplinati* showed a greater social consciousness and that during times of communal unrest they sought to promote civic peace.[10]

Medieval chroniclers reveal, however, that both types of confraternity managed to function more or less autonomously when local ecclesiastical authority was hampered by interdict. During these times when the sacraments were forbidden the activities continued, in effect taking the place of the proscribed liturgical functions. An anonymous Florentine chronicler of the fourteenth century thus relates that in 1376, when the city was under interdict and the divine offices suppressed,

> some Catholics began to form processions with the *disciplinati*, carrying the standard of the Church throughout the land, singing *laude* and litanies and other prayers. Many such companies were newly formed at the time, companies of men, boys, and children. Also, at that time other societies of *laudesi* originated as well, singing . . . in the evening for the glory of God.[11]

The failure to distinguish between the two types of confraternity, however, is the source of unnecessary confusion about the origin and function of popular hymnody. It is thus very important to distinguish between these two types--the *laudesi* and the *disciplinati*--which disseminated the *laude*. The *laudesi*, or Marian confraternities, had quite simply been founded with a different purpose in mind from the *disciplinati* or penitential companies. Many scholars, especially around the turn of the century, only increased confusion by indiscriminate use of the terms *laudesi* and *disciplinati,* which at times have been used interchangeably.[12] An example of such muddling of nomenclature may be found in Girolamo Mancini's article "Laude Francescane dei disciplinati di Cortona" (1889) in which he announced his discovery of the Cortona *laudario* and attempted to build a case for its *laudesi* origin.[13] Unfortunately, therefore, the standard textbook treatment of the subject too often perpetuates the error, over-emphasizing the association of *lauda*-singing with the practice of flagellation, especially with the penitential outbreak of the so-called *gran devozione* in 1260, whereas indeed there is very substantial evidence of such singing activities from before the *flagellanti* period. Because of the problems inherited from earlier scholarship, it would seem advisable to examine each of the two main types of confraternity in turn in an effort rigorously to distinguish their respective contributions to popular hymnody and ritual of the late Middle Ages.

Laudesi. In his study of the *laudesi* and *disciplinati* of Florence, Henderson demonstrates that while the two types of companies had a complementary development, the *laudesi* in fact flourished earlier. The majority of the *laudesi* confraternities in that city were established during the last sixty years of the thirteenth century, while after 1300 the number of new groups began to decline so that by 1400 almost no new *laudesi* were being established. Conversely, throughout that same period and particularly after the Black Death *disciplinati* account for the vast majority of the new confraternities.[14]

Perhaps the most prominent characteristic of the early *laudesi* was their origin as Marian confraternities. As we know, the various religious orders, especially Franciscans and Dominicans who achieved such a high level of popular support in the thirteenth century, founded Marian companies of lay people and gave them statutes which were adapted to the time and locality.[15] Unfortunately, we do not know with precision at what date certain of these Marian societies began the practice of singing songs in praise of Mary. The earliest such company recorded in Florence was known as the Societas S. Maria Virginis S. Maria Novella, which was founded in 1244 by Peter of Verona (Piero Martire) and which later adopted his name.[16] Soon similar organizations were established at other conventual churches: at the Servite church of Santissima Annunziata (1273),[17] at the Franciscan church of Santa Croce (before 1278),[18] at San Gillo dei Sacchiti (1278),[19] at the Carmelite church of Maria del Carmine (1280),[20] and at the

Augustinian church of Santo Spirito (before 1328).[21] In addition, Marian societies were founded at the cathedral and in churches which were not affiliated with the mendicants or any other religious order. Of these the two most important were the company of Santa Reparata, which was founded in 1271 at the cathedral,[22] and the company of Orsanmichele, established in 1291.[23]

Similar developments were recorded elsewhere in Italy as well. Meersseman cites a document of 2 September 1273 which is a letter of Bernardo Gallerani, Bishop of Siena, granting an indulgence to the Marian company in the church of St. Dominic in that city. According to the letter, by this date the group was meeting regularly every evening to pray and sing *laude* to Mary. Meersseman argues that such daily practice indicates an already well-established custom.[24]

The origin of these companies in Marian devotion is attested over and over again through the naming of the Virgin as their primary patron, though usually a second saint was added--e.g., in the instance of the Societas Sanctarum Marie et Agnetis de laudibus in ecclesia domus beate Marie florentini ordinis fratrum Carmelitarum. However, the addition of a second patron sometimes took on a different signification, since such designations as Confraternitas in honorem B. Mariae Virginis et B. Francisci confessori are merely meant to identify the Marian confraternity according to the respective church in which it was established through mention of the religious order serving that church. If Meersseman's suggestion is correct, by the middle of the fourteenth century the addition of a second patron may also have represented an effort to revitalize the diminishing ardor of the company.[25]

That which most decidedly sets the *laudesi* apart from the *disciplinati*, however, is the absence of the practice of self-flagellation. Not only does this distinguish their ritual practices, but it also colors the texts of their *laude* and eventually leads to divergent practices in the performance of the *lauda*. The *lauda* repertoire clearly was shared by several different groups, but, as we would expect, there are distinctive characteristics which mark the texts associated with organizations with differing purposes and devotional practices. Nowhere is this more evident than in those *laude* which are found in both *laudesi* and *disciplinati* manuscripts. Liuzzi calls attention to one example, the text of *Madonna santa Maria*, which is included in the Cortona *laudario* and which is found also in the *laudario* of the *battuti* of Udine where it contains four added strophes describing in graphic manner the act of self-flagellation:

Strophe 11   Io si son stado pecadore
                 et ai offeso al mio signore
                 battome per lo suo amore
                 ch'el me debia perdonare.

                 (I have been a sinner
                 and have offended my Lord,
                 and thus I scourge myself for his love
                 so that he will pardon me.)

Strophe 12   Et alegro e gaudente
                 battome le spalle e'l ventre,
                 per descazar quel serpente
                 che me volea devorare.

                 (And joyously and happily
                 I scourge my shoulders and belly
                 in order to escape the serpent
                 who wants to devour me.)

Strophe 14   Oimè, carne topinella,
                 come tu è fresca e bella,
                  tu dei andar sotto la terra
                 e li vermi t'averà manziare.

                 (Alas, miserable flesh,
                 how fresh and beautiful you are,
                 but you must go under the earth,
                 and the worms will have you to eat.)

Strophe 15   Non sia nessun sì duro
               che si vergogni d'andar nudo
               Gesù Cristo fo batudo
               per li peccatori salvari.

               (Let no one be so hard
               that he is ashamed to go naked.
               Jesus Christ was beaten
               in order to save sinners.)[26]

Nevertheless, the problem of identifying a company as either of one type or of the other is sometimes more confusing than might at first appear to be the case since some existing *laudesi* confraternities actually assumed the practice of flagellation after 1260. An example is the confraternity of Santa Maria delle Grazie in Faenza, which adopted the discipline and took the habit of the Bianchi.[27] In Florence a further complication is evident in the company of San Gilio, which divided into cells of flagellants and *laudesi* though both continued to function within the same fraternity.[28]

Nor should we assume that the confraternities were entirely the domain of men. There is evidence that women were in fact admitted to *laudesi* in some capacity. An undated inventory of San Zenobi, Florence, declares among its belongings "two books in which are written the names of all the men and women of the society."[29] Similarly, the statutes of Annunziata del Borghetto, Florence, stipulate the payment of dues thus: "The men pay five soldi, the women three, and children under fifteen years of age pay one."[30] And a 1338 redaction of the statutes of Orsanmichele states that "every member of the company, male or female, must confess often and receive communion once a year."[31] Such documents, however, do not necessarily indicate that women participated in the same manner as men. Very possibly their membership was such that it entitled them to share only in the spiritual benefits of the group.

Paraliturgical Exercises. The surviving ordos, account books, inventories, and other miscellaneous accounts make possible the constructing of a more complete picture of the way in which the *lauda* was performed within the context of the paraliturgical exercises of these confraternities. *Laudesi* companies were distinguished from other types of fraternities by virtue of their daily services, which were held in the evening and at which the singing of *laude* played such an important part. The statutes of Orsanmichele expressly state that "the evening of the *lauda* service should be illuminated with burning candles in hand, before the image of the Blessed Virgin Mary, and at the expense of the confraternity."[32] Similarly, the statutes of San Gilio in Florence ordain that "each member of the company, when he sees the church of San Gilio lit by candles in the evening, should enter the said church and in singing and responding should obey his captain."[33] The rule of San Gilio further charges the treasurer with the responsibility of preparing for these evening meetings: "The treasurer of this company must be solicitous of coming to the church of San Gilio and preparing the lectern and the book of the *laude* and other things which are used for the singing of the *laude*, placing two burning candles in two candlesticks in front of the altar and one before the standard when . . . the *laude* are sung."[34] The importance of these meetings is underscored by the many references in various statutes which prescribe the recitation of specified prayers by those who for some legitimate reason are not able to attend. At San Gilio, such persons were admonished to say the Our Father and Hail Mary three times in place of the service.[35] The rule of the *laudesi* of Sant'Agnese at the Carmine was more severe, for here the member who had been absent was required to pay a fine.[36]

Quite clearly there was considerable care taken to maintain a respectable level of performance, for various statutes allude to schools which were held on Sundays in order to teach the *laude* to members, while a number of inventories mention books for teaching *laude* to children.[37] The *laudesi* of Orsan-michele decreed that one of the major responsibilities of the prior was to provide for such a school: "The office of the governors of the *laude* is to determine and to ordain how the *laude* should be sung before the image of the Madonna on the pillar under the loggia each evening, and to provide a school on Sundays in order to learn to sing the *laude* in the houses and in the shops of the company."[38] In the company of Sant'Agnese, the brother who taught the *laude* also had full responsibility for arranging the processions, choosing the cantors, and deciding which *laude* should be sung. He was an elected officer who held the keys to all the objects needed for the evening services: the lectern, the candles, the table, a lantern, and a blackboard.[39]

In addition to these daily prayer meetings, the *laudesi* frequently held processions which in some companies were regular monthly events, while special high feasts and civic celebrations might also be occasions for public processions. Meersseman notes that sometimes, as in Pisa, Marian compa-nies combined efforts to form a grand procession on the major feasts of the Blessed Virgin: the Annunciation, the Assump-tion, the Purification, and the Nativity. The companies assembled at the cathedral, which was the location from which the procession originated. According to the revised statutes (1312) of the *laudesi* della Vergine of Pisa, a vigil was ob-served as well: "Our priors must hold a vigil for these four feasts of the Virgin Mary and recommend to the members that they should go to the cathedral to participate in the procession, and that they should take a candle and make an offering for it and go two by two."[40]

Apparently there was a certain degree of cooperation between confraternities in the matter of scheduling processions and sermons. In Florence, for example, the *laudesi* of San Zenobi held their procession on the first Sunday of the month,[41] and this may explain why those of Santa Maria Novella held theirs on the second Sunday while the *laudesi* of

San Gilio scheduled theirs on the final Sunday of the month.[42] Since sermons were also of great importance to the *laudesi* spiritually, much care was given to the scheduling of preaching so that the maximum number might be able to attend. And those present were often rewarded with the granting of indulgences.[43]

In Florence, by the late thirteenth or early fourteenth century, the companies of San Piero Martire and San Gilio began to carry in procession wax images called *ceri* which represented their respective patron saints.[44] Those companies which did not produce or own such wax images carried other devotional objects such as banners, canopies, and elaborate stars (*stelle*).[45] The multiplication of such objects by the later fourteenth century seems to indicate a greater emphasis upon the elaborateness of the festival. Greater complexity is also suggested by the appointment of a master of ceremonies who was given the title of *festaiuolo* and also by the common employment of professional singers and instrumentalists.[46]

A revision of the rule of the company of San Zenobi, dated 1508, provides some indication concerning the processions at the beginning of the sixteenth century, for this document speaks of singing *laude* in the midst of the cathedral "with lights and with angels hanging from the star in the usual manner . . . and with organ and trumpet, according to the old custom."[47] The earlier statutes (1326) of this company make it very clear that on one Sunday of each month the procession was actually incorporated into the celebration of the Mass, with the *laudesi* forming the Offertory procession and thus becoming participants in the rite.[48]

The desire to participate more actively in the religious services was already apparent among the early Marian confraternities, whose processions with prayers and songs in the vernacular were evidence of a creative response to this urge among laymen to be more involved in worship experiences. The participation of the confraternities in the Mass and Office of the clergy would necessarily have been limited, and there is evidence that many were not able to understand the Latin of the liturgy. Meersseman attributes the desire for active participation to the growing self-awareness of the free citizen of the commune who was no longer content to be a mere spectator or auditor. Thus the paraliturgical activities of the *laudesi* were a healthy solution introduced to rectify an apparent lack in the Latin rites which had been formerly available.[49]

The problem of Latin was solved, however, by practices reported in various statutes such as those of the *laudesi* of Pisa which decreed that, while the clergy were required to recite the Divine Office and literate lay people were to say the votive Office of the Blessed Virgin Mary in Latin, the others were permitted to substitute twenty-five Our Fathers and Hail Marys--prayers preceded and followed by the *lauda Sia benedetto il nome di Nostro Signor Gesù Cristo.*[50] An additional recommendation specified the distribution of these prayers throughout the day in the manner of the Office with five each said for Matins and Vespers and three each for the minor hours.[51] *Laude* were likewise sometimes appended to prayers at meals.[52]

By far the most revealing expenditures related to ritual and music in the account books of the *laudesi* are those which provided for the proper performance of the *laude* through the employment of experienced musicians to sing and play. D'Accone's studies of the records of the companies of San Piero Martire, San Zenobi, Santa Trinita, and Orsanmichele reveal a wealth of information not only concerning salaried musicians but also implying important elements of performance practice.[53] Although the names of certain singers and instrumentalists recur frequently enough to suggest more or less continuous employment, these musicians may not have been professionals in the modern sense since the records seem to indicate that their main employment may still have involved other work--e.g., as weavers, cobblers, cabinet makers, tanners, and, in a few instances, priests. Some also were children. At Santa Maria Novella the company of San Piero Martire employed such professional singers as early as 1312.[54] While the earliest record showing expenses for music by the company of San Zenobi dates from 1337 when the accounts list a disbursement for flowers, wine, and fruit for the *cantori* who conducted a singing school on the feast of the patron saint,[55] the first indication of singers being hired for the actual services is not recorded until 1345.[56] By 1428 when the statutes of San Zenobi were revised, they were altered to include provisions for the employment of "certain *laudesi* and instrumentalists" as deemed necessary for the services.[57]

From the extant documents it is apparent that singers were sometimes employed in pairs, that some were hired for daily services while others were reserved for special high feasts. Likewise, instruments were used to accompany the singing. Numerous entries record payments to players of the viol and *trombe*, to *pifferi*, and, later, to *organiste*. Of these, certain names such as Chellino della viuola stand out for the frequency with which they occur, though others, such as Squarcialupi, are important by virtue of their significance in the development of the art music of the period.[58]

The accounts of the *laudesi* of Sant'Agnese in the Carmine indicate that paid singers and players were common to the *oltrarno* as well. Interestingly, many of the payments in this case are contained in the accounts showing expenses for the Ascension plays mounted during the fifteenth century in the church of the Carmine by the Compagnia of Sant'Agnese.[59] Thus we are able to verify the participation of the musicians in the religious spectacles of the time and to suggest the close connection between the music under discussion in the present study and the vernacular drama. The *laudesi* of Sant'Agnese, like the other companies noted above, employed performers in different numbers as funds were available[60] or depending on such other contingencies as the depletion of the ranks of the confraternity by death.[61] Even the company of Orsanmichele, perhaps the wealthiest of all the Florentine confraternities, from time to time fluctuated in the number of musicians employed. The accounts from 1380-90 reveal that the number varied between five and ten but that these included at least two instrumentalists.[62] The number of musicians hired for a given performance cannot often be ascertained with precision, but D'Accone demonstrates that as early as 1365 Orsanmichele was using at least three singers for the regular evening service; by the beginning of the next century their number was increased to as many as ten, supplemented by three instrumentalists.[63]

The increase in the number and the simultaneous use of voices and instruments invites speculation concerning the possible performance of polyphonic music. Exactly how the instrumentalists interacted with the singers is not known. They may have performed in unison or antiphonally, or possibly were used merely to support the singing of the congregation. However, D'Accone suggests that the employment of instruments may very well indicate that they were used to double and support the lines of polyphonic compositions--a theory which is reinforced by the mention of motets in the records of the company of Piero Martire in 1325 and also by the association for eight years of the Florentine composer Gherardallo with the company of San Zenobi. It is thus reasonable to speculate that during those years Gherardallo may have composed works for the group--or at least he may have made some *travestimenti* of popular music.[64] There is also the testimony from c.1400 of the Florentine poet-composer-singer Andrea Stefani, who confirms the existence at that time of polyphonic *laude*. Several of his texts are contained in Florence, Biblioteca Marucelliana, MS. C 152, in which he also tells us that "all of these *laude* have been harmonized in three parts and notated in my own hand along with the words."[65] Unfortunately, Stefani's music is not extant.

Further support for the argument for polyphonic *laude* comes from the records of San Zenobi which in 1502 list the names of newly hired *laudisti*, four of whom are designated as *cappellani* since they were also members of the cathedral choir, which at this time had recently been reactivated and which was singing polyphony.[66] The deliberations of the Cathedral Chapter clearly establish that "the said chapel is obliged to sing figural music . . . and *laudi* in the same chapel on the evenings of all feast days as they have begun to do and as is customary. . . ."[67]

The account books of the companies also begin in the fifteenth century to identify singers by their voice types: tenors (*tenori, tenoriste, tinoriste*), sopranos (*sovrani, sobbrani*), and even contraltos (*choltro*).[68] To be sure, the sopranos to which reference was made in the records were young boys, who were sometimes led by an adult singer.[69] The company of Sant'Agnese on occasion sang with the boys of San Giorgio,[70] and by the beginning of the sixteenth century this company was employing treble voices from the company of the *fanciulli* of Sant'Alberto.[71] An entry of 1506 states that although the boys "sing willingly," they are lacking a tenor. And since the company of Sant'Agnese deems it a praiseworthy thing to sing *laude* thus (presumably in parts) on feast days, one of their own members, Antonio di Lucha, was hired to "hold the tenor [*tenere il tenore*] and to teach *laude* to the boys."[72]

Salaries for *laudisti* varied from one company to another, and depended upon the wealth of the fraternity and also upon the nature and frequency of services rendered. For example, the company of San Piero Martire in 1455 paid thirty soldi per month to those who sang on feast days and forty soldi to those who sang for the daily services.[73] Between 1431 and 1433 the company of San Zenobi was paying thirty-five soldi per month for daily singing,[74] while in the same period Orsanmichele paid as much as two lire (forty soldi).[75] Even within the same company salaries varied--a fact which suggests that quality of performance and seniority were rewarded. Indeed, in 1518 Orsanmichele rewarded Sano di Giovanni for fifty years of service by granting him a pension.[76] In the company of Sant'Agnese, which always paid lower salaries, a certain

Raffaello di Giovanni who had served the company by singing *laude* for about two years without pay was granted a stipend of ten soldi per month in 1492 and was given in addition three lire "partly in remuneration and partly because he is poor."[77] It appears that this company also recognized effort and rewarded ability, for an entry of the same date raises the salary of Giovanni di Francesco from ten to fourteen soldi per month because "he improved his voice and sang better."[78] Generally the payments of this company in the late fifteenth and early sixteenth centuries ranged from ten to twelve soldi per month for a beginning singer up to fifteen for those who had served longer.[79]

In the case of professional instrumentalists there is reason to believe that they had some further responsibilities to the confraternities in addition to playing for services. Upon the death of a certain Loysius Macteis, *soniter viole*, who had served the company of Orsanmichele by playing *laude* for its processions, the *Capitani* announced that they had engaged in his place Paulum ser Ambroxii whom they described as "the best performer on the viol, rebec, lute, and other instruments." The document describes his duties, which include not only playing for services in the oratory but also "at the table of the lord prior."[80]

Signs of Decline. The reduction in the number of *laudesi* companies after 1300 was accompanied by a change of emphasis in their activities. There would appear to have been a diminishing of spiritual fervor that accompanied a departure from the pristine ideals of the early Marian confraternities. To a certain extent, the elaborate performances suggested in the account books are symptoms of this change, which is marked in its earliest stages by the proliferation and diversification of the companies. In some respects the change may have been indicative of a desire to escape from the paternalistic attitudes of the religious orders from which their spiritual directors were drawn. The consequences of this development were a gradual departure from the concern for genuinely spiritual interests and a substitution of a growing preoccupation with social issues.[81] The spiritual directors were now sometimes appointed from among the secular clergy rather than from religious orders, and meetings might be held at a church chosen by the *governatore*--thus weakening the ties to the parent convent, monastery, or parish. As a consequence, the ecclesiastical prior began to function in more of an honorary capacity.[82]

Secularization had its effect upon the ritual and the music of the *laudesi* and hence was reflected in the *laude* and in the manner in which they were performed. With the advent of the professional singer, *lauda*-singing was becoming more a virtuoso vehicle approaching the *bel canto* tradition for which Italian singers would later become justly famous. The elaborate *fiorature* of the Magliabechiano collection (Mgl[1]) provide musical evidence of this tendency already in the fourteenth century.[83] But perhaps the most important effect of this transformation was the change in the function of the *lauda* itself, since it now tended to lose its participatory function as paraliturgical expression in which the faithful might join, while it instead became a performance only to be heard.

By the fifteenth century, Florentine *laudesi* in particular had become more and more involved in the staging of religious spectacles in which *laude* still remained the main musical component, though as we might guess this form now became absorbed in the theatrical mode of presentation. Such spectacles were mounted not merely for the members of the companies but also for the general public, and their purposes were edification and devotion as well as entertainment.

Festivals. Descriptions of the elaborate and colorful religious festivals in *quattrocento* Florence which have come down to us suggest that they may have been the Church's answer to the competition offered by the more secular humanistic festivities, including those promoted by the Medici at this time.[84] However much such elaborateness may have departed from the original aims of the Marian confraternities, the participation of the *laudesi* in mounting and performing theatrical representations in the churches constitutes an important contribution to the development of the scenic element so necessary to the *sacre rappresentazione*. The *carri* and *trionfi* of the carnival now have their religious counterpart in the *mandorle* honoring some mystery of the life of Christ or the patron saint of the confraternity.

Several valuable eye-witness accounts of these performances have been preserved. The earliest is that of Paolo di Matteo, who provided a brief description of the Ascension play which he witnessed in Florence:

> On Thursday, May 21, 1422, during the day of the Ascension and the night before it there was a solemn and beautiful festival in the church of the Carmine. And a living man instead of [i.e., representing] Our Lord went up into heaven. He was pulled from the arches to the platform and reached the roof going straight upward. All episodes were represented in the likeness of [the life of] Our Lady, of S. Mary Magdalene and the twelve Apostles. This festival was considered to be very beautiful on account of the many devices around the *nuvola* [cloud] so that when the *nuvola* came down and united with [the figure of] Christ ascending, then many candles burst at once into light, reflecting also on other figures of angels. [This] will be seen by those who witness the festival if it pleases God to let it be performed.[85]

A somewhat later and much more detailed description of the Ascension play is included in the *Itinerario* of the Russian Bishop Abraham of Suzdal who accompanied Isidore, the Metropolitan of the Eastern Church, to the Ecumenical Council held in Florence in 1439. Bishop Abraham describes the climax of the play, that moment when Christ ascends and is greeted by God the Father who awaits him high above.

> Seven cables . . . rise up to the heavens opening above the Mount of Olives. And a young man representing . . . Christ

is in the act of ascending [to heaven] by means of them. At the crest of the mountain God the Father is seen surrounded by a blinding light which is diffused from an infinite number of lamps. The children who represent the angels move around him. The larger angels above are painted on discs which revolve and thus appear to be alive. From heaven where God is seen, a beautiful cloud descends by means of the seven cables, surrounded by the revolving discs. To the right and to the left are angels with golden wings.[86]

The active participation of the *laudesi* of Sant'Agnese in the mounting of the play is amply documented in the account books of the confraternity which contain many expenditures for costumes, flowers, cables, ropes, and other equipment as well as salaries to craftsmen and to artists. The artists even included men of the stature of Masolino da Panicale, who painted the angels "who go around the cloud."[87]

A still later description is contained in Vasari's account of the Florentine engineer Francesco d'Angelo, better known as Cecca (1447-88).[88] Vasari provides a lengthy description of the intricate apparatus designed by Cecca for use in the Ascension plays at the Carmine, and mentions also that Brunelleschi had designed similar machines for the Annunciation play mounted in the little church of San Felice in Piazza. Vasari's account is valuable in making clear how intimately the confraternities were involved in these presentations.[89]

Bishop Abraham, in his description of the Florentine spectacle, makes several references to music and specifically notes the "sweet songs resounding through the church."[90] Given the non-liturgical nature of these representations, the popularity of the *lauda* in Florence at that time, and the close association of the *laudesi* with the plays, we may surmise that the "sweet songs" would indeed have been *laude*. The contemporary *rappresentazione* of Feo Belcari, who was then also active in Florence, sometimes call for the device of music to embellish climactic points in the plays. In his Annunciation drama, at the moment when the heavens open and God the

Father speaks to Gabriel, Belcari indicates that a "*lauda* is sung by the angels who accompany Gabriel." The entire text of the *lauda* then follows, and at the end another rubric indicates that Gabriel now has a solo *lauda*: "Truly from heaven I have been sent by the Father."[91] Belcari uses this musical device again in his Resurrection play at the point when the Apostles learn that Jesus has risen: at this moment they express their joy by singing a *lauda*.[92] Hence in the play described by Abraham the inclusion of *laude* would have been quite in keeping with local practice.

The complexity of these religious spectacles was such that preparations were ongoing throughout the year,[93] and hence also some of the companies responsible for them began to specialize, choosing particular feasts and adding more effects to their presentations as their technical skills increased. Thus the *laudesi* of Sant'Agnese concentrated efforts on the complicated mechanism for the Ascension and also the Assumption, a development which may have been conditioned at least in part by the suitability of the Carmine with its unusual height.[94] Unfortunately, since none of the extant descriptions of the plays were written by the members of the confraternity itself, they do not provide any information about their effect on the company that staged the spectacles. However, by addressing a wider public the confraternity may have altered its "more self-contained and private way of life." In any case, such elaborate festivities certainly must have created a strain on the company's financial resources, for in one year (1425) the company spent sixty-one percent of its annual income on the Ascension spectacle alone.[95]

The records nevertheless show that often equipment, costumes, and properties required refurbishing or replacement. While such expenditures were not necessary every year, a more thoroughgoing restoration of costumes and properties occurred in those years which were marked by the state visit of some special foreign dignitary or by a Church function such as the Council of 1439.[96] The fact that the government of the city of Florence was willing to grant a subsidy in the form of a *gate gabelle* to the company is further evidence that the Medici took a favorable view of the spectacle and that they perhaps in fact used it to lend pomp and celebrity to their administration.[97] Government subsidies nevertheless were not the main source of revenue for the companies. Often the confraternities inherited property, the rental of which in some cases became the primary income. In return, testators bequeathing property to a company required certain obligations, including services which sometimes multiplied to such an extent that a company could almost be dominated by the fulfillment of testamentary obligations.[98] Not surprisingly, the preoccupation with these contracts as well as with the plays and festivals seriously altered the original intentions of the *laudesi*.

The many letters of bishops granting indulgences for daily singing of *laude* in the fifteenth century appear to have held out such spiritual rewards as incentives for renewal. One such letter--from Gaspare, the Bishop of Imola, to the Societas della V. Mariae in 1455--indicates that the daily singing of *laude* had declined to a weekly observance occurring now only on Sundays and feast days.[99] But attempts of this kind to revive the devotion appear to have been relatively unsuccessful, especially after the passing of the plague. Meersseman cites as evidence of this decline a document of the Provincial Chapter of the Dominicans of the Observance in the province of Lombardy. This document records that the confraternity paid the religious to sing in their place on Sundays and feast days after Vespers and Compline, and specifies *Ave maris stella* and *Ave regina coelorum* or some other hymn to the Virgin. As compensation the company paid to the convent forty lire annually, and thus it freed itself of any obligation with regard to singing. The change signalled here is significant, for by now many groups had become wealthy and preferred to dedicate their efforts instead to charitable works.[100] And although their meetings were sometimes still held in the chapter rooms of the orders, they became more or less ritualistic formalities lacking the kind of devotion which had animated the early Marian confraternities.[101]

By the sixteenth century, the extent of the decline is reflected in the remarks of the Dominican friar Serafino Razzi (1531-1611), who complained that the custom of daily *lauda*-singing had ceased until "in 1563 when a new publication . . . caused a revival of the practice."[102] This "new publication" was, of course, his own collection, the *Libro primo delle laudi*, which bears on the title page the words "for use in the churches of Florence after Vespers and Compline for the consolation and entertainment of the devout servants of God, with proper music and manner of singing each *lauda* as it was used by the ancients and is used in Florence."[103] Judging from the subsequent proliferation of *lauda* collections, and especially those of Matteo Coferati in the seventeenth century,[104] Razzi's efforts were successful, for once again the *lauda* flourished in the churches of Florence and presumably in other churches throughout the region as well. However, discussion of the later Counter-Reformation practice is outside the scope of this study. On the other hand, an investigation of the singing activities of the *laudesi* must be supplemented by a consideration of the parallel history of the practice among *disciplinati* societies of the period leading up to the early sixteenth century.

2

Non-Musical Documents: *Disciplinati*

The *laudesi* and *disciplinati*[1] are distinguished from each other by the terms by which they are designated and which declare their *raisons d'être*. The *lauda,* when compared to its use by the *laudesi* for whom it was of very great importance, might at first seem to be given a subordinate and supporting role by the *disciplinati*, for whom it was more or less accessory to the primary devotion of penance in the form of self-flagellation. Nevertheless, the *lauda* was in fact an essential part of *disciplinati* piety from the time of the penitential movement of the 1260's, when the flagellant confraternities originated, and it remained essential through the fifteenth century. As important as the *gran devozione* of 1260 was, its relation to the musical activities of these penitent companies has tended to be overemphasized, and hence there often has been a failure to understand the differences between the practices of the two types of confraternity.

The spontaneous outbreak of religious devotion in 1260 must thus be considered within the context of contemporary piety which placed great emphasis upon the humanity of Christ, for, as noted above, it was the example of his suffering and death which motivated the penitent companies to participate in the redemptive act by means of self-flagellation in order to expiate their own sins. Such stress on the human Christ and his mother was very familiar to the people through the popular preaching of the mendicants, and the tendency of flagellant companies to identify with martyred saints is further evidence of their high regard for those who suffered for the love of Christ.[2]

Soon after the *gran devozione*, therefore, some of the pious laymen who had been caught up and inflamed with the zeal of penitential fervor began to form confraternities. Documents as early as 1261 provided for the granting of indulgences to the faithful for taking the discipline,[3] and by 1262 the Penitents of Bologna, for example, were already recognized as a confraternity.[4] The groups proliferated rapidly, and there is evidence that in some respects they were confused with the *Penitenti*[5] though in reality the two were quite different. The *disciplinati* did not constitute a federation as did the *Penitenti*: instead, each group had its own set of statutes which were admittedly similar though not identical. More important, they did not take vows and thus did not have the right of ecclesiastical immunity, and hence too they were more readily welcomed in certain quarters.[6]

While the medieval chroniclers who describe the flagellant processions instigated by Raniero do notice the presence of singing, it cannot even be verified that what these early flagellants actually sang were *laude*. Several chroniclers record the invocations used and mention singing specifically. And the *Chronicon Patavini* insists not only that these lugubrious songs of the penitents were the only music allowed at this time, but also that both musical instruments and love songs were silenced. Only "the angelic songs of the penitents were heard over and over again."[7]

Salimbene of Parma, with his usual eye for detail, has left a vivid account of the phenomenon of the *flagellanti*. He describes their singing thus: "In their mouths sounded the words of God and not of men, and their voice was as the voice of multitudes. Men walked in the way of salvation and composed [*componebant*] godly songs of praise in honor of the Lord and the Blessed Virgin Mary. And these they sang as they went and scourged themselves."[8] The use of the verb *componebant* here is ambiguous, since we do not know if it is being used in the modern sense.   In the opinion of Meersseman, the supplications of the penitents (*clamori di compuzione*) were more likely short invocations repeated over and over on a monotone in litany fashion.[9]   Indeed, the chroniclers' descriptions at times seem to support this theory. The writer of the *Annales Genuenses* claims that the penitents repeated again and again the words *Pax, pax*[10] and the cry *misericordia e pace, Signore, date a noi.*[11] However, the same chronicle also contains a stanza which was sung by the flagellants:

> Domina Sancta Maria
> Recipite peccatores
> Et rogate Jesum Christum
> Ut nobis parcat.[12]

The vernacular equivalent of this text is found in several manuscripts of *laude*, most notably the Cortona *laudario* in which it is preserved with musical notation and seven additional stanzas.[13]   Whatever the exact nature of the link between the singing of the flagellants as described by the chroniclers and the use of *lauda* by the *disciplinati*, it is nevertheless certain that these confraternities did not initiate the practice of singing *laude*.

Full membership in *disciplinati* confraternities was reserved to men alone, although women sometimes enjoyed a limited association which entitled them to a share in the spiritual benefits.   In certain cases this association provided for a funeral with full honors of the confraternity--that is, with all members in attendance and in the habit.[14] In some companies, women were required to recite the same prayers as the men.   The statutes of the *Battuti* of Cividale del Friuli, for example, state clearly that upon the death of a brother each member of the company, "whether man or woman," must say for the deceased twenty-five Our Fathers and Hail Marys and must make an offering for the candles used at the funeral.[15]

The practice of flagellation was not in fact new at the time of the processions of 1260,[16] for it had existed in the Church previously, first as a punitive measure and later as a voluntary form of penance practiced by devout individuals. Various monastic rules and constitutions of women religious had embraced the custom and admonished their members to discipline the flesh in pursuit of perfection. But lay people also had been known to have adopted the practice privately, as is evident from the canonization process of Elizabeth of Thuringia (d. 1231) which brought forth evidence that this married noblewoman had regularly taken the discipline.[17] However, though women were known to have espoused this form of corporal penance in private and long before 1260, it is inconceivable that they should have done so within the *disciplinati* confraternities. Modesty alone would have precluded their participation in a practice which necessitated exposing the bare back.[18] One late-fifteenth-century source, a revision of the statutes of the *Battuti* of Bergamo, leaves no doubt about this matter: "All the women who wish to enter our rule . . . are obligated to do all the things which are required in the statutes, just as the men do, save that obligation of taking the discipline, that is, the self-scourging of the men."[19]

The *disciplinati* wore a sort of religious habit[20] (figs. 1-2) which consisted of a loose-fitting tunic belted at the waist with a cord and which had a hood with holes provided for the eyes. A large circular opening between the shoulders allowed the brother to scourge his bare back with the leather thongs that hung from his belt.[21] As the customary payment for the garb and the scourge, the newly received brother was often required to make an offering such as a pound of pure wax.[22] The documents show that the habit was regarded with great respect and that it was not worn at all times as was the case in a canonically established religious order. But the garment was reserved for the times when the companies assembled for their meetings, at which the habits and scourges were distributed by the sacristan whose duty it was to maintain them.[23] The garb was bestowed on the new member only at the time of his formal reception into the company, which usually occurred after a novitiate or some established period of trial.[24] In most cases, anyone seeking admittance was required to undergo serious scrutiny and to subject himself to an examination by the prior in the presence of all the *fratelli*.[25] The ceremony often ended with a *lauda* proper to the occasion--e.g., the following item from the *laudario Oliveriana* intended for the investiture ceremony:

> Guarda bene, disciplinato,
> Tu ch'a Cristo mostre amore,
> Che de Dio no sie inganato.
> Sia fondato en caritade
> Tucto pieno d'umilitade.[26]

> (Be attentive, disciplinato,
> You who show your love for Christ,
> That you be not led away from God.
> Be rooted in charity
> And be all filled with humility.)

Once inducted into the company, the member was bound by a set of rules, the infraction of which might bring censure or even expulsion, depending upon the gravity of the offense.[27] Penalties ranged from the simple recitation of a specified number of prayers or the payment of a fine to more severe and humiliating chastisements. Extreme measures of castigation were as a rule reserved as punishment for those infractions of the statutes which reflected unfavorably upon the confraternity. The company Gesù pellegrino in Florence, for example, compelled the errant brother to don a black habit (instead of the usual white habit) and to stand before his brothers in the oratory during the service. He also might, if warranted by the seriousness of the infraction, be required to kneel as each brother passed by him and struck his bare back with a whip. If a brother proved intractable, he was allowed one last opportunity before being expelled from the company: dressed in a black habit signifying his shame, he was to walk to another church and, while services were being held there, was to scourge himself. The distance he was required to go was determined by the gravity of his fault; those who were regarded as the most guilty were ordered to walk as far as San Miniato al monte. Punishments such as these were imposed for frequenting taverns, breaking silence during meetings, or missing services on Good Friday.[28]

Strict rules of secrecy prohibited discussion of activities and even the disclosure of the names of other members of the company. Many statutes contain provisions which deny membership to any person already belonging to another confraternity of *disciplinati*.[29] That this secrecy provoked suspicion and fear on the part of the local government is evident in the actions of the Florentine commune, which in the fifteenth century established a commission to investigate these companies.[30] The secrecy, the severity of the statutes, and the harshness of the punishments exacted for breaking the rules all tend to underscore the fact that the flagellant groups, unlike the *laudesi*, preserved the purity of motivation which initially had animated them. If any change may be noted, it was in the formation of new *disciplinati* groups called *compagnie delle notte* which exacted an even stricter devotion; these groups met during the night for long periods of prayer.[31]

With regard to our understanding of the *laude*, the examination of *disciplinati* sources provides considerable information concerning the function of the *lauda* within the activities of the companies and reveals that four occasions in particular were consistently embellished by the singing of such music. These were the *devozione*, funerals and suffrages of the dead, processions, and Holy Week services.

The *devozione*. The most frequent use of the *lauda*

appears to have been in conjunction with the *devozione*, the penitential exercises held in the privacy of the oratory during which the brothers scourged themselves.   Unfortunately, however, some of the contemporary references to the manner in which these hymns were incorporated are vague and hence do not actually clarify the question of who did the singing or of how it was rendered. The preferred day seems to have been Friday, in commemoration of the Passion of Jesus. In some cases, however, this penitential service was held twice weekly, while in other instances it was less frequent, sometimes only twice each month.[32]   In Florence, where meetings seem to have occurred in pairs, the first was the occasion of the discipline and the second was more apt to be a prayer meeting at which the prior might correct the brothers for any infractions of the rule.[33]

The *devozione* was typically conducted in the dark and partially disrobed in order to facilitate whipping the bare back. The account preserved in the statutes of the Compania di San Zenobi in Florence is representative:

> The said devotion is conducted in this manner: at the conclusion of the office the sacristans reverently give the scourges to the brothers . . . and the prior says some words encouraging the brothers to do penance. Having said this, the lights are extinguished and some stanzas of the Passion are spoken, and then some brief words are said exhorting the brothers to do good. Then, keeping silence, they scourge themselves for the space of ten Our Fathers and Hail Marys. After that a prayer is said, and when this is done, a psalm is said, the *Miserere mei Deus* or the *De Profundis* . . . or actually the psalm is sung, or a *lauda* or a hymn, depending upon the will of whoever is in charge.[34]

The way in which the *lauda* was used in this type of penitential service is more clearly established in an early-fourteenth-century Ordo of the Confraternita di San Stefano in Assisi which prescribes that the brothers should first pray in silence and then, at the sound of the bell, begin to scourge themselves. Thereafter,

> immediately they rise and sing *laude* in the vernacular. He who sings them moves the hearts of the brothers to tears more than words move the mind.
>
> The *laude* are performed in this manner: on Fridays or any other day when the Passion is commemorated, or in preparation for the Passion, *laude* in honor of Our Savior Jesus and his most sorrowful mother are sung. But on Sundays or feast days the *lauda* of the day or of the feast is sung. If the discipline is to be taken in the habit, all of the verses are sung. At the end of each stanza they scourge themselves. But while the cantor sings the *lauda* they rise, and at the sound of the bell or some other signal, they cease the discipline. And thus it proceeds until the aforesaid *lauda* is completed by the singer.[35]

The context into which this devotion was incorporated was a species of popular Office that not only reflects the larger design of the liturgical cycle of the Church but also betrays the influence of the liturgical practices of the religious order with which the respective company was affiliated.[36]

Funerals and Suffrages for the Dead. *Disciplinati* statutes are noticeably interwoven with supplications for the deceased, and some identify an Office of the Dead.[37] It was, of course, an era which after 1348-49 was afflicted with periodic visitations of the plague, and hence a certain preoccupation with death should not be surprising. However, there apparently was other motivation as well, for a member of the confraternity who died in the good graces of his company was deemed worthy of burial with full honors and was thus assured of a large funeral with all the brothers in attendance and in the habit.[38] Furthermore, in Florence the confraternities were exempt from the sumptuary laws which prohibited the use of "richly worked cloth" or "excessively large candles" at funerals.[39]

The proper exequies of a deceased brother are generally described in some detail in the rule, and invariably the service includes both the discipline and the *lauda*, allowing for some slight variants in the ceremony in the case of different companies.[40] In *disciplinati* companies, a member who had been faithful to the rule was usually buried in the garb of the confraternity, his arms folded across his chest, and with scourge in hand.   The statutes of the Compagnia di San Giovanni Battista in Florence prescribe that "if it pleases our Lord Jesus Christ to call to himself one of our company, he must be dressed in his robe with his cincture, with his scourge in his hand, barefoot, and uncovered."[41] A delegation of the *fratelli* went to dress the corpse--four who continued to scourge themselves on the way and one who carried the robe of the brother. After they had dressed the body for burial, they returned to the company, and the funeral procession pro-gressed, as described in the rule, "with candles and the cross, each one holding a burning candle in his hand when they leave the house of the dead to go to the burial place. . . . [Then] at the tomb they must sing those prayers and *laude* which are suitable for that sad occasion."[42]   The rule of the Compagnia di San Domenico in Florence provided that at the funeral service the prior should intone the *lauda*, which would then be sung by all. At the end the lights were extinguished, and the brothers took the discipline--after which there was "a short sermon on the misery and fragility of our life and a prayer for the soul of the dead *fratello* and for all those of our company. [After this,] they again dress themselves and sing *laude*."[43]

In Cortona, the brothers of the confraternity of Santa Croce, whose statutes are dated 1300, appointed several members to carry the bier while singing "the *lauda* on death." The remainder of the company walked before the cross and disciplined themselves all the way to the church, where they were to stand silently at the side of the priest as he gave the sermon.   At the grave site the brothers continued to scourge

themselves until the burial was completed.[44]   Possibly the
"*lauda* on death" to which reference has been made may have
been the hymn *Chi vol lo mondo despreççare* that is preserved
with musical notation in the Cortona *laudario* of the preceding
century.[45]   However, nowhere in the accounts are there
specific incipits indicating exactly what was sung.

Nevertheless, there are numerous examples of suitable
funeral *lauda* texts to be found in other manuscripts, particularly from Umbria, during this period. Thus, near the end of
the well-known *laudario* of the *disciplinati* of Sant'Andrea in
Perugia[46] several examples of texts appear (Nos. 110-20)
which are labeled *pro defunctis*. The other great Perugian
collection belonging to the company of San Simone e
Fiorenzo[47] likewise contains a section of eleven *lauda* texts
that are so designated. One small manuscript in the Cathedral
Library in Assisi (MS. 36/ii) is made up entirely of *laude* on
the subject of death; five of the seven contained in it are
dialogues between the Body and the Soul or between Life and
Death. Bound with this manuscript is a modest set of funeral
lamentations.[48] A single *lauda* on death is also contained in a
manuscript, formerly the Frondini Codex, from Assisi (Rome,
Biblioteca Nationale Centrale Vittorio Emanuele II, MS.
478).[49] Yet another isolated example is the text *Levate gl'ochi
o peccaturi et retornate a penetenza*, which occurs in Assisi,
Biblioteca Comunale, MS. 705 (formerly the Illuminati
Codex); this item bears the rubric "This *lauda* is sung when
the body of the deceased is carried to the grave." Each verse
is designated *homo devoto*.[50]

Processions.   The *gran devozione* of 1260 had been
characterized by penitential processions, as we have seen.
Chroniclers provide vivid descriptions of these lugubrious
devotions in which men and women, clergy and laity, and civil
and ecclesiastical officials alike were said to have participated.
According to one account,[51] these demonstrations lasted for
thirty-three days[52] and were continued throughout the night,[53]

even in rain and cold.[54]   Solemnly the penitents walked from one church to another[55] while scourging themselves and singing.[56]   Little imagination is required to comprehend the kind of reaction such a spectacle would have elicited from the curious and less fervently inclined.   But Salimbene indicates that a certain amount of social pressure was brought to bear on those not naturally disposed to take such penances upon themselves.[57]

Rulers--e.g., Manfred and Uberto Palavicino--sometimes received the flagellants harshly and legislated against their disturbances,[58] perhaps more for the sake of order than out of impiety as some contemporary chroniclers charged.[59]   While it is true that certain social benefits may have resulted from the flagellant movement--e.g., the freeing of prisoners and the abandonment of some long-standing vendettas--the more lasting and significant result was the impetus given to the formation of new confraternities.

Even after the *disciplinati* companies settled into the quieter and more peaceable routine of taking the discipline in the privacy of the oratory, processions continued to be a very important part of their devotional practices.   Processions were especially important on the patronal feast of the confraternity or of the city.   In Florence, for example, on the feast of the city's patron, John the Baptist, all of the major companies walked in procession carrying standards adorned with their insignias.   However, various statutes demonstrate that on these occasions when the flagellants left their oratories to join in public processions they were to conduct themselves with the greatest modesty and decorum, "dressed in habits with their cowls well down over their faces in order to avoid recognition."[60]

Holy Week Observances. Processions during Holy Week were also a very important element of devotion in some areas. In fourteenth-century Cortona, for example, processions took on a curiously competitive aspect.   Here the confraternity of

Santissima Trinita sponsored an elaborate procession on Holy Thursday at which a statue of the Scourging with Christ tied to the pillar was carried throughout the city, while the company of Maria della Manna on Good Friday transported the image of the dead Christ, which was placed in a coffin, through the streets. A more joyous climax came on Holy Saturday when the confraternity of Maria della Misericordia anticipated the events of Easter morning by bearing in procession an image of the risen Christ. Among these three companies there appears to have been a kind of friendly rivalry, for we are told by the historian Ridolfini that there was "a contest to determine which of them could produce the most smoke [presumably incense] and the most music [almost certainly *laude*]."[61]

Especially important for understanding how the *laude* were incorporated into the ritual of the *disciplinati* are the accounts of their services for Holy Thursday and Good Friday. Since on Good Friday no Mass was celebrated, the confraternities' desire to amplify their own ceremonies presumably was heightened at this time. This was especially the case since the flagellant companies identified their voluntary penance so closely with the sufferings of Christ, especially with the scourging.

Among Florentine companies, however, Holy Week devotions seem to have reached their dramatic climax with the washing of the feet on Holy Thursday. This service, called the *mandato*, was not merely a symbolic gesture commemorating Christ's voluntary act of humility at the Last Supper, for it also constituted a reversal of the social order in the companies as the prior washed the feet of all the brethren.[62] The ritual was traditionally incorporated into the recitation of a kind of popular Office of *tenebrae*--that is, Matins and Lauds for Wednesday and Thursday of Holy Week. Nevertheless, in keeping with the commemoration of the Last Supper, the devotion was accompanied by a symbolic meal shared by the members of the company, and also there was singing of *laude*.[63]

The Office of *tenebrae* as conducted by the Florentine Compagnia di San Giovanni Battista tra le arcore is typical of the manner in which the companies in Florence observed the occasion. After assembling in their oratory at five o'clock in the afternoon, the brothers were admonished to make a perfect act of contrition for their sins in preparation for this solemn Office. Some portions of the Passion of Christ were read, after which the *governatore* intoned the Office of the day and the penitential psalms. As in the Divine Office of the Lenten period, the *Gloria Patri* was omitted at the end of the psalms, and instead the versicle *Christus factus est pro nobis obediens usque ad mortem* was said. At this point, the sacristan brought forth the candelabrum containing fifteen tapers, which would each in turn be extinguished after the recitation of the designated psalms until the entire oratory was enveloped in darkness and the traditional noise was made. The climax of the service was the *mandato* prescribed by the rule: "The *governatore* with great reverence and humility, following the example of Our Lord Jesus Christ, washes the feet of all the brothers and kisses the feet of each. He washes [them], and the councilors dry [them] . . . and then a most devout meal is had."[64]

Holy Week Services: Umbria. An important example of the *mandato* is found in the rule of the Compagnia di San Lorenzo in Assisi which describes the gathering of the brothers in the oratory

> to celebrate with devout reverence and profound humility the example of the Divine Majesty who humbled himself to wash the feet of the fishermen and servants, thus showing us an example of our Lord and Master. So we, with the discipline and in charity and humility of a servant, serve one another thus by the greater washing the feet of the lowlier. The prior begins with the sub-prior and the other officials, down to the lowliest and poorest, thus providing a *mandato* for those who are gathered in our place on that most holy night in expiation, weeping tears blessed by God.[65]

This directive, however, first appeared elsewhere, in the rule of the Compagnia di San Stefano, also in Assisi, which likewise possessed an ancient *laudario* (Assisi, Biblioteca Comunale, MS. 705) that contained a *lauda* clearly intended for the *mandato.* The item bears the rubric *La lauda per lo di de Jovedi Sancto commença cosi. Homo devoto.* The second stanza in particular repeats almost verbatim the words found in the statutes: *la divina maesta a lavare i piede di pescadure.*

> Avemo assempio dumilitade.
> Per Dio ciascun depona el core
> Vedere quell alta maiestade
> Lavare i pie ai pescadure.
> Quil che fra nui e piu onorato
> De essere piu humilitate.[66]

> (We have an example of humility.
> In God's name let each of us humble his heart
> At the sight of the high majesty
> Who washes the feet of the fishermen.
> The most honored one among us
> is the most humble.)

Although the Offices of the Florentine *disciplinati* manifested a tendency toward the dramatic in their re-enactment of the events of the Last Supper, these Offices should not be regarded as *rappresentazione.* At most the actions of the participants seem to have been patterned in imitation of similar ritual movements found in the liturgy of the Church for Holy Week. And there is no evidence to suggest the use of costumes or stage furnishings of any sort. However, numerous sources from Umbria indicate that there the ardor of the penitent groups reached a height in Holy Week which manifested itself in true dramatizations. *Lauda* collections from such major Umbrian centers as Perugia and Orvieto are well known for their dramatic *laude* which by the fifteenth century had become fully theatricalized productions.[67] But lesser Umbrian centers, which have received very little scholarly attention, are the repository of a treasury of incipient dramatic *laude* that document the mutations of the genre from lyric to dramatic. Compared to the magnitude of the *lauda* collections from Perugia and Orvieto, the holdings of Assisi may seem truly minor, yet they are impressive because they upon occasion contain informative subtitles or rubrics that are either incomplete or entirely missing in the Perugian codices containing the same texts. When supplemented by ordos and rituals of the same companies which owned the *laudari*, these Assisi sources provide useful insights into the metamorphosis of the dramatic *lauda* from *devozione* to *rappresentazione.*

The most amply documented of the confraternities at Assisi is that of San Stefano. The Latin statutes of this company bear the date of their approbation and promulgation, 23 August 1327, though the company must already have been in existence at this date, for another document in the Cathedral Archives states that the group originated in May of 1324 under Pope John XXII.[68] This confraternity was apparently looked upon as something of a model since its statutes were copied by a number of other companies both in Assisi and in nearby Gubbio. Though these companies' statutes were in the vernacular, they are exact in following the text of the company of San Stefano even to the extent of using the appellation "protomartyr."[69]

Among the manuscripts which had belonged to the confraternity of San Stefano at Assisi are two missals, both in the Cathedral Library at Assisi (MSS. 27 and 13). The first of these is dated 1482, while the second is a late-thirteenth-century manuscript that, though it had once belonged to the Friars Minor, had been acquired by the company in 1338 for the price of seven gold florins and forty soldi contributed by members of the fraternity whose names appear on an inserted leaf. From other documents of the company also we are able to verify that the *lauda* played an important part in its devotions. An inventory of 1427, for example, records among its belongings "four books for singing laude."[70] Of the *laudari* identified as having once belonged to San Stefano, the oldest is the Codex Illuminati of the Biblioteca Comunale (MS. 705) at Assisi, now housed at the Sacro convento, San Francesco.[71] Five other *laudari* of the confraternity appear in the Cathedral Library at Assisi under the shelf mark 36/i/ii/iii/iv/v.[72] Neither Bartholomaeis nor Galli seems to have known these important manuscripts, each of which contains some *laude* as briefly described in the following list:

> MS. 36/i: the smallest of the manuscripts, since it contains only three *laude*, all of which are in dialogue. The third of these is a lengthy 260 verses.

> MS. 36/ii: dated 1388 at the top of fol. 2. The manuscript contains seven *laude* for the dead, of which five are in dialogue form.[73]

> MS. 36/iii: a small collection of five *laude*. It is noteworthy since it contains *Segniore escribe or que faciemo*, the Passion *lauda* common to several other important sources.[74]

> MS. 36/iv: by far the most important, since it contains fifty-seven *laude*, mainly dramatic in form, which are disposed according to the liturgical cycle from the first Sunday of Advent to Easter.

> MS. 36/v: a small manuscript of paper with vellum covers. It consists entirely of funeral laments. Thirteen pages (five blank).

Another *laudario*, Rome, Biblioteca Nazionale Centrale Vittorio Emanuele II, MS. 478 (già Frondini),[75] contains sixteen *laude,* seven of which are dramatic, as well as Latin orations and an Office of the Dead. Tenneroni, Galli, and Fortini believed it to have belonged to the Confraternita di San Stefano, but more recent research by Del Pozzo and Terruggia has established that it was owned by the Compagnia di San Pietro in Assisi.[76]

Detailed directives for the ceremonial of the *disciplinati* exercises are contained in the ordines of the company of San Stefano, now MSS. 20 and 21 in the Cathedral Library at Assisi.[77] When studied in conjunction with the statutes of the confraternity, these manuscripts demonstrate that its paraliturgical services evolved along two distinctly different lines of development. In contrast to the discreetly private devotion of the Ordo already cited above, the statutes instead prescribe that on Good Friday a *rappresentazione* of sorts was to be performed for the people. Thus the rule and the Ordo clearly distinguish between (1) those religious functions intended for the members and confined to the oratory, and (2) those designed for apostolic life and the inspiration of the public outside of the oratory. These two types of activity are termed respectively *della congregatione* and [*della*] *processione* in the rule.

The "representation for the people" by the confraternity of San Stefano thus may usefully be placed in its proper place in the chronology of events at the culmination of the Holy Week observances. The statutes describe the differences between these public events and the private devotions of the company. From nightfall on Holy Thursday to Good Friday morning all of the brothers were required to gather in the oratory to take the discipline and to re-enact the ancient custom of the ritual washing of the feet as in the *mandatum* of the Mass for that day. In the early hours of the morning, those *fratelli* who wished might be permitted to return to their homes, but with the strict admonition to return to their oratory at the hour of Prime to hear the Passion and the "sad sighs of Christ." Then, at the hour of Prime, they will go, wearing their habits to the Church of St. Francis and the Blessed Virgin Mary of the Angels (the Porziuncula) where they will "sing tearful *laude*, sad songs, and bitter laments" of the Blessed Virgin Mary bereft of her Son. "These," the document explains, "are enacted with reverence *for the people* who understand above all more with tears than with words. After singing the laude,

47

all must return to our place."[78]   This is undoubtedly one of the earliest references to a simple kind of *rappresentazione.*   And the "tearful *laude,* sad songs, and bitter laments" to which reference is made here are in fact to be found in Assisi, Biblioteca Comunale, MS. 705, the oldest of the *lauda* collections belonging to San Stefano.[79]

While the number of *laude* contained in MS. 705 is small, the collection is unique because within its modest dimensions it chronicles several stages in the development which would eventually culminate in the fully developed plays of later manuscripts.   Among the Passiontide *laude* in this small collection are examples of the *planctus* or lament of the Virgin Mary (Nos. 1, 8), which are written in pure monologue, as well as dialogues that result from the addition of *homo devotus* as interlocutor (No. 2) and the exchange between Mary and the Holy Women (No. 3).   A more truly dramatic level is achieved through the gradual inclusion of other characters of the Passion story; these at first address the audience, but eventually they engage in dialogue with each other (Nos. 11/7, 15).

One *lauda* text in particular deserves special mention here for its inherent dramatic qualities.   This item is *Levate gl'ochi e resguardate* which, judging from its inclusion in several other *laudari,* must have been among the most widely disseminated *laude* of the period.[80]   In MS. 705 it is preceded by the rubric "This lauda is sung in memory of the Passion, and begins with the sisters of Mary."

> Levate gl ochi e resguardate
> morto e cristo ogi per nui
> le mano e i pie en croce a chiavate
> aperto el lato o triste nui
> piangiamo et feciamo lamento
> e nariamo del suo tormento.[81]
>
> (Lift your eyes and see:
> Christ has died for us today.
> His hands and feet are nailed to the cross,

His side is opened. Oh, sad are we!
Let us weep and lament
And tell of his torments.)

The stanza which follows is spoken by the Virgin and contains what appears to be a very early allusion to actual gestures and costumes, for Mary asks the holy women to bring her a black mantle so that she may don it as a symbol of widowhood in order to express her sorrow at being robbed of her Son:

O sorelle della scura
or me daite uno manto nero
a quilla che giamai non cura
ne bei drappo ne buon velo
puoi chio so si abandonata
e del mio figlio vedovata.[82]

(O sorrowful sisters,
Now give a black mantle
To her who cared
Neither for beautiful silk nor good veil.
For I am so abandoned
And widowed by my Son.)

Then in the third stanza the holy women respond to the sorrowing Mary by bringing to her the mantle that she has requested:

O di pien de vedovanza
pien de pena e de dolore
mort e la nostra speranza
cristo nostro salvadore
ciascun facia novo pianto
e a Maria date esto manto.[83]

(Oh, day of widowhood,
Filled with pain and sorrow.
Dead is our hope,
Christ our Savior.

Let us make a new lament
And give to Mary this mantle.)

The text of *Levate gl'ochi* thus deserves special attention for its repeated references to the mantle brought to the Virgin and the implied action involving the holy women. Examination of the *lauda* text cannot provide more than circumstantial evidence or grounds for speculation, but, when supplemented by the information contained in the inventories of the confraternity that owned the *laudario,* these clues take on substance. The following entries extracted from these inventories include repeated references to the black mantle for Mary, the black coverings for the crucifix, and other items used for these devotions:

1412:
Also a book for saying the little Office. Also two books of *laude.*
Also one black mantle for Our Lady.

1427:
one black mantle for Our Lady and the black covering for the crucifix.

1429:
Also a black cover and black wrappings for the crucifix.
Also a black mantle for Our Lady.[84]

The entry for 1442, which specifies "also a sealed chest inside of which is the black mantle for the madonna," suggests that special respect was given to the costume now securely locked away.[85]

A similar set of documents exists from Gubbio, whose *disciplinati* had copied the statutes of San Stefano including the phrasing requiring the representation for the people and the mandato.[86] As in Assisi, the brothers could either remain and pray all night at the oratory, or they might go home, provided that they return promptly for the morning Office and the singing of *laude*.

Although various inventories of the Gubbian confraternities list a number of books of *laude*, the sole surviving *laudario* from this municipality is now MS. Landau 39 in the Biblioteca Nazionale in Florence.[87] Seven of its fifteen *laude* are common to one or more of the Assisi collections. The text *Levate gl'ochi* as it appears in the Gubbio version, however, is considerably longer than in MS. 705 from Assisi, but like its model it is supported by the inventory of the company which lists the properties needed for the *devozione,* including the black veil. While this inventory is clearly dated 1428, it is described by the copyist in the manuscript as "the new inventory," thus providing a confirmation of the existence of a previous one, now apparently lost.[88] The approximate date of the *laudario* is suggested by certain of its contents, which indicate that it was no earlier than 1337 since it contains three *laude* to Tomasso of Costacciaro, who died in that year and whose cult very quickly became popular in Gubbio where a church was erected in his honor.[89]

Extracts from the Gubbian inventory are usefully indicative of the extent to which these dramatic presentations had developed by the time of the *quattrocento*:

> Also two books of *laude* on vellum.
> Also one book of vellum which begins *Domina labia*.[90]
> Also two crosses of wood.
> Also one wooden dove.
> Also four pairs of wings.
> Also two crowns for the king and twelve crowns for the apostles.
> Also one book of *laude* on paper of cotton-wool.
> Also four beards.
> Also one black veil.
> Also one piece of black cloth to put over the crucifix.[91]

In addition to this fifteenth-century document, there exist from nearly a century earlier records which suggest an active musical life within the Gubbian company of Santa Maria della misericordia (del marcato).[92] The accounts of this company note payments to professional singers (*cantoribus* or *cantadore*) for singing *laude* at various services. There were also payments of wine for singers whose names recur repeatedly: Massolo (nicknamed "*delle laude*"), Sabatuccio, Ceccolo, Petruccio, Mattei, and Andrea. These men are also identified as "the singers who sing the Passion on the day of Good Friday."[93]

Such records not only corroborate the dramatic developments suggested by the texts of the *laude*, but also underscore the real necessity in our methodology of consulting documents and other non-musical sources. However, remarkable as these indications of dramatization are, exaggerated claims for involvement in religious theater should be avoided, for the rule of San Stefano, like those patterned after it, demonstrates that such *rappresentazione* were the exception and that they occurred only once each year on Good Friday.[94]

The number of dramatic *laude* contained in the earliest of the Assisi collections is small, yet the ordines (Cathedral Library, MSS. 20 and 21) decree that while *laude* of the Passion should be sung on Fridays and other days commemorating the sufferings of Christ, on Sundays or feast days the *lauda* proper to the day or feast should be sung.[95] MS. 36/iv from Assisi may have been compiled in an effort to provide such a liturgically complete cycle for the use of the confraternity of San Stefano.[96] It is the only known example from Assisi to be thus organized, and, like the large Perugian manuscripts, it distinguishes between the *laude liriche* for feasts of saints and *laude evangelici* which are dramatic texts elaborating on the Gospel of the day. This proliferation of new *laude*, now representing different types and functions, necessitated the compilation of ordines and rituals to codify the ceremonial aspects of worship. Thus the *lauda* repertoire became to the laity what the Missal and Breviary were to the clergy. Gradually Marian hymns of the early repertoire were outnumbered by the *laude* to the saints and the dramatic representations of the Gospel, and, like the liturgy of the Church, the observances of the *disciplinati* began to manifest a sense of ritual arrangement over a broad expanse of time. In effect, the *fratelli* now possessed what might be described as a marginal liturgy with its own Office and its own music.

The largest and most significant collections of dramatic *laude* are contained in the two Perugian *laudari* of the fourteenth century (Perugia, Biblioteca Comunale Augusta, MS. 955, and Rome, Biblioteca Vallicelliana, MS. A26) and the early-fifteenth-century *laudario* from Orvieto (Rome, Biblioteca Nazionale Centrale Vittorio Emanuele II, MS. 527).[97] All three manuscripts manifest a sense of liturgical progression and allow for some slight variations in the conception and also for occasional interpolations in the form of such confraternity business as registers or necrologies.[98] Although the two Perugian manuscripts share many texts in common, the Sant'Andrea *laudario* is believed to provide the most authentic readings.[99] The distinction between texts intended for devotion within the oratory and those directed to a general audience is even more clearly delineated in these collections where the lyric *laude* were evidently reserved for the use of the brothers sequestered in the privacy of their own meeting place, while the dramatic *laude* were motivated by a broader apostolic concern since they were intended for the general public. The confraternity records as well as civic records demonstrate that by the third decade of the *trecento* the flagellants in Perugia were regularly performing these dramatic *laude* in public on Sundays and holy days throughout the year.[100]

The extent to which the dramatic elements were developed by this time is illustrated by the impressive Last Judgment scene in the Advent play of the Sant'Andrea manuscript. The play begins with an Antichrist episode (96 verses) which includes a dramatization of the Signs of Doomsday, then moves to the central segment of the drama which takes place at the judgment seat of Christ (240 verses), and finally is completed by a hell scene (54 verses). It has been suggested that the dimensions of the play and the unusual stage effects which it required were inspired by the subject matter, which would need to be impressive to be effective--"its large and varied cast that includes several choruses--the People of Jerusalem, the Blessed, the Damned, the Demons; for its *messa in scena* that involves a three-level acting area for its simultaneous representation of heaven, earth, and hell; and for its many unusual theatrical effects." Further, "[i]n the course of the Antichrist episode, for example, rubrics and text indicate the following: the sun darkens, the moon turns to blood, stars fall from heaven, withered trees blossom, thunder sounds, [and] Gabriel strikes Antichrist with a fiery sword."[101]

These dramatizations are hardly mere excuses for theatrical indulgence--i.e., for a spectacle--for the works themselves have merit as skilfully fashioned dramatic structures. While the didactic intent of the message was important as a means of conveying to the people the lessons of repentance through, for example, the Last Judgment, such a play was also closely linked to the devotional life. The scenes of the drama were intended to motivate individuals to thoughts of their own personal penance and thereby to a richer spiritual existence.

The longest drama contained in the Sant'Andrea manuscript is *Signore scribe*, a Passion play intended to be performed on Good Friday. Although this drama is generally faithful to the scriptural account of St. John's Gospel which is the prescribed reading for Mass in the liturgy of that day, it does at times substitute episodes from the synoptic Gospels with the effect of occasionally scrambling the chronological sequence of events.[102] Here, as in the Judgment play, the scenes move from place to place--the cenacle, the Mount of Olives, the Court of Pilate. Often the movement takes place with very little or no dialogue at all--a characteristic that suggests the possible use of mime.[103] In contrast to the rapid traversing of time and space in the first portion of the play, the second part (120 verses) is more static and consists of lyric lamentations in which Christ, Mary, John, Magdalene, and the holy women participate. Thus this segment has much in common with the laments which figure so prominently in the *lauda* collections of Assisi.[104]

Curiously, neither this long play nor the shorter Passion play in the same manuscript dramatizes the central act of Good Friday, the Crucifixion. The shorter play, *Quista vesta*, indeed begins after Christ's death with the casting of lots for his garment. As Kathleen Falvey has pointed out, however, the scourging of Jesus becomes the pivotal point, a "carefully choreographed transition between the two parts of the play," which serves to emphasize that very aspect of the Passion that constituted the primary devotion of the *disciplinati*, the act of flagellation."[105] It is no wonder, then, that *Signore scribe* should be included in so many other Umbrian collections that belonged to *disciplinati*. Not only does it appear in the other large Perugian collection (Rome, Biblioteca Vallicelliana, MS. A26), but it is found in at least three of the main sources from Assisi--Cathedral Library, MSS. 36/ii and 36/iv, and Rome, Biblioteca Nazionale Centrale Vittoria Emanuele, MS. 478. While there are some differences, a comparison of the texts reaffirms the important position of the Assisi versions as a transitional stage in the development of the play. The reading in MS. 478 enumerates fewer characters than the Perugian versions, but it specifies seven choruses: Jews, Scribes, Pharisees, Priests, Ministers, Disciples, and Holy Women. However, the version contained in the Sant'Andrea *laudario* is unique because of its extensive marginalia which not only identify characters but also provide some stage directions-- e.g., "here the judges move Christ to Pilate," "then the cock crows," "here Pilate washes his hands"[106] (see fig. 3).

The large number of characters required in the dramatizations of the Perugian *laude*, and also the numerous rubrics which tend to fragment stanzas into more diversified exchange of dialogue than is common in the Assisi manuscripts, may suggest some questions concerning the performance of these texts. Is it possible that the more rapid exchange of dialogue might have necessitated the spoken recitation of the *lauda* rather than the actual singing of the text? Because no music was ever written out for these sources, we may be tempted to inquire whether they were in fact entirely sung or whether they included spoken dialogue. However, the Perugian *laudari* and the somewhat later *laudario* of Orvieto (Rome, Biblioteca Nazionale Centrale Vittoria Emanuele, MS. 527) contain evidence that at least some of the texts were actually sung, since the rubrics frequently prescribe melodic types--e.g., *ad modum paschalem* (for Sundays and joyful feast days) and *ad modum passionalem* (for times of penitence). The Orvieto manuscript contains seventeen examples of *laude* in the paschal mode and thirteen in the Passion mode. Those bearing the rubric *pasquale* most often are written in the form of the *ballata maggiore* with alternating septenaries and hendecasyll-ables having a rhyme scheme of aBaBbCcX, while those indicated *passionale* follow the pattern of the *sestina semplice*, having eight or nine syllables to a verse, with a rhyme scheme of ababcc). Since no musical notation as such survives in these manuscripts, the meaning of the designations cannot be reconstructed with precision, but there is reason to believe that the melodies intended here were derived from the respective liturgies of Easter and Holy Week.[107]

Since the number of characters indicated in the rubrics of certain of the dramatic *laude* was large, the confraternities sponsoring these dramatic representations began to accumulate a store of properties and costumes, the extent of which is indicated by the surviving inventories and account books. The Archivio Pio Sodalizio Braccio Fortebracci in Perugia is a rich depository of such documents, which help to illustrate the theatrical activities of the three major companies of *disciplinati* in that city--San Agostino, San Domenico, and San Francesco.[108] The oldest of the inventories of which we know was that of 1339, though this is now lost; fortunately, extracts from it were preserved by Ernesto Monaci.[109] While there is no way of ascertaining whether there was a line of unbroken continuity in theatrical practice by the confraternity of San Domenico which owned it, a much later document belonging to the same company nevertheless suggests that these dramatic representations remained an important part of its apostolate. A set of deliberations from 20 March 1513 charges the company to elect two qualified members who, along with the prior, should provide for the construction of "a theater in the church of St. Dominic . . . for the presentation of the Passion of Our Lord Jesus Christ."[110]

Another manuscript, dated in the fifteenth century, from the same archives, the *Libro di prestançe* of the company of Sant'Agostino, lists theatrical furnishings--equipment, costumes, and properties--which were owned by that confraternity but which were available to other companies on loan. Representative entries are extracted as follows (see figs. 4-5):

> 1427:
> These are the things which we loaned to the men of the confraternity of San Domenico. . . .
> Four tunics: green, yellow, and blue, and the other of red and blue.
> One small blue curtain with blue fringe.
> Three small red and blue striped curtains.
> One hat of rabbit fur for the king.
> One crown of brass for the king.
> One golden orb with a scepter for the king.
> Five beards and five wigs.
> One pointed hat of silk painted with lilies.
> Three silk veils with beautiful hats for the Marys.
> One beautiful veil of cotton wool with a cap.
> One long black beard with a wig.[111]

> 1441:
> These are the things taken by the fraternity of San Domenico for the *devozione* or *rappresentazione* of death. . . . In the first place,

> The cloak
> The scythe
> an hour glass   } Death
> the hand

And for the *devozione* of the Passion:
>Four short tunics [?surplices].
>One yellow cope.
>Two albs without collars, with an amice.
>Ten wigs: five beautiful, five ordinary.
>Seven beards.
>One flesh-colored garment with stockings.
>One pair of flesh-colored stockings of leather.
>Seven gold angel crowns.[112]

Summary. In spite of the lack of any major collection of *laude* with musical notation from the fifteenth century, there is sufficient evidence that the singing of *laude* remained an unbroken tradition among the *disciplinati* as well as the *laudesi* throughout those years. Documents surveyed in this study support such a view and also furnish evidence of the growth of the practice as the religious confraternities themselves developed. In spite of some signs of decline in the popular singing of *laude* among the *laudesi* as outlined in the previous chapter, the activities of the lay confraternities were expanding throughout the late fourteenth and fifteenth centuries. The *laudesi* continued their processions, which were by this time frequently held in church. And, in Florence particularly, the participation of the confraternities in the mounting of religious spectacles, which were elaborately staged and enriched with both singing and instrumental music, is a well-documented fact. Moreover, the records of the *laudesi* testify to their concern for the quality of performance. Significantly, among the expenditures for professional singers and instrumentalists noted in the present chapter and the previous one, all except one payment are by the *laudesi*, not by the *disciplinati*.[113] The *disciplinati,* however, left a legacy of a different sort from the *laudesi*. Their activities fell into two categories, as we have seen: the private *devozione* in the oratory which in time gave rise to a fully developed Office including the singing of *laude*, and their dramatic representations, involving some theatrical innovation, for the public. Ceremonials, ordines, and other documents of the *disciplinati* confraternities yield considerable information about performance practice--e.g., indications of solo, responsorial, and antiphonal singing. While it is true that the *laudesi* also contributed to the development of the *rappresentazione*, their dramas were more focused on theatrical spectacle and less concerned with the object of inspiring penance than were the productions of the Umbrian *disciplinati*. Moreover, while many of the texts of the flagellant plays have survived, there is nothing in the records to suggest that these were mounted with the sumptuousness and splendor of the spectacles staged by the Florentine *laudesi*. Conversely, the *laudesi* documents are rich in details that illustrate their contribution to the scenographic aspect of the Italian theater.

A careful distinction is to be made between the role of the *lauda* itself in the theatrical productions of the *laudesi* and the function of this music in the representations of the *disciplinati* confraternities. To equate the dramatic *laude* of the Umbrian school with the *lauda* in the *sacre rappresentazione* of Florence would constitute a serious error. The *laude drammatiche* of the flagellant companies of Umbria gradually effected an organic change in the genre itself, for they apparently moved from monologue to dialogue performance and eventually became fully staged. Thus the dramatic *lauda* became the play, while the hymns of the *laudesi* companies were, on the contrary, inserted into the *rappresentazione* as embellishments left intact--a desirable ornament, a musical moment employed to heighten the climactic points of the drama to which it remained only ancillary. Yet both types of production--and both types of *lauda*--were to be important to the history of the theater in Italy.

3

The Musical Documents: Cortona 91

The number of extant *lauda* manuscripts has been esti-
mated to be well over two hundred, and there are more that are
still preserved in small provincial towns that once were the
seat of some confraternity.[1] The place of primacy among the
manuscripts must, of course, be accorded to the two that are
unique in containing melodies to which the *laude* were sung--
the thirteenth-century Cortona *laudario*, Cortona, Biblioteca
del comune, MS. 91,[2] and the fourteenth-century codex
Magliabechiano (Mgl[1]), Florence, Biblioteca nazionale
centrale, MS. II I 122 (Banco Rari 18).[3] Those manuscripts
which preserve only the words without the music are nevertheless invaluable for the collating of texts, and often the adapta-
tions and emendations which occur in them reflect important
transformations occurring within the confraternities themselves.

Although the two manuscripts which contain music have
customarily been discussed together, they are in some respects
very different. Both, to be sure, utilize a rather enigmatic
musical notation, the interpretation of which has been the
subject of some controversy, and both have a number of *laude*
in common.[4] The earlier of the two, the Cortona *laudario*, has
been vested with a certain degree of mystery since 1876, when
it was discovered by Girolamo Mancini, curator of the
Biblioteca del comune.[5] The manuscript, in poor condition,
was found in a tiny room used for the storage of coal and
kindling wood. The book was disbound, and lacked title page
or identification; the years of neglect and abuse had taken their

toll, as may be observed from the badly deteriorated first folios (see fig. 6).

The Cortona manuscript, which comprises 171 folios in two discrete sections, is written in a large gothic hand. The earlier portion (fols. 1r-120v) contains forty-five *laude* which, with the exception of No. 5, are all provided with musical notation and are all in the same hand. Folios 121-22 are virtually blank, though they contain discernible traces of some rather primitive drawings. Folios 123-32 contain two additional *laude* with music, *Benedicti e llaudati* and *Salutiam divotamenti*, which are the work of a different scribe. Though included in the first section, these laude were not part of the original design, for folios 133r-135v contain an index of the collection which ends with No. 45, *Amor dolce, sença pare*, the final *lauda* in the hand of the original scribe.

The second section of the manuscript, written by a less accomplished scribe and without music, contains the texts of nineteen *laude*[6] (see fig. 7). The poems are varied in form and subject, and they do not reflect any particular plan with regard to the order of their presentation. Several have dialogue, and No. 57, *Un piangere amoroso lamentando*, is a plaint reminiscent of the Umbrian laments to which reference has been made above. Franciscan influence is evident in several examples (Nos. 51, 58, 62), and although there is no mention of flagellation to suggest the use of the manuscript by a *disciplinati* company, No. 52 on death reaches a level of realism not found elsewhere in the collection.

Neither segment of the manuscript contains illuminations, although the first (and presumably older) part of the book is ornamented with initials executed alternately in red and blue. The musical notation, found only in the earlier section, is written in square black notation resembling plainsong, on four-line staves of red with vertical lines of red marking off the margins. Graceful arabesques of red decorate the left-hand margins above and below the initials. The first strophe of the text appears in each case as underlay with the music, and all the subsequent stanzas are then placed at the end of the piece.

The organization of the first part of the manuscript into four distinct sections provides that sixteen Marian *laude* appear first, possibly on the basis of chronology since their style suggests early origin. These are then followed by two seemingly misplaced *laude* (Nos. 17-18) to St. Catherine of Alexandria (fols. 36v-38r) and St. Mary Magdalene (fols. 38v-39v). *Lauda* No. 19 begins the second section, the liturgical cycle from Christmas through Trinity Sunday. The absence of any *laude* for Advent may at first seem curious, but the Last Judgment theme of the liturgy for the first Sunday in Advent is developed primarily in *disciplinati* manuscripts of the *trecento*, often in dramatic fashion, and is rarely found in the *laudesi* repertoire. However, the Marian *laude* which precede the liturgical cycle may nevertheless have functioned as Advent hymns, for they are filled with allusions to the Virgin birth, stressing the role of Mary in the Incarnation. On the other hand, the placement of the *lauda* honoring St. Catherine may also be significant, for her feast was celebrated on 25 November, four weeks prior to the feast of the Nativity and therefore coinciding approximately with the beginning of Advent. No such easy explanation comes to mind for the *lauda* to Mary Magdalene, however, since her feast occurs in July. Thus Varanini[7] advanced the theory that the inclusion of these two *laude* was a scribal mistake: since the *lauda* to Catherine begins with the words *Vergine donçella*, possibly the scribe mistakenly thought that it was a hymn in praise of the Blessed Virgin Mary. The *lauda* to the Magdalene then might have been added in order to provide another item of the same type and to insure that the one *lauda* would not stand in isolation in the collection. There was, however, a lively devotion to both Catherine and the Magdalene among the early Franciscans, and their importance in this regard may have been a factor in the choice of these *laude*.[8]

Following the *lauda* to the Trinity which concludes the liturgical cycle is the third section, a group of four *laude* which are distinctly different from the others in both content and style. Because of their didacticism and for lack of a better term, they might be called "homiletic." Yet such a designation does not denote a homogeneous grouping, for the four hymns are quite different from each other. Although they are probably the most affective of the entire manuscript, they are nevertheless removed from the realism found in the *laude* of some of the later flagellant confraternities. Finally, there is a fourth section, a group of miscellaneous *laude* to saints. Unlike most fourteenth-century collections, including the Magliabechiano codex, which are rich in hymns to saints, the Cortona *laudario* contains only a few--too few to resemble anything like a sanctoral cycle. In addition to those already noted, the only saints represented here are either figures from the New Testament or Franciscan saints. The hymns honoring such biblical figures as John the Baptist or John the Evangelist adhere closely to Scripture, whereas those to the other saints lean heavily on popular legend. The two *laude* to St. Francis exhibit a familiarity with both the historical accounts of the saint's life and popular legends, while that to St. Catherine and one of the two to Magdalene are unmistakably indebted to the *Legenda Aurea* of Jacobus de Voragine.[9]

The texts included in the Cortona *laudario* represent an effort to set something down in writing that had been essentially an orally transmitted poetry and to do so in a tongue which was not yet established as a literary language. As will be found to be characteristic of writings in the emerging vernacular, the orthography is irregular. Similarly, the amanuensis of the music was forced to adapt neumes derived from Gregorian notation. The music abounds with inaccuracies arising from the lack of proper alignment of the text underlay with the musical notation, and from misplaced clefs and lack of agreement between clef and custos. But a far more complicated problem facing the transcriber of the music was the lack of symbols denoting duration--a circumstance which has led to various theories and some dubious solutions that will be taken up below.

The shapes of the *virga* and *punctum* are presented more or less indiscriminately, and the ligatures employed are *binariae, ternariae, quaternariae*, and sometimes larger--up to *nonariae*. These longer ligatures are less frequent, however, and attempts to transcribe them into modal rhythm have not proven satisfactory. Some of the variations in ligature forms which are used to express exactly the same melodic figure are shown in Example 1, below.

Example 1: Variations of Ligature Form in Cortona 91

A. *Lauda* No. 10

fol. 22ᵛ--first system

fol. 22ᵛ--second and third systems

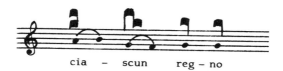

fol. 22ᵛ--third and fourth systems

B. *Lauda* No. 27

    fol. 58r--second system

    fol. 58r--third system

C. *Lauda* No. 39

    fol. 96v--third system

    fol. 97r--first system

Table 1.A (pp. 68-70 below) lists the *laude* contained in Cortona 91, in the order in which they appear in the manuscript. The first portion of the codex--the *laude* with musical notation--is tabulated in 1.A, while 1.B lists the *laude* in the second part of the collection. While the numbering of the *laude* is in agreement with that of Varanini, Liuzzi's numbering is nevertheless included here for reference. The discrepancy arises from Liuzzi's failure to assign a number to No. 5, *Ave Maria, gratia plena*, which lacks music, nor does he provide any numbering for the second portion of the manuscript, which also is without music.

Provenance. Although the Cortona *laudario* has been established as having belonged to the Confraternita di Santa Maria delle laude attached to the church of San Francesco in Cortona, the *laude* contained in it have not been identified as distinctively Cortonese in origin. Varanini argues that Cortona 91 is likely to have been copied from the *protolaudario* which he believes to have been of Sienese origin.[10] Thus the *laudario* should probably be regarded as a collection of popular hymns from the general area of Siena, Arezzo, and Cortona which was compiled by a scribe associated with the confraternity. He was more than likely a cleric of some erudition and almost certainly a Franciscan. However, other internal evidence in the texts also will shed a certain amount of light on the question of origin and the dating of the manuscript--evidence which was not fully explored by Liuzzi.

The study of the provenance of the Cortona *laudario* must begin with a consideration of the history of the city of Cortona, which, though dating from Etruscan times, enjoyed a significant development in the first half of the thirteenth century. This period of development was also contemporary with the early years of the Franciscan establishment there not very long after the inception of the Order in Assisi.[11] In 1210 Francis himself had gone to Cortona to preach to the people of the city, among whom was Guido Vagnotelli who, according to the annals of the Order, in the following year distributed his possessions to the poor, donated his property outside the city to Francis for use as a hermitage, and received the habit from the saint himself.[12] The vitality of the Order in Cortona is attested by both material monuments and documents that establish the transference of property to the Franciscans. Throughout the thirteenth century and well into the next century the activities of the Friars Minor there were closely linked with the growth of lay confraternal life in the city, and the records sometimes provide a link with the

Table 1.A. - Cortona *Laudario*: Table of Contents

Part I: *Laude* with Text and Music

Number in: Varanini	Liuzzi		Incipit	Argument	Manuscript Reference	Final R	F
1	1		Venite a laudare	Praise of Mary	1r-3v	g	g
2	2		Lauda novella sia cantata	Praise of Mary	3v-5v	d	d
3	3	*	Ave, donna santissima	Praise of Mary	5v-8v	d	d
4	4		Madonna santa Maria	Prayer to Mary	8v-10r	e	
5	4bis †		Ave Maria, gratia plena	Annunciation	10r-12v	-	-
6	5		Ave, regina gloriosa	Praise of Mary	12v-14v	d	d
7	6	*	Da ciel venne messo novello	Annunciation	14v-17r	d	d
8	7	*	Altissima luce--col grande splendore	Praise of Mary	17r-19v	f	d
9	8		Fami cantar l'amor di la beata	Praise of Mary	19v-22r	d	d
10	9		O Maria--d'omelia	Praise of Mary	22r-24r	c	g
11	10	*	Regina sovrana--de gram pietade	Praise of Mary	24r-25v	f	d
12	11		Ave, Dei genitrix	Praise of Mary	25v-27r	d	d
13	12		O Maria, Dei cella	Praise of Mary	27r-29r	f	f
14	13		Ave, vergene gaudente	Praise of Mary	29r-32v	f	f
15	14		O divina virgo, flore	Praise of Mary	32v-34v	g	g
16	15		Salve, salve, virgo pia	Praise of Mary	34v-36v	f	f
17	16	*	Vergine donçella da Dio amata	Catherine of Alexandria	36v-38r	c	b
18	17	+	Peccatrice, nominata	Mary Magdalene	38v-39v	d	f
19	18	+	Cristo è nato--et humanato	Nativity of Christ	39v-43v	g	g
20	19	+	Gloria 'n cielo e pace 'n terra	Nativity of Christ	43v-44v	f	c
21	20		Stella nuova 'n fra la gente	Epiphany	45r-46r	g	g
22	21		Plangiamo quel crudel basciar(e)	The Passion of Christ	46v-47v	g	g
23	22	+	Ben è crudel e spietoso	The Passion of Christ	47v-51r	f	f
24	23		De la crudel morte de Cristo	The Passion of Christ	51r-53r	d	d
25	24		Dami conforto, Dio, et alegrança	The Passion of Christ	53r-55r	c	c
26	25	*	Onne homo ad alta voce	The Holy Cross	55r-57v	a	a
27	26	*	Iesù Cristo glorioso	The Resurrection	57v-60r	g	g
28	27	+	Laudamo la resurrectione	The Resurrection and Ascension	60r-63r	g	g
29	28		Spiritu Sancto, dolçe amore	The Holy Spirit	63r-64v	g	g

Number	in:		Incipit	Argument	Manuscript Reference	Final	
Varanini	Liuzzi					R	F
30	29	+	Spirito Sancto glorioso	The Holy Spirit	64ᵛ-68ʳ	f	f
31	30	+	Spirito Sancto, dà servire	Pentecost	68ʳ-69ᵛ	d	d
32	31	+	Alta Trinità beata	Holy Trinity	70ʳ-72ʳ	c	c
33	32		Troppo perde l tempo ki ben non t'ama	The love of Christ	72ʳ-82ᵛ	d	d
34	33		Stomme allegro et latioso	Admonition to penance	82ᵛ-85ʳ	f	g
35	34		Oimè lasso e freddo lo mio core	Admonition to penance	85ᵛ-88ᵛ	d	d
36	35	+	Chi vol(e) lo mondo despreçcare	Death	88ᵛ-90ʳ	f	f
37	36		Laudar vollio per amore	St. Francis	90ᵛ-93ʳ	d	d
38	37	*	Sia laudato San Francesco	St. Francis	93ʳ-96ʳ	g	g
39	38	*	Ciascun ke fede sente	St. Anthony of Padua	96ʳ-100ᵛ	d	d
40	39		Magdalena, degna da laudare	Mary Magdalene	100ᵛ-110ᵛ	d	d
41	40		L'alto prençe archangelo lucente	Michael the Archangel	110ᵛ-112ᵛ	f	f
42	41	*	Faciamo laude a tutt'i sancti	All Saints	112ᵛ-114ᵛ	a	g
43	42		San Iovanni al mond'è nato	John the Baptist	114ᵛ-116ʳ	g	f
44	43	+	Ogn'om canti novel canto	St. John the Evangelist	116ʳ-117ᵛ	f	f
45	44	**	Amor dolçe sença pare	The love of Christ	117ᵛ-120ᵛ	g	g

Added *laude* with music

46	45		Benedicti e llaudati	The Apostles	123ʳ-131ᵛ	d	d
47	46		Salutiam divotamente	The Annunciation	131ᵛ-132ᵛ	f	g

* Music and text in Mgl¹ (normally with variants)

+ Text in Mgl¹ (abbreviated and with different music)

** Music in Mgl¹ (with different texts)

† Incomplete

Table 1.B. - Cortona *Laudario*: Table of Contents

Part II: Texts lacking music

Varanini	Incipit	Argument	MS Reference
48	Alleluia, alleluia--alto re di gloria	Praise of the Father, Son, and B.V.M.	136[r]
49	Salutiamo divotamente	The Annunciation	137[r]
50	Ave Maria, gratia plena	Virgin Mary	138[r]
51	Allegramente e de buon core con fede	Margaret of Cortona	139[r]
52	Quando t'alegri--homo d'altura	Death	141[r]
53	Innante che venga--la morte si scura	Death	142[r]
54	A voi, gente, faciam prego	Call to penance	143[r]
55	Gente pietosa--amirate a Maria	Marian lament	144[r]
56	Salve, regina di gran cortesia	Prayer to Mary	144[v]
57	Un piangere amoroso lamentando	Marian lament	146[r]
58	Laudiamo Iesu, lo figliuol de Maria	Mary and various saints	160[r]
59	Chi vole che'l suo amare accepto sia	Prayer to Mary	161[r]
60	A tucte l'ore sia laudato	Michael Archangel	163[r]
61	Ciascuno canti novello canto	Eucharist	164[r]
62	Nuovo canto sia cantato	Guido Vagnotelli	164[v]
63	Onne homo laudi con amore	St. Mark the Evangelist	165[v]
64	Tucti del buono core	Virgin Mary	166[v]
65	Vergene conçella sete	The Life of Mary, the Annunciation to Crucifixion	167[v]
66	Ben voiglio laudare tucta la mia vita	Praise of St. Lucy	170[v]

enigmatic figure of Brother Elias of Cortona (d. 1253), whom Francis had appointed as his successor in 1221.[13]   Certain details of Elias' life are thus of some importance to this study.

After Elias had been deposed as general of the Order in 1239, he passed his time alternately between his home town of Cortona and the court of Frederick II. At one time he had been sent by Gregory IX as papal legate to the Emperor. Attracted by the intellectual climate of the Emperor's court, Elias sought asylum there after his great humiliation. By 1240 he was fighting in the ranks of Frederick's army--an open transference of allegiance from the Pope to the Emperor which resulted in his excommunication.[14] On his periodic returns to Cortona, Elias was followed by various intellectuals of the court of Frederick--a fact of some significance because the court was the center of the so-called Sicilian school of poetry and had also become, after the siege of Toulouse in 1218, the refuge of several troubadours. But there were others who followed Elias to Cortona as well. *The Chronicle of the Twenty-Four Generals* reports that some friars remained faithful to the deposed general,[15] and that among them was one Giovanni *delle laude*, so designated because of his ability to compose in that genre.[16] The identity of this lay brother is well established in various sources of early Franciscan history, and he is perhaps best known for having been selected by Francis himself to care for him after he had received the stigmata.[17] In spite of his close association with Francis, however, he would remain a faithful follower of Elias, and very probably his sojourn in Cortona corresponded with the time when the *lauda* repertoire was developing there.

Salimbene speaks of several other Franciscan friars in the region who were gifted in both performance and composition, and specifically names Enrico da Pisa, Vita Lucchese, Giovanni da Parma, Giacomino Olle da Parma, Bonagiunto da Fabriano, Guidolino da Parma, and Guglielmo Piemontese.[18] Elsewhere he gives vent to his dislike of Elias, however, and makes numerous allegations against the deposed general. Though Salimbene engaged in a certain level of distortion of the facts with regard to him, there is some truth in his assertion that Elias showed favor to the laity. But this favor brought him support from the townspeople, who gave donations to the early friars. Under Elias, the Franciscans in Cortona cared for the sick of the city, buried the dead in the cemetery of the Order, assumed the direction of a group of *laudesi,* and supplied an oratory for them.[19]

This oratory was incorporated into the church of San Francesco which Elias built in Cortona. In 1244, shortly after his second excommuncation, Frederick sent him on a mission to Constantinople from whence he brought back to Cortona a large relic of the true cross.[20] Upon his return, the people of the city presented to him the plot of land known as Bagno della Regina; here with characteristic dispatch Elias set about building a church that was to enshrine the relic which, according to the Bollandists, was reputed to be one of the largest known. The church, which would be dedicated to St. Francis, was under construction already before the end of the year 1245.[21]

The oratory beneath the church seems, however, to have been abandoned and eventually forgotten until its rediscovery in 1887. The commune had ordered a search for the bones of Luca Signorelli (1450-1523), a native son who was believed to have been buried in the church of San Francesco. While the excavations failed to discover any remains of this artist, the digging nevertheless led to the small subterranean chapel of the *laudesi*. The chapel was identified as part of the original building which had been completed between 1245 and 1250. Like the great basilica of St. Francis in Assisi which Elias had also built, the little church is a double structure. The lower portion had been walled up in the sixteenth century when the interior of the upper church was renovated and four large altars installed along the lateral walls of the nave.[22] After the excavations of 1887, the oratory was again closed, but one small reminder of it still may be seen in the slightly rounded arch of a door frame protruding above the pavement to the left of the entrance of the church (fig. 8).

Thus the question of the identity of the confraternity to which the oratory belonged becomes important. The town of Cortona had a number of such societies, which are noted in Ridolfini's *Historia di Cortona*, while the communal library contains statutes and other documents of various confraternities, among them one which called itself the Compagnia di Santa Croce del 1300.[23] The very name of this company of the Holy Cross invites speculation concerning its possible relationship with the *laudario* which contains a splendid hymn (No. 26) in honor of the Holy Cross (see Example 2, below). Both the refrain and the first stanza of the *lauda* take note of *la verace croce*, while the final strophe gives mention to the fraternity. It is very likely that the words *verace croce* were intended quite literally to refer to the relic of the true cross at Cortona. However tempting such a connection may seem, the statutes of the Compagnia di Sancta Croce demonstrate that the fraternity was one of *disciplinati*.[24] The *laudario*, on the

Example 2

Lauda No. 26, Cortona 91, fols. 55r-57v

To preserve the mode, the clef before the word *verace* in the last system required moving from the second to the third line, thus making it analogous to the second line of the refrain.

other hand, contains no mention of flagellation, and further-more the hymns are of the devotional type characteristic of *laudesi* confraternities.   Unfortunately, no statutes of the company of Santa Maria delle laude which owned the *laudario* have survived.

Four of the *laude* in the Cortona codex (Nos. 8, 14, 30, 45) contain reference at the end to one Garço who is believed to have been the author and who, according to Liuzzi and Nino Pirrotta among others, may have been the paternal great-grand-father of the poet Petrarch.[25]   The recent research of Varanini and his colleagues, however, challenges this theory since if the "Gartius" referred to by Petrarch in the third book of the *Familiari* were the same Garço of our manuscript, he would have been over ninety years of age at the time when the *laude* were composed.   His name appears in the text *Santa Chiara sia laudata* (in Florence, Biblioteca Riccardiana, MS. 1802) which expressly speaks of St. Clare's canonization, an event that occurred in 1255.[26]   Moreover, the name Garço (Garzo, Garso, or Garçone) appears in various other manuscript sources as well.[27]   The evidence accords with Varanini's belief that Siena was most likely the center from which the *laude* were dissemi-nated, that Garço, probably a talented poet-composer, was active in the early development of the *lauda* repertoire, and that his name was simply retained in the poems as they were copied by a later scribe.

Liuzzi thought that the *lauda Troppo perd'l tempo ke ben non t'ama* (No. 33) was the work of Jacopone da Todi, and noted as well that No. 26, which breaks into dialogue in stanzas 8-13, bears resemblance to that author's famed *Donna del Paradiso*. The latter *lauda* text, which is representative of the type of complaint of the *Madre afflitta*, is preserved, though in texts that involve a number of variants, in various *lauda* collections.   However, it should be remembered that there is a large body of pseudo-Jacopone literature from the Middle Ages.   More important than actual ascription of individual *laude* to Jacopone, therefore, is the matter of the many clues to Franciscan influence to be found in the *laudario*--clues which reveal an affinity in subject matter and even in imagery to much early Franciscan preaching and devotional literature. As noted above, the theology of the early Franciscans placed great emphasis upon the humanity of Christ and upon the important role of Mary in the redemptive plan. Of the forty-five *laude* in the first portion of the Cortona manuscript, fully two-thirds are devoted to such mysteries as these.

In the thirteenth century, religious orders retained the right to alter their liturgical practices and to make changes in the ordinances by which they were governed. Perhaps the best-known influence of the Franciscans upon the liturgy was the abridgement of the Roman Office, a change which was necessitated by the nature of mendicant life.[28] Also important was the introduction of new feasts, which eventually found their way into the Roman calendar as a result of having been popularized by the Franciscans. The Visitation (see *lauda* No. 43), for example, was observed by the Order for nearly a century and a half before Urban VI extended it to the universal Church in 1390. And while the actual celebration of the feast of the Trinity has been traced as early as the seventh century and Stephen of Liège composed an Office for it in the tenth century, the Franciscans must be given credit for revising that Office and for popularizing it in the Middle Ages.[29]

The texts of the two *laude* that treat St. Francis display fidelity to historical and legendary sources, and thus repeat the well-known tales of the saint's love of the Creation, his sermon to the birds, and other famous stories. Additionally, both texts refer to the establishment of three orders, while *Sia laudato San Francesco* (No. 38) even devotes a complete stanza to each, including one to the Third Order Secular, the tertiaries.

Strophe 7   A laude de la Trinitade
              l'ordine tre da lui plantate

75

per lo mondo delatate
fanno fructo cun alore. (fol. 94ᵛ)

(He founded three orders
in praise of the Trinity.
They flourished and bore fruit
throughout the world.)

Strophe 8   Li povari frati minori
de Cristo sono seguitatori:
de le gente son doctori
predicando sença errore. (fol. 94ᵛ)

(The poor Friars Minor
are followers of Christ,
teachers to all men,
preaching without error.)

Strophe 9   L'altre sono le pretiose
margarite gratiose,
Vergeni donne renchiuse
per amor del salvatore. (fol. 95ʳ)

(The others are the precious
and beautiful flowers,
virginal ladies, cloistered
for the love of the Savior.)

Strophe 10   E li frati continenti,
coniugati penitenti,
stand'al mondo santamente
per servire al Creatore. (fol. 95ʳ)

(And the celibate brothers,
married penitents, remain
saintly in the world, in order
to serve the Creator.)

Perhaps even more important in establishing Franciscan connections in the *laude* in the Cortona *laudario* is *Ciascun ke fede sente* (No. 39), in honor of St. Anthony of Padua. The anonymous poet responsible for this text not only betrays familiarity with the events of the saint's life but also actually borrows language from some of the earliest sources of Franciscana. Anthony's story is not told in the *Legenda Aurea*, but it was available through the *Legenda Prima seu Vita Antiqissima* as well as in the account of Julian of Speier in the work published in the *Acta Sanctorum* under the title *Vita auctore anonymo valde antiquo*.[30]

At the time that the Bollandists compiled their *vita* of Anthony, the oldest and most authentic legend of the saint had not yet been uncovered. Indeed, this legend was not to be found until 1888 when a Capuchin friar, Hilary of Paris, made the discovery in a monastery at Lucerne of the ancient copy of what now is known as the *Legenda Prima*. The manuscript had been copied in a woman's hand, probably by a poor Clare, and contains an inscription in Old High German declaring it to be the work of Katherine von Purchlausen. The manuscript is dated on the eve of the feast of St. Bartholomew (23 August) 1337.[31] Hilary's initial opinion was that the legend should be regarded as the the work of John of Peckham--an authorship which would have placed it as late as 1272. But it is now apparent that Vincent of Beauvais drew upon this old legend for his *Speculum Historiale*, as did Julian of Speier for his *Lives and Liturgical Offices of St. Francis and St. Anthony*.[32] Julian reproduced whole passages of the *Legenda Prima* in metric measures in the same manner as he had borrowed from Celano's *Legenda Prima* of St. Francis. Since Vincent died in 1264 and Julian in 1250, the legend must necessarily be dated prior to the middle of the thirteenth century. Also, the rhythmic Office was already in use in 1249, for John of Parma refers to it in a letter of that year, and it was likewise known to John Parenti who was Minister General of the Order from 1227 to 1232.[33] Moreover, as Raphael Huber points out in his excellent study of the sources for the life of St. Anthony, the chronicler Rolandino, who knew this saint personally, remarks in his *Liber Chronicarum de factus in Marchia Tarvesina*[34] (written about 1260) that the saint actually lived in the manner depicted "in his legend"--i.e., according to Huber, the *Legenda Prima*. Hence, Huber speculates, the *Legenda Prima* was very likely written at the time of Anthony's canonization in 1232.

The above digression demonstrates that the author of the *lauda* to St. Anthony had knowledge of at least one of these earliest sources, for the hymn shows strict fidelity to the legend in content, in the order of the presentation of the events in the narrative, and even in the actual language of the *Legenda Prima*. Of course, because Julian also borrowed from this source, we cannot be certain exactly which of the two versions was known to the poet of the *lauda*. But reliance on one of these sources rather than on later accounts is further demonstrated by the poet's failure to treat the active years of Anthony's apostolate in anything but the most general terms. It is noteworthy that the first stanza of the *lauda* refers to Anthony's origin in Portugal and cites in an off-hand way a pre-existing source: "D'Ulisbona si parte, se con'suna la legenda, la unde fo nato" ("He left Lisbon, so says the legend, there where he was born"). One of the most striking points of resemblance between the *lauda* and the early legend occurs at line 65 (fol. 99r), the point at which Anthony is called *archa testamenti*. The *Vita Antiquissima* reads: "Nempe enim talia et tam profunda de Scripturis facundo eructabat eloquio ut ab ipso domino papa, familiari quadam praerogativa, Arca Testamenti vocaretur."[35] Julian of Speier's text echoes the wording of the older legend: "Quam profunda vero de sacris eloqiis eructaret, summus ipse Romae Sedis Pontifex testabatur, a quo vir sanctus Arca Testamenti, peculiari quodam nomine, vocabatur."[36] The knowledge of Scripture, theology, Franciscan history, and legend required in order to produce these *lauda* texts, therefore, argues for strong Franciscan influence on the Cortona collection.

Since the discovery of the Cortona *laudario* a little more than a century ago, scholars have advanced various theories concerning its date. Its discoverer, Mancini, logically established the *terminus a quo* by citing the *laude* to Francis and Anthony as proof that the manuscript could not be dated prior to their deaths in 1226 and 1231 respectively. His argument for a *terminus ad quem* is less tenable. Since the segment which contains music contains no *lauda* for either Guido or Margaret--local saints whose cults were already very popular soon after their deaths[37]--he held that the earlier part of the *laudario* necessarily was copied during their lifetimes. Guido's *vita* in the *Acta Sanctorum* states that he was twenty years of age when he received the habit in 1211 and that he died at the age of sixty, which would fix the date of his death around 1247.[38] This accords with Wadding's statement that by 1250 there was already a vigorous cult in Guido's honor. From this evidence, Mancini deduced that the first part of the manuscript must have been compiled after the death of Anthony in 1231 and before that of Guido in c.1247, while the final segment of the manuscript would have been compiled after the death of Margaret in 1297.[39] The first scholar to object to Mancini's dating of the Cortona manuscript was Rodolfo Renier, who, on the basis of paleographic interpretation which has been now been discredited, assigned it to fourteenth-century *disciplinati* origin.[40] Shortly thereafter, Guido Mazzoni published an edition of texts, and in his notes he affirmed Renier's attribution of the manuscript to a flagellant confraternity. Mazzoni cited as evidence soiled spots on the manuscript which he believed to be wax drippings resulting from use during penitential processions.[41] Even if the spots are in fact wax, processions were one of the principal activities of the *laudesi*; hence his theory would seem to have been very shaky indeed. Appropriately, Mazzoni's theory was quickly challenged by Enrico Bettazzi who, like Mancini earlier, assigned the *laudario* to a group of *laudesi*.[42]

These disputes, typical of scholarship of the late years of the nineteenth century, are marked by an almost total disregard for that feature which above all sets Cortona 91 apart from all other *lauda* manuscripts of the period--that is, the presence of

79

musical notation. It is utterly amazing that De Bartholomaeis, writing nearly half a century after the discovery of the manuscript, should complain of the "absence of one of the most helpful instruments of critique which would be able to resolve so many doubts, that is, the knowledge of the music which accompanied these songs."[43]

Following the vigorous controversies of the late nineteenth century, however, Cortona 91 was given little attention by scholars until taken up in the 1930's by Fernando Liuzzi. His articles, published in numerous Italian journals of that decade, presaged the luxurious facsimile publication of both the Cortona and Magliabechiano manuscripts which make him deservedly famous.[44] In an article published in 1930 in *Archivum Romanicum*,[45] Liuzzi quoted generously from the Cortona *laudario* and thus provided the first satisfactory sampling of this music, though a few brief examples had been transcribed by Ludwig in 1924.[46] A discussion of Liuzzi's highly questionable rhythmic transcriptions will be deferred until the treatment of the Magliabechiano manuscript in which his more or less procrustean methods may be more easily observed. However, whatever the faults of his theories, Liuzzi deserves great credit for at last bringing this treasury of early Italian music to public notice.

More germane to the present discussion of the origins of the *laudario* is Liuzzi's belief that the codex was compiled some time after 1270, a date established on the basis of his attribution of some of the texts to Jacopone whose conversion occurred only in 1268. Like Liuzzi's other theories, this has not found general acceptance. To rely simply upon the presence or absence of a *lauda* in the manuscript is to ignore the rather obvious fact that in the case of an oral tradition it simply is not possible to know how long the music had been known and sung before it was actually written down. Thus, if other evidence is set aside, we might speculate that the musical portion of the manuscript could have been assembled as late as the beginning of the *trecento*.

In his discussion of the date of the Cortona manuscript, Varanini addresses the arguments of earlier writers who based their theories, as we have seen, upon such fragile premises as the lack of *laude* to either Margaret or Guido--a lack which, it was believed, indicated composition prior to their deaths. Varanini points out that the earlier portion of the manuscript with musical notation contains a *lauda* honoring St. Michael the Archangel who was patron of the city of Cortona prior to 1261, whereas St. Mark, designated as the city's patron only after 1261, is represented in the second portion of the manuscript which also contains texts in honor of Margaret and Guido. This evidence therefore suggests that the first part of the manuscript reflects saints venerated in earlier times, while the second part may have been put together in an effort to bring the collection up to date by including more modern devotions.[47]

Varanini's theories are postulated upon the assumption of an early and active tradition of *lauda*-singing in Siena, and are now substantiated by the researches of Meerssemann who has produced significant evidence to support his claim that the earliest *laudesi* company whose activities can be documented originated in that city.[48] Hence Siena may be the center from which the *lauda* repertoire was disseminated to the nearby cities of Cortona, Florence, and Lucca where the hymns were adapted and modified to reflect local linguistic and musical differences. Moreover, in the opinion of Varanini, Siena was a more active intellectual center than Cortona in the early thirteenth century and hence was a more likely source for the diffusion of the *lauda*. However, in view of the fact that no statutes (only the *laudario*) of the Cortonese company survive and no *laudario* (only the statutes) of the Sienese company remains, Varanini's suggestions probably cannot be proven. Nevertheless, his theories have an element of plausibility lacking in some of the earlier theories about the date and provenence of Cortona 91.

Poetic Form and Language. Although the four-line octosyllabic strophe is most common in the *laude* of the Cortona *laudario*, the hendecasyllabic stanza and strophes of uneven verse length do appear with some frequency. The greatest stylistic uniformity is found in the beginning of the manuscript, while the homiletic *laude* and those to the saints manifest a greater individuality in both style and form.

The form most often employed in this repertoire has been described as *lauda-ballata*, a hybrid which applies the structural scheme of a secular form, the *ballata* (roughly equivalent to the French *virelai*), to the popular sacred lyrics of the *lauda*. Since the *lauda* consists of a refrain and stanza, its poetry conforms nicely to the formal elements of the *ballata*, which is characterized by alternate statements of the *ripresa* (refrain) and strophe (stanza) in much the same manner as the round dance. The stanza of the true *ballata* in its strictest form consists of *piedi* (two feet of identical versification) and *volta*, having the same structure as the refrain and retaining the same music. Hence the melody of the refrain and the first *piede* are simply repeated for subsequent stanzas. This alternation of refrain and stanza causes the *ballata* to be very well suited to group singing and consequently makes it adaptable to the evangelizing purpose of the *lauda*.

The adaptation of the secular form of the *ballata* to the sacred repertoire took place in fact before the compilation of the oldest surviving manuscript of *laude*. To be sure, only texts survived from the earliest history of the *ballata*--again an indication of the presence of an oral tradition of music. By the end of the thirteenth century, the poets of the *dolce stil novo* had perfected the versification of the *ballata*, for which they preferred the eleven- and seven-syllable line. Pirrotta believes that "the new *ballata* was first introduced as a literary translation of the alternation between soloist and chorus, as a refinement of the dance song, soon transferred to purely lyrical poems mainly because of its musical effectiveness."[49]

While it is characteristic of the *lauda* to repeat one or

more of the melodic members of the refrain in the strophe, such repetition is more often a derivation than a direct restatement. Whenever the last lines of the stanza do utilize the melody of the refrain exactly, the melody is said to turn in upon itself. Thus the scheme may be reduced to that of the *ballata*:

Text	A B	ccab	A B	ccab	A B
Music	A	bba	A	bba	A

Only a relatively small number of *laude* follow this scheme strictly, however, and the tendency toward variation rather than repetition lessens the dance character found in the *ballata*. Hence the term *lauda-ballata* more accurately describes its behavior and is indicative of greater variety in the internal organization of the melodic material.[50]

The dialect employed in the codex is a curious kind of mixture of mutations characteristic of a language still in evolution from Latin to the vernacular. Latin training is revealed throughout in the borrowing of entire Latin words, though not to the extent of the Middle English macaronic carol which actually alternates Latin and vernacular verses. Latinisms are revealed too in the many suffixes and hypercorrections. A thorough study of the linguistic behavior of the language of this poetry, some of the earliest in the Italian vernacular, is long overdue. Such an investigation is beyond the scope of the present study and in any case is the province of the romance philologist rather than the musicologist, but some comment nevertheless may be required with regard to certain aspects of the language utilized in the Cortona manuscript. The *laude* contained in this codex show a fairly consistent tendency to the following usage:

1. *The homorganic m (or n)*. Before labials, p or b, and m, the n becomes an m. Conversely, before dentals, t and d, the m becomes an n.

2. *The sibilant ç.* When c precedes a palatal vowel, it is written with the cedilla and appears thus: *merçede, dolçe, dolçore.*

3. *The use of g for c.* Common in words such as *seguro*, for *securo.* The same is true of the use of the d for t and of the v or b for p. For example, *emperadore* for *emperatore, savia* for *sapia.*

4. *The intrusion of n or m before -gn.* E.g., *ongne.*

5. *The use of ecclesiastical Latinisms.* These may be in the form of Latin word endings such as *-entia* or *-antia* or in the borrowing of entire words such as *juxta, lux,* etc.

6. *The preservation of the tonic o.* Throughout the codex the tonic o is rarely transmuted into a diphthong. For example, *fuoco* remains *foco, cuore* remains *core,* and *uomo, omo.*

7. *Frequent substitutions.* The e for i, and vice versa; the ll for gl; and the sc for g.

The rhyme schemes of the *laude* in Cortona 91 are diversified; the majority of the texts contain a refrain of two lines and a stanza of four with a rhyme such as xx a a ax or a simple variant thereof. A greater degree of complexity is reached in those texts which employ a rather intricate system of internal rhyme--e.g., *O Maria, d'omelia* (No. 10) and *Cristo e nato et humanato* (No. 19). Following are examples of internal rhyme in these *laude*:

Lauda No. 10, fols. 22^r-24^r:

O Maria--d'omelia	(x)	x
se' fontana--fior e grana	(y)	y
de me aia pietança!		z
Gram rein'a--chi inchina--ciascun regno	(a)(a)	b
sì m'affina--la curina--quando segno	(a)(a)	b
i' ò non degno!--'N core tegno	(b)	b
tuo figure--chiar' e pura	(c)	c

ch'ongne mal m'è 'n obliança   z

Lauda No. 19, fols. 39ᵛ-43ᵛ:
  Cristo è nato--et humanato   (x)   x
  per salvar la gente   y
  k'era perduta--e descaduta   (z)   z
  nel primer parente!   y

  Nato è Cristo--per fare aquisto   (a)   a
  de noi peccatori,   b
  k'eràm partiti--e dispartiti   (c)   c
  dai suoi servidori   b
  perké fallenti--e non serventi   (d)   d
  ma deservidori   b
  eràmo facti--da cului tracti   (e)   e
  k'è tutor fallente   y

Some of the texts employ assonance rather than rhyme, and a few of the poems also use the device of *anadiplosis*, which effects an interlocking pattern between the last word of the strophe and the beginning of the next, as in *Lauda* No. 1 (fol. 1ʳ-1ᵛ):

> Venite a laudare
> per amore cantare
> l'amorosa vergene Maria!
>
> Maria gloriosa, biata
> sempre sia molto laudata;
> Preghiam ke ne si' avocata
> al tuo filiol, virgo pia!
>
> Pietosa regina sovrana,
> conforta la mente ch'è vana;
> grande medicina ke sana,
> aiutane per tua cortisia.
>
> Cortese ke fai grandi doni. . . .

Within Cortona 91, the scheme of melodic repetition may vary from an exact reiteration of the tune, as in *Iesu Cristo glorioso* (No. 27; Example 3), to a type which is almost literally through-composed, as in *Gloria 'n cielo* (No. 20; Example 4). Midway between these two *laude--laude* which set the limits with regard to handling melodic repetition--are those in which the melodic material of the refrain is more freely adapted or elaborated upon in the strophe--e.g., *Plangiamo quel crudel basciar(e)* (No. 22), in which the last line of the strophe employs material from the beginning of the first line of the refrain but combines it with the end of the second line of the refrain (Example 5). In almost every case the end rhyme of the refrain is repeated in the last verse of the stanza. This relationship of rhyme and musical scheme may be observed in the following examples, all different in length and formal scheme:

No. 26: *Onne homo ad alta voce*   No. 39: *Clascun ke fede sente*   No. 23: *Ben è crudel e spietoso*

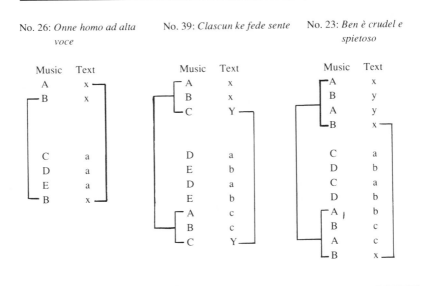

Example 3

Lauda No. 27, Cortona 91, fols. 57ᵛ-60ʳ

Refrain

Ie – sù   Cri – sto   glo – ri – o – so,

a   te   sia   lau – de   e   çe – chi – men – to,

ké   per   noi   sur – re – xi – men – to,

fa – ce – sti   vi – cto – ri – o – so!

Strophe

Vi – cto – ri – o-so   el   ter – ço   di – e

fa – ce – sti   sur – re – xi – men – to;

per   un – ger   le   tre   Ma – ri – e

lo   tu – o   cor – po   al   mo – ni – men – to

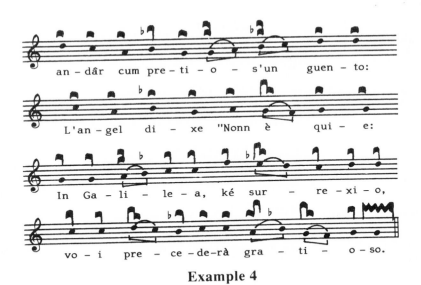

Example 4

Lauda No. 20, Cortona 91, fols. 43ᵛ-44ᵛ

Refrain

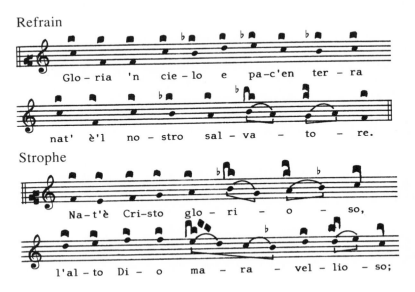

Fact' è hom de - si - de - ro - so

lo be - ni - gno cre - a - to - re!

Example 5

Lauda No. 22, Cortona 91, fols. 46ᵛ-47ᵛ

Refrain

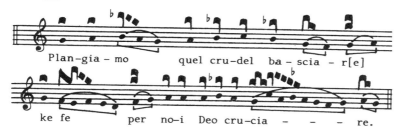

Plan–gia – mo   quel cru–del ba – scia – r[e]

ke fe   per no–i Deo cru –cia – – – re.

Strophe

Ven – ne Iu – da tra – di – to – re,

ba–scio li di – e – d'e gran do – lo – re;

lo qual fa–ciam noi per a – mo – re a

lu–i   fo si–gno di pe–na – – re.

The melodies of the *laude*, then, are characterized by a considerable degree of variety, and they range from repetitive formulae (almost like a litany) to through-composed compositions. Although they are rooted in modal practice, there is a strong suggestion of popular song in the modulations, inner cadences on the dominant, and the feeling of tonic-dominant polarity resulting from numerous triadic figures. These characteristics are especially marked in the melodies in the *tritus* and *protus* modes which require a b-flat, thus resulting in a distinctly major or minor tonality.

The refrain and the stanza most often have the same final. Of the forty-seven *laude* with musical notation, thirty-six follow this pattern with the following distribution of finals:

> 15 on d and d
> 10 on g and g
> 8 on f and f
> 2 on c and c
> 1 on a and a

Examples with refrain and stanza having different finals are:

> 2 on f and d
> 2 on f and g
> 1 on d and f
> 1 on f and c
> 1 on g and f
> 1 on a and g
> 1 on c and g
> 1 on c and b
> 1 incomplete, on e

The finals of each lauda are identified in the right-hand column of Table 1.A above (p. 68), while Table 2 (below) tabulates the musical form.

Table 2. Musical form of *Laude* from the Cortona *Laudario*

Number	Refrain	Strophe
1	a b	c d a^1 b^1
2	a b	a^1 c d b^1
3	a b	c d e b^1
4	---	a b c d
5	no music	
6	a b	c b^1 a^1 b^1
7	a b	a a c b^1
8	a b	c c^1 d e
9	a b	a b^1 a b^1
10	a b	c c d c^1
11	a b	c d e d^1
12	a b	c c d b^1
13	a b	c d a^1 b
14	a b	c d e a
15	a b	c b^1 a^1 b^1
16	a b	c d c^1 e
17	a b	c d e f
18	a b	c c d e
19	a b c d	e f c^1 d g h c^1 d^1
20	a b	c d e f
21	a b	a b a b
22	a b	c d e b^1
23	a b a b	c d c d a b a b
24	a b	c c^1 d--(last line missing)
25	a b	a b c b
26	a b	c d e b^1
27	a b c d	e f e^1 f^1 a^1 b^1 c^1 d^1
28	a b	c d c^1 d^1
29	a b	c c d b^1
30	a b	c d e f
31	a b	a c a b
32	a b	c c a^1 b
33	a b	c b^1 c b^1
34	a b c d	e f g h a^1 b^1 c d
35	a b c	a^1 a^1 b^1 c
36	a b	a^1 c a^1 b^1
37	a b	c c a b

Number	Refrain	Strophe
38	a b c	a b a d
39	a b c	d e d e d e a b c
40	a b	b^1 a^1 c b
41	a b	c c^1 d e
42	a b a^1 c	d b d b d b a^1 c^1
43	a b	c c^1 a c^1
44	a b	c d e f
45	a b	c d e d
46	a b a^1 b^1	c d e d
47	a b c d	a b^1 a b^1 c^1 d^1

Prime numbers here indicate some alteration in the melody in place of a true repetition of the phrase.

Conclusion. The problem faced by the music copyist was not unlike that of the poet and/or scribe who set down the text. As the one was forced to record in writing the sounds of a spoken language not yet taught or codified, so also the amanuensis of the music was faced with the task of how to capture the aural impression of an essentially unwritten musical repertoire and to represent it to the eye. The latter task of necessity still employed the tools of a past style. The notation therefore bears close resemblance to the square, black notation of plainsong. While no mensural indications are found in the *laude*, quite certainly these simple hymns, some of which probably derived from actual popular song in the first place, were given rhythmic interpretation in performance, very likely determined by the meter of the texts.

The *lauda* repertoire, existing in a sense independently from the manuscript, depended largely for its popularity upon oral dissemination, which admits of a certain degree of variation between one transcription or collection and another. Textual variants are, of course, the rule rather than the exception in the numerous manuscripts that lack notation, which manifest innumerable differences in the same item between one city or region and another. Many of these differences are the result of adaptation to new locations and circumstances-- e.g., the borrowing of a *laudesi* text by a *disciplinati* confraternity.

As Higinio Anglès aptly reminds us, the monophonic *lauda* testifies to the fact that the art of improvisation flourished among the lower (and middle) classes as well as the literati.[51] Hence some allowance must be made also between the written sources which survive and the actual performances lost on the soundwaves of the past. For all of these reasons, the *laude* defy reduction to absolute, fixed note values of modern mensural notation. So too do the *laude* in the Cortona codex elude researchers who would like to know the exact date of composition, which cannot be discovered on the basis of paleographic or notational practice alone. The repertoire may have existed long before it was written down in the *laudario*. Cortona 91 nevertheless remains a testimony to the mind of the medieval Christian whose religious and musical experience must often be sought in the remaining artifacts which record his thought, actions, and feelings.

4

The Musical Documents:
Magliabechiano II I 122
and Other Manuscripts

The second and only other complete manuscript preserving the monophonic *lauda* in the vernacular is the fourteenth-century *laudario*, which has the shelf mark Magliabechiano II I 122 (Banco Rari 18) in the Biblioteca Nazionale Centrale, Florence.[1]   Like the Cortona *laudario*, it contains musical notation, but otherwise there is no visual resemblance between the two manuscripts, for the Magliabechiano manuscript (Mgl[1]) is an elegant codex which stands in contrast to the appearance of the earlier collection of music and texts. Comprising 153 folios and bound in a brown leather binding that is probably from the seventeenth century, the Magliabechiano collection appears to be a coupling of two disparate manuscripts, the first of which contains ninety-seven *laude* written in a fine large gothic hand on four-line staves inked in red.   Each individual *lauda* begins with an illuminated initial, and successive stanzas commence with colored initials executed alternately in red and blue.

The two parts of the manuscript are identified by different systems of pagination. The *laudario* was originally marked in Roman numerals at the bottom of the page, while Arabic numbers were later added in the upper right hand corner of each folio. However, the second portion of the codex, which contains an incomplete collection of sequences in two gatherings (fols. 136ʳ-153ᵛ), uses a different system, beginning the pagination again on the fourth folio. And unlike the *laudario* in which the scribe used guide words at the end of each fascicle to indicate the first word of the next, no such guide words are found in the section containing the sequences.[2]

The manuscript follows a hierarchical arrangement, beginning with *laude* to the Godhead and proceeding through the Temporal, Marian, and Sanctoral Cycles. Table 3 lists the *laude* in the order in which they appear in the codex.

But without doubt the most immediately impressive aspect of the manuscript is its profusion of illuminations, though they are uneven in quality. They also differ in size, ranging from full-folio paintings in the hand of the master to smaller figures of indifferent quality contained within the initials presumably of workshop production. The finer examples were once thought to be the work of Beato Angelico (1387-1455), an attribution which has been disproven by art historians who now agree in dating them c.1340-50.[3] Indeed, the miniatures themselves may have been an obstacle to the examination of the *laudario* as an integrated work containing music, text, and pictorial representations--i.e., as a well planned and carefully thought out manuscript. Earlier in this century, art historians tended to examine the illuminations without much attention to the significance of their placement within the scheme of the codex, while at the same time other scholars who studied the text and/or the music took note of the miniatures but did not consider the implications of their size, position, quality, and narrative elements as embellishments of the text.[4] However, recent musicological research has given attention to the importance of the sequence of the *laude* in a given manuscript,[5] while Vincent Moleta in his careful examination of both text and painting in the Magliabechiano manuscript has demonstrated the close collaboration between scribe and artist in the planning and layout of this codex. In Moleta's view, a carefully worked out decorative plan was coordinated with musical considerations.[6] This conclusion seems to be borne out by those

Table 3 - Index of *Laude*, B. R. 18, in Order of Presentation

Number	Liuzzi's Number	Folio	Concordance	Incipit	Argument	Final Refrain	Final Strophe
1	1	2v	+	Spirito sancto glorioso	Pentecost	f	a
2	2	4r	+	Spirito sancto da servire	Gifts of the Holy Ghost	f	a
3	3	5v	+	Alta Trinità beata	Holy Trinity	f	f
4	4	6v	†	A voi gente facciam	Jesus as Judge	-	f
5	5	8r	+	Del dolcissimo Signore	Jesus as Savior	c	c
6	6	9r	+	Gloria in cielo	Nativity of Christ	d	d
7	7	11r	+	. . . dori/perche fallenti (Fragment)	Nativity of Christ	-	c
8	8	11v	U	Sovrana si' ne' sembianti	Redemptive role of B. V. M.	d	f
9	9	13r		Lamentomi et sospiro	Lament over human failing, trust in God	d	d
10	10	15v		Tutor dicendo di lui	Praise of Jesus as Savior	d	-
11	11	17r	U	Nova stella apparita	Epiphany/Magi	f	e
12	11bis	19v	+	Ben è crudele	Passion	-	-
13	11ter	21v		Ogne mia amica	Passion/Lament	-	-
14	12	22v		Piange Maria cum dolore	Passion/Lament	g	g
15	13	23v		Iesu Cristo redemptore	Passion	d	d
16	14	25r	*	Ogne homo ad alta boce	Holy Cross	a	a
17	15	25v		Voi ch'amate lo criatore	Passion/Lament	d	d
18	16	26v		Or piangiamo che piange Maria	Passion/Lament	e	e
19	17	28r		Davanti a una colonna	Passion/Lament	-	d
20	18	29r		Alleluya, alleluya	Crucifixion/Resurrection	-	a
21	19	30r		Co la madre del beato	Resurrection	a	a
22	20	31r	*	Geso Cristo glorioso	Resurrection	a	c
23	20bis	33r		Or se' tu l'amore	Resurrection/Hortulanus	-	-
24	21	35r		O Cristo 'nipotente	Reputedly by Jacopone, on his wife's death	f	f
25	22	36v	+	Laudate la surrectione	Resurrection/Ascension	g	f
26	23	37v		Ave Maria, stella diana	Nativity of Mary	c	f

Number	Liuzzi's Number	Folio	Concordance	Incipit	Argument	Final Refrain	Final Strophe
27	24	39ʳ	U	Nat'è in questo mondo	Nativity of Mary	b	f
28	25	40ᵛ	*	Da ciel venne messo novello	Annunciation	d	d
29	26	42ʳ		Ave Maria, gratia plena	Annunciation	a	a
30	27	43ʳ	*	Altissima luce	Praise of Mary	a	g
31	28	44ᵛ		Sancto Symeom	Purification	d	f
32	29	45ᵛ		Altissima stella	Praise of Mary	c	c
33	30	47ʳ		Con umil core	Praise of Mary	f	f
34	31	48ᵛ	*	Ave, donna sanctissima	Praise of Mary	d	d
35	32	50ʳ	U	O humil donçella	Assumption of Mary	f	g
36	33	51ʳ		Regina pretiosa	Praise of Mary	f	f
37	34	52ᵛ	U	Vergine donçella	Praise of Mary	f	f
38	34bis	53ᵛ	U	Ave, Virgo Maria	Praise of Mary	-	-
39	35	54ᵛ	*	Die ti salvi, regina	Redemptive role of B. V. M.	d	d
40	36	55ᵛ		Regina sovrana	Praise of Mary	f	f
41	37	57ʳ		Dolce Vergine Maria	Praise of Mary	d	e
42	37bis	58ʳ		Laudate sempre sia	Praise of Mary	-	-
43	37ter	59ᵛ		Venite ad orare	Prayer to Mary for Peace	-	-
44	38	60ᵛ		Vergen pulçella	Praise of Mary	d	d
45	39	61ᵛ	†	Exaltando in Iesu	Angels/Archangels	g	g
46	40	63ʳ		Sancto Iovanni Baptista	John the Baptist	d	d
47	41	63bis		Pastore principe	The Call of Peter	a	a
48	42	64ᵛ	U	Con humilità di core	Conversion of Paul	f	f
49	43	66ʳ	U	Andrea beato laudi	St. Andrew. Apostle	d	d
50	44	67ʳ		San Giovanni amoroso	St. John, Apostle	d	f
51	45	68ʳ		Di tutto nostro core	St. James the Greater	a	c
52	46	69ᵛ		Apostolo beato	St. Bartholomew. Apostle	f	f
53	47	71ʳ	U	Ciascuna gente canti	St. Phillip. Apostle	f	f
54	48	73ʳ	U	Apostol glorioso	St. James the Lesser	f	f
55	49	75ʳ	U	O alta compagnia	SS. Simon and Jude, Apostles	f	e

				Incipit	Description		
56	50	76r	U	Di Gesu Cristo dolce	St. Matthew, Apostle	g	g
57	71	77v	U	Novel canto, dolce santo	St. Thomas, Apostle	c	c
58	52	78v	U	A Sancto Mathia	St. Matthias, Apostle	f	f
59	53	80r	U	Sancto Luca da Dio amato	St. Luke, Apostle	d	d
60	54	81r	U	Sancto Marco glorioso	St. Mark, Apostle	c	c
61	55	82v		Lo signore ringraçiando	All the Apostles	d	c
62	56	84r		Stephano sancto	St. Stephen, protomartyr	g	g
63	57	85v		Sancto Lorenço	St. Lawrence, Martyr	d	d
64	58	86v	U	Martyr glorioso	St. Lawrence, Martyr	d	g
65	59	88r		Martyr valente	St. Peter of Verona, Martyr	c	c
66	60	89r		Sancto Vincentio	St. Vincent, Martyr	d	d
67	61	90v	U	O sancto Blasio	St. Blaise, Martyr	f	-
68	62	92v	U	Sancto Giorgio martyr	St. George, Martyr	c	c
69	63	94v		Laudia'lli gloriosi	All Martyrs	d	e
70	omitted	95v		Ave Maria gratia plena	B. V. M., fragment	-	-
71	64	96v		Gaudiamo tucti quanti	St. Augustine of Hippo	f	f
72	65	98r	†	Sancto Augustin doctore	St. Augustine of Hippo	b	d
73	66	99v		A la grande valença	St. Ambrose	f	f
74	67	100v		Alla regina divota	St Peter Pettinagnolo	a	-
75	68	101v		Da tucta gente	St. Nicholas of Bari	a	f
76	68bis	103r	U	Con divota mente	St. Paul, Hermit	-	-
77	69	106r	*	Ciascun che fede	St. Anthony of Padua	f	f
78	69bis	107v	U	Sancto Allexio stella	St. Alexis	-	-
79	70	109r	U	A sancto Jacobo	St. James the Greater	c	c
80	71	110r	U	Sancto Bernardo amoroso	St. Bernard	d	d
81	72	111r		Novel canto tucta gente	St. Zenobio	c	c
82	73	112v	+	Og'omo canti novel canto	St. John Evangelist	d	d
83	74	113v		Vergine e Sancta Maria	Prayer to the Virgin	g	g
84	75	114v		Salve, virgo pretiosa	Praise of Mary	d	d
85	76	116r		San Domenico beato	St. Dominic	d	d

Number	Liuzzi's Number	Folio	Concordance	Incipit	Argument	Final Refrain	Final Strophe
86	77	117ᵛ	U	Allegro canto, popol cristiano	St. Dominic	f	f
87	78	119ʳ	*	Sia laudato San Francesco	St. Francis of Assisi	c	c
88	79	120ᵛ	U	Radiante lumera	St. Francis of Assisi	c	c
89	80	122ʳ	U	Lo'ntellecto divino	St. Augustine of Siena	f	f
90	81	125ʳ	*	Peccatrice nominata	Mary Magdalene	g	g
91	82	125ᵛ		A Sancta Reparata	St. Reparata	f	f
92	83	126ᵛ	U	A tutta gente	St. Margaret	f	f
93	84	128ʳ	*	Vergine donçella	St. Catherine of Alexandria	f	c
94	85	129ᵛ		Sancta Agnesa da Dio amata	St. Agnes	d	d
95	86	130ᵛ	U	Canto novello et versi co laudore	All Virgins	c	d
96	87	133ʳ	*	Facciam laude a tuct'i sancti	All Saints	c	c
97	88	134ᵛ	+	Chi vuol lo mondo dispreçare	On death	d	c

* Music and text in Cortona *laudario*
+ Text only in Cortona, with different music
†Music in Cortona, with different text
U *Unicum*

examples in which the illumination encroaches on the space needed for the music, since the miniaturist carefully drew around the area required for the notes and left sufficient space for the music to be entered.

The paintings indeed seem to have been of the greatest importance in the planning and arrangement of the signatures. Accordingly, the number of strophes included in each case was determined by the amount of space available after the illumination was designed. Moleta argues that the sequence of events that occurred in the production of the *laudario* was as follows: (1) the selection of the *laude* to be included and the grouping into signatures; (2) the determination of length, taking into account the amount of space required for the notation of the refrain and first stanza as well as the size of the miniature; (3) the outlining of initials, drawing of miniatures, and ruling of staves; (4) the writing of the text; (5) the painting of the miniatures and historiated initials; and (6) the entering of the musical notation.[7] This theory would account for the extreme truncation of the text--a peculiarity of the Magliabechiano codex. While emphasizing the vigor of oral tradition in the dissemination of the music, such a theory also suggests that the manuscript was not intended as a repository to preserve the hymns in their entirety but that it instead may have been intended as a votive work.[8]

Not surprisingly, analysis of the *laude* in the manuscript will reveal certain cycles and sub-cycles arranged at times in a symmetrical pattern. The pairing of meditative and narrative laude at key points in the codex is clearly marked by a change in the scale of the decorations.[9] Table 4 (p. 103, below), which is indebted to Moleta's analysis, is intended to demonstrate the cyclic nature of the plan of the manuscript as well as to point up certain parallels in the decorative scheme.

Unlike Cortona 91, the Magliabechiano manuscript (Mgl[1]) poses no great problem with regard to provenance. Its identity as a Florentine manuscript is certified again and again by the *laude* honoring local saints and patrons of the oldest churches of the city.[10]   Further, the second of the dedicatory *laude* specifically refers to "la tua compagnia di Florentia," which we know to be the Compagnia di santa Maria delle laude in the Augustinian church of Santo Spirito in the *oltrarno*.   Ownership by the group is clearly confirmed in the opening *lauda* with its lavish illumination of the descent of the Holy Ghost upon the Apostles at Pentecost (fig. 10).   A second *lauda* on the same subject immediately follows, and the hierarchical order of the opening set of *laude* is rounded out to form a group of five hymns described by Moleta as "non-meditative" since they do not touch "upon the humanity of Christ or the Blessed Virgin in affective terms" or voice "the soul's emotional response."[11]

The Augustinian affiliation of the church is commemorated in the two *laude* in praise of St. Augustine of Hippo, the first of which contains a large illumination representing the saint in glory, flanked by tonsured friars in the Augustinian habit, while below are figures of laymen in secular attire, who probably represent the members of the company.[12]   The position of these two illuminations at the opening of the Cycle of Confessors is significant.   Although the order followed in the Sanctoral Cycle corresponds generally to the Litany of the Saints, the sequence here is altered.   For example, Ambrose, who is credited with the conversion of Augustine and whose name occurs first in the Litany, now follows that of the patron of the order serving the church that was the seat of the company owning the *laudario*.

Text. The *laude* of the Magliabechiano codex (Mgl[1]) are characterized by a greater diversity of both poetic and musical forms than those of Cortona 91. Although the *ballata minore ottonario* predominates, the hymns of the latter part of the manuscript tend especially to have the longer stanzaic formulae of the *ballata mezzana* or *ballata maggiore*, and they frequently employ verses of unequal length. Seventy-seven of the ninety-seven texts retain the familiar end rhyme of the refrain in

Table 4 - The Decorative Scheme of Mgl[1]

Major Cycle	Sub-Cycle	Number	Folio	Subject	Comments	Symmetrical Schemes
Dedication	Opening non-meditative cycle	1	2ᵛ	Holy Spirit	Opening dedicatory *laude* honoring patron of the Company. *Paired*	
		2	4ᵛ	Holy Spirit		
		3	5ᵛ	Trinity	Complete the trinitarian Godhead	
		4	6ᵛ	Christ, Judge		
		5	8ʳ	Christ, Lord		
Temporal Cycle	Nativity Cycle	6	9ʳ	Nativity of Christ	Large illumination on fresh recto	
		7	11ʳ	Nativity	Forms an opening *pair*	
		11	17ʳ	The Three Epiphanies	Text constitutes a transition to Passion Cycle	
	Passion Cycle	12	19ᵛ	Christ's sacrifice in becoming man	No major illumination	
		20	29ʳ	Praise of Christ as Redeemer	Text constitutes a transition to Resurrection Cycle	
		21	30ʳ	Resurrection	Large illumination on fresh recto	
		22	31ᵛ	Resurrection	Forms opening *pair* balancing Nativity Cycle	
		25	36ᵛ	Resurrection and Ascension	Large illumination rounds off calendar cycle on the scale of the opening.	

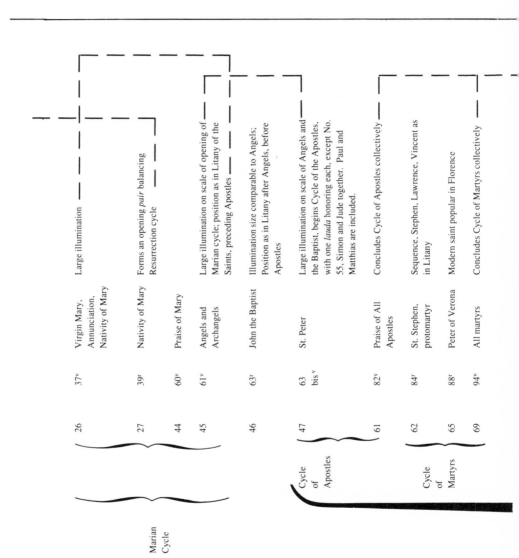

26	37ᵛ	Virgin Mary, Annunciation, Nativity of Mary	Large illumination
27	39ʳ	Nativity of Mary	Forms an opening *pair* balancing Resurrection cycle
44	60ᵛ	Praise of Mary	
45	61ᵛ	Angels and Archangels	Large illumination on scale of opening of Marian cycle; position as in Litany of the Saints, preceding Apostles
46	63ʳ	John the Baptist	Illumination size comparable to Angels; Position as in Litany after Angels, before Apostles
47	63 bis ᵛ	St. Peter	Large illumination on scale of Angels and the Baptist, begins Cycle of the Apostles, with one *lauda* honoring each, except No. 55, Simon and Jude together. Paul and Matthias are included.
61	82ᵛ	Praise of All Apostles	Concludes Cycle of Apostles collectively
62	84ʳ	St. Stephen, protomartyr	Sequence. Stephen, Lawrence, Vincent as in Litany
65	88ʳ	Peter of Verona	Modern saint popular in Florence
69	94ᵛ	All martyrs	Concludes Cycle of Martyrs collectively

Marian Cycle

Cycle of Apostles

Cycle of Martyrs

		Folio	Saint	Description
Sanctoral Cycle	Cycle of Confessors			
	71	96v	St. Augustine of Hippo	Large illumination on scale of opening of calendar cycle
	72	98r	St. Augustine of Hippo	The two form a *pair* as in opening of Marian and Temporal Cycle. Apostles James Greater and John are included again here
	89	122r	St. Augustine of Siena	Cycle opens and closes with the two Augustines
	90	125r	Mary Magdalene	Included with Virgins as in Litany
	91	125v	St. Reparata	Popular local saint
	95	130v	All Virgins	Concludes cycle of Virgins collectively
	96	133r	All Saints	Concludes the entire cycle of saints collectively. Large illumination on scale of the opening of the Sanctoral Cycle
	97	134v	On death	Large illumination on scale of opening of Cycle of Confessors (See fig. 9)

the last line of the strophe. Also, twenty-four *laude* are constructed with internal rhyme, sometimes only in a single line but upon occasion extending to the entire poem. Of these items with internal rhyme only two are texts found also in Cortona 91; seven are unique to the Magliabechiano codex, and fifteen of them occur in the *laude* of the Sanctoral Cycle which are later compositions thought to have been composed specifically for this manuscript.[13]

Music. In spite of the proliferation of *fiorature*, especially in the *laude* to the saints, the formal outlines of refrain and stanza are still present in the music. However, only approximately half (forty-nine) of the melodies contain a repetition of the music of the refrain in the strophe, and even in instances of melodic repetition of all or even part of the refrain occurring in the stanza it must often be considered a variation of the first statement instead of an exact reprise. The sometimes extensively ornamented cadences and long internal melismas tend to obscure the true dance character of the *ballata* much more than in Cortona 91.

In addition, the widening of the vocal range which often results from these elaborations sometimes alters the modal behavior of the music and results in interior modulations or often creates a melody that fluctuates between the authentic and plagal ranges of the same mode. In fifty-eight of the eighty-eight musically complete items, the refrain and stanza share the same final (see Table 3, col. 7). In general, as in the Cortona *laudario*, the *protus* and *tritus* modes predominate, but they appear with extended ranges which tend to occur most often in *piedi* and *volta* that would have been sung by the soloist. No judgment can be made as to whether this phenomenon was a cause or a result of the employment of professional singers by the *laudesi* companies.

Variation in melodic behavior in *laude* of the Magliabechiano manuscript defies reduction to the usual formulae. Hence in Table 5 the indication of recurrence of melodic mem-

Table 5 - Musical Form and Intonations of *Laude* from MGL[1]

Repeat of entire Refrain in Stanza

Number	Refrain	Piedi	Volta	Intonation of second Stanza
84	a b	a^1 a	a b	----------
79	a b	a b	a b^1	----------
21	a b	a c	a b	2 lines, s, d
47	a b	a c	a b	1/2 line, s
30	a b	c c	a b	6 notes, d
6	a b	c c^1	a^1 b	1 line, s
17	a b	c c^1	a b	2 notes, s
31	a b	c c	a b^1	2 notes, s
35	a b	c c^1	a^1 b^{1*}	----------
68	a b	c c^1	a b^1	1-1/2 lines, s
94	a b	c c	a b	----------
16	a b	c b^1	d b^2	----------
14	a b	c b^1	a^1 b^2	1/2 line, d
59	a b	c d	a b^1	8 notes, d
64	a b	c d	a b^1	5 notes, d
8	a b	c d	a b^1	entire, d, d, s, s
18	a b	c d c^1 inc	a^1 b^1	----------
49	a b	c d c d	a b	4 notes, s
63	a b	c d c d	a b	7 notes, d
92	a b	c d c d	a^1 b	----------
57	a b	c d c d c d	a b	3 notes, s
9	a b	a b	a b	----------
56	a b	c d $c*$ d^1	a^1 b^1	3 notes, s
57	a b	c d c d c d	a b	3 notes, s
73	a b a^1 c	d e d^1 e	a b a^1 c	----------
96	a b a c	d b d b	a^1 b^1 a^2 c	----------
48	a b c d	e f e^1 f	a b c d	----------
51	a b c d	e f e f	a b c d^1	----------
52	a b c d	e f e f	a b c^1 d	1 line, inc. s
53	a b c d	e f e^1 f	a^1 b^1 c d	1 note, s
58	a b c d	e f e^1 f	a b c d	----------
81	a b c d	e f e f	a b c d	2 lines, s, d
60	a b c d	e f e f	a b c d^1	4 notes, s
88	a b c d	e f g f^1	a b c d	----------
22	a b c d	e f g h	a^1 b^1 c^1? d ↓	----------
89	a b c d	e f g e^1 f g^1	a b c d	----------
87	a b c	a	b^1 d c^1	----------
91	a b c	d d^1 d	a b c^1	----------
85	a b c	d d e	a b c	1 line, inc. s
66	a b c	d e d e	a^1 b^1 c^1	----------

107

Number	Refrain	Piedi	Volta	Intonation of second Stanza
69	a b c	d e d e	a^1 b^1 c^1	----------
71	a b c	d e d^1 e^1	a b c	----------
33	a b c	d e d^1 e^1	a^1 b^1 c^1	1/2 line d
36	a b c	d e d^1 e	a^1 b c^1	----------
77	a b c	d e f e f^1 e	a^1 b^1 c	1/2 line like f
39	a b c	d e f d^1 e f	a b c	----------
86	a b c	d e f d^1 e f	a b c	----------
61	a b c	d e d^1 e^1 e^2 f g h	a^1 b^1 c^1	----------

Melody of last line of Refrain repeated in Stanza

Number	Refrain	Piedi	Volta	Intonation of second Stanza
28	a b	a^1 a^2	c b^1	----------
40	a b	c c	d b^1	6 notes, d
34	a b	c d	e b^1	8 notes, d
32	a b	c b^1	c b^1	----------
29	a b	c c	c b^1	1 line + 3 notes,
80	a b	a c	d b	s
90	a b	a* c	d b^1	1-1/2 lines, 1, s,
97	a b	a c	d c	1/2 d
44	a b	c c	d b	5 notes, s
65	a b	c c	d b^1	----------
82	a b	c c	d b^1	2 lines +, d
62	a b	c a^1	d b	6 notes, s
50	a b	a^1 c	d b^1 ↑	1/2 line, d
54	a b	c d c^1 d c d	e b	entire, d, d, s, s
75	a b c d	d f d f	g h c^1 d ↓	2 lines, s, d
			or g b^1 c^1 d ↓	7 notes, s
24	a b c b^1	d e	d^1 e f b	----------
45	a b c d	e f e f	g b^1 f? d^1	----------
16	a b	c b^1	d b^2	----------

Melody of first part of Refrain repeated at the end of the Stanza

Number	Refrain	Piedi	Volta	Intonation of second Stanza
15	a b	c d	a d	1 line, d
95	a b c	d e f d^1 ↓ d^2 ↓ [ ]	a b* g	----------
27	a b c d	e f g h e^1 f g h	a b c e^2	----------
11	a b c d	d f inc f ↓	a^1 g h i	2 lines, d, s*

Incomplete or not in Refrain, Stanza form

Number	Refrain	Piedi	Volta	Intonation of second Stanza
74	a b	c d c d¹ c [ ]	[--]	----------
67	a b c d	e f g h	a b c inc.	----------
19	----------	a b c b¹ d		2 lines, d only cadence
4	----------	a b c b d e		same entire d, 3rd
10	----------	a d e		stanza,
20	a b	a b		7 notes, d
70	fragment			1 line, s

No melodic repetition of Refrain in Stanza

Number	Refrain	Piedi	Volta	Intonation of second Stanza
5	a b	c b¹	d e	1 line, inc. s
46	a b	c c¹	d e	----------
2	a b	c d	e f	1 line, d
3	a b	c d	e f	----------
26	a b	c d	e f	----------
93	a b	c d	e f	5 notes, s
1	a b	c d	d¹ d¹	entire, d, s, s, s+ cadential
25	a b	c d	e f	extension
37	a b	c d	c d¹	7 notes, d
83	a b	a b a b	c d	1/2 line, s
41	a a¹ b	c d	e f	----------
55	a b c	d e d¹ f	d² e² f	2 notes, s
72	a b c	d e d e¹ d e	f g h	----------
				2 notes, d

The following symbols are used in the above table:

*	Same melody, different final
↑	Same melody, transposed up
↓	Same melody, transposed down
inc.	Lacking part of melodic member
s	Same ⎫ in reference to
d	Different ⎬ intonations of
+	Added notes ⎭ second stanzas
[ ]	Lacking entire melodic member

bers does not signify exact repetition. In the scheme employed here the repeated phrase may thus include minor alterations such as added passing notes or neighbor notes that do not significantly alter the melody. For those instances in which the phrase involves a greater elaboration of the tune while retaining the original statement recognizably, prime numbers are also employed.

On the other hand, a phrase that has been very extensively or excessively altered is indicated as new material. Occasionally a melodic member may be transposed, in which case it is interpreted as a repetition with the resulting new final indicated (see the explanatory legend placed at the end of table). At times the melodic fluctuation is of such character that the line of distinction between repetition and elaboration is admittedly difficult to establish, and hence an element of arbitrariness may necessarily have been introduced at such points in spite of efforts to provide systematic and careful description. Those *laude* in which a portion of a phrase may be repeated while the remainder of it is different present a particular problem. If the dissimilar portion is longer than the part repeated, it is indicated as new material. For this reason, the student of the music will need to be warned that in the case of these *laude* there is no substitute for first-hand examination of the items in the manuscript itself.

Forty-seven *laude* in the Magliabechiano codex have musical notation for the intonation of the second and occasionally even part of the third stanza. This is a unique feature. Perhaps, as Moleta believes, the scribe may have desired to fill up any portion of the staff which remained empty after the refrain and first stanza had been notated. Whatever the reason, some provocative questions with regard to performance practice are raised in the instance of these intonations, which range from entire second strophes to as few as one or two notes. Surprisingly, in only a small number of *laude* is the intonation of the second stanza identical to the music of the initial strophe (e.g., No. 6; Example 6, A). Frequently the second strophe may begin with a melodic member not found in the opening line of the first stanza but derived from a later verse, as in *Lauda* 14 (Example 6, B). Still others may serve as a melodic extension of the mode, as in No. 21 (Example 6, C).

Example 6

A. *Lauda* No. 6, fol. 9ᴿ

Intonation as identical repetition

Strophe 1, verse 1

Na – t'è Cri – sto glo – ri – o – so

Strophe 2, intonation

Del – la Vir – gi – ne so – vra – na

B. *Lauda* No. 14, fol. 22ᵛ

Intonation borrowed from the second line of the first stanza

Strophe 1, verse 1

Fu – e cum gau – di – o

Strophe 1, verse 2

or so – no tri – sta

Strophe 2, intonation

Ri – ce – vet – ti   la

C. *Lauda* No. 21, fol. 30ʳ

Intonation as an extension of the modal range

Strophe 1, verses 1-2

Su – sci – ta   –   t'e l'al – ta vi – ta

Strophe 2, intonation

Su–sci – ta – t'e'l sal – va – to – re

che mo – ri – o per no – stro

The dedicatory *lauda* which stands at the head of the collection, like the first of the two items honoring St. Augustine, is intricately wrought with festoons of rhomboidal shaped notes almost as if the elaborate melodic ornamentation were intended as a measure of honor designed to rival the sumptuousness of the accompanying illumination depicting the dedicatee. Furthermore, in the opening *lauda* to the Holy Spirit, the entire second strophe is notated: line 1 is completely dissimilar, line 2 is a transposition, line 3 is identical, while

the fourth line is similar but with a cadential elaboration
(Example 7).

Example 7

Lauda No. 1, Mgl[1], fols. 2ᵛ-4ʳ

Refrain

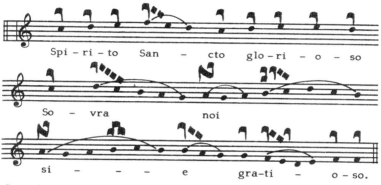

Spi – ri – to   San   –   cto   glo – ri – o – so

So – vra   noi

si – – – e   gra-ti – o – so.

Strophe 1

Che con gran   dol–çor   ve – ni – sti,

Strophe 2, intonation

Co la tu – a   vir-tù   po – ten – te

La   pen – te – co – ste   con – pie-sti,

The exact significance and method of performing these curious intonations cannot be fully treated in this study. Nevertheless, the mosaic-like construction of the *laude* derived from what often appear to be pre-existing melodic fragments, which then may be assembled in different order, suggests a kind of composition based on principles similar to centonized chant. At other times, the melody is retained intact but with inserted fragments needed to accommodate the text of successive stanzas in the manner of the type-melodies of Gregorian chant. Very possibly the phenomenon of melodic elaboration as present in these *laude* from the Magliabechiano manuscript might be a clue to improvisational ornamentation such as would have been practiced in the fourteenth century.

The Contribution of Liuzzi and Others. No treatment of the *lauda* repertoire could be complete without further examination of the contribution of Fernando Liuzzi (1884-1940), whose work, as noted above, constitutes the first scholarly approach not only to the Magliabechiano manuscript but also to the entire musical repertoire of *laude* and reflects his training in both literature and music. Significantly, as a young student in Bologna he had attended the lectures of the venerable poet Giosuè Carducci, whose love of music once had prompted him to complain that Italy had never produced a figure of the stature of Coussemaker to investigate its earliest musical documents.[14] During his adult life, Liuzzi was active as researcher, writer, conductor, composer, and teacher--often simultaneously.[15] But his appointment as Professor of Music History at the University of Florence marked a growing concentration of energies in that area for which he would later become so famous--i.e., the study of early Italian monophonic music, specifically the *lauda* and the liturgical drama. Although today his work seems flawed by certain misconceptions and his resolution of the problem of the rhythm of the *laude* may be erroneous, he nevertheless was a pioneer working without benefit of previous musicological opinion in these areas. Above all, as his obituary in *The Musical Quarterly* recognized, he contributed greatly to reducing the gap in our knowledge of the era between Gregorian chant and the first flowering of the music of the early Italian Renaissance.[16] Yet even today it is appropriate to remember Einstein's caveat in his 1939 review of Liuzzi's *La lauda* that "Nobody is capable of reproducing these tunes quite unambiguously in modern notation."[17] In the period of nearly half a century since these words were written by Einstein, various theories concerning the rhythm of the monophonic *laude* have, to be sure, been developed, but none has been convincing in every way. The current trend toward diplomatic editions also underscores the validity of Einstein's proclamation.[18]

It may, however, be necessary to review briefly earlier attempts at understanding the notation of the *laude*, which were examined by the German musicologists Ludwig, Besseler, and Gennrich. Ludwig, who had long advocated the use of the rhythmic modes in the transcription of medieval monophonic music, published (in 1924) three *laude* using instead Riemann's *Vierhebigkeit* method by which the melodic line was reduced to four accents or measures.[19] One of Ludwig's transcriptions was then reproduced in 1931 by Besseler,[20] who also included an item actually taken from Liuzzi. Then, in the following year, Gennrich, whose theories were strongly influenced by Ludwig and whose notation of the rhythm was indebted also to Beck and Aubry, published his famed *Grundriss einer Formenlehre* in which he claimed liturgical forms to be the models of secular music.[21]

At the outset Liuzzi rejected Franconian rhythm as the solution to the problem of the rhythm of the *laude* since he believed such notation was primarily intended for use in polyphonic music, and he also noted that the *laude* contained none of the usual Franconian symbols which would justify its application.[22] His idiosyncratic method postulates fidelity to the rhythm of the words above all. In the usual disposition of the elements in the *lauda*, a musical phrase normally coincides in length with a verse of text. Such a phrase in turn falls into four smaller rhythmic groups comparable to four measures in modern notation. Each of these groups then comprises two units of time, one strong and one weak. Upon this alternation of *thesis* and *arsis* Liuzzi bases his theory of transcription. He manipulates the music, alternately stretching or contracting it, in such a fashion that the tonic accent of the verse coincides with the strong pulse of the music. Whatever lies between these stressed beats must accommodate itself to the amount of space remaining. Depending upon whether the first syllable of the text is accented or not, the musical phrase accordingly begins with a stressed beat or with an anacrusis. In spite of his critical stance toward the *Vierhebigkeit* theory, therefore, Liuzzi nevertheless produces a transcription which is strongly reminiscent of Riemann's practice. Admittedly, the system is adequate when applied to syllabic melodies with texts that conform to the regular recurring stress of the *ottonario*, but in asymmetrical strophes with hyper- and hypo-metric verses, the resulting groups of short note values can only be described as sounding contrived.

The harmonizing of syntactic structure with musical sound is one of the basic laws of form in all early music. It was Luizzi's highly personal resolution of the problem of words and music that immediately drew sharp criticism from Yvonne Rokseth, whose approach to transcription places the integrity of the melody first, the meter second, and only thereafter the alignment of beat and word accent--the reverse of Liuzzi's procedures.[23] She believed that in an accentual language such as French the inflexible rhythmic modes could serve to support and underscore the text, while such an approach to the Italian *lauda* texts would do violence to the poety.[24] She goes directly to the heart of the matter when she addresses what is perhaps the greatest weakness in Liuzzi's transcriptions--i.e., the failure of his system to accommodate successive stanzas. To her a melody that is not able to maintain its character in repeated strophes is inconceivable, a veritable "hérésie musicale."[25] In this regard Jacques Handschin is in agreement with Rokseth and in fact notes that even within the first stanzas of Liuzzi's transcriptions there are melodic repetitions which frequently need to be altered to force the music into conformity. This "going contrary to the text occurs more times than one would think from reading [Liuzzi's explanations]."[26]

For Rafaello Monterosso, neither Liuzzi nor Rokseth produced a convincing transcription of this music. He charges Liuzzi with erring, like Riemann before him, in the attempt to impose the modern concept of regular recurrence of strong and weak beats to medieval music. But whereas Riemann's approach at least results in a mechanical application to the music, Liuzzi's "discretional" approach--an approach that demands attention to each individual case--terminates in a transcription in which the exceptions are more numerous than the rules he so laboriously had set up.[27]   In a word, Monterosso considers the work of Liuzzi to be a "useless reaction against the tendency . . . to extend the application of modal theory indiscriminately as a kind of good key to open the closed door of any melody in which the notation remains imprecise."[28] Using examples from both Liuzzi and Rokseth, he accuses them of utilizing methods that result in a mensural transcription. Of course, in fairness to Liuzzi and Rokseth, it should be remembered that mensural transcription was the prevailing scholarly practice of their era.

A more recent and in some respects more satisfying solution to the problem of the notational problem of the *lauda* is that of Ludwig's pupil, Higinio Anglès, whose approach may be described as modified-mensural. In his monumental study of the *cantigas* attributed to Alfonso El Sabio, Anglès found that more than sixty *cantigas* were written in equivocal notation--"simple notes taken as either *virgae* or *puncta*"-- which led him to a quasi-mensural solution based upon the theory that a single note, a *ligatura binaria*, and a *ternaria* each occupy a single beat. Thus a *quaternaria* would occupy two beats, as would also a *quinaria*, with two notes given to the first beat and three to the second.[29] The result is a smooth alternation of two- and three-note groupings that produces a kind of undulating movement instead of the jarring juxtaposition of rapid sixteenth and even thirty-second notes found in Liuzzi.   Anglès disapproves of reliance on preconceived systems since he believes instead that the "mensural but non-modal" notation of the *lauda* repertoire represents an early stage in the development of notation and is "perhaps the most ancient among the known systems."[30]

As Grossi points out in his study of the Magliabechiano codex, the fact that such divergent renditions of the music are possible only emphasizes the very equivocal nature of much notation prior to the *Ars Nova* as well as of some early *Ars Nova* notation itself. The current trend in favor of diplomatic editions provides better groundwork for purposes of analysis, but of course cannot answer all the questions raised by previous scholars and their transcriptions. Grossi correctly insists that we need especially "in the evaluation of transcriptions published in the earlier part of this century . . . to ascertain if the editor has gone beyond a mere assignment of metric values . . . which are, in themselves, mere speculation when applied to the *lauda*."[31]

Liuzzi's method, when weighed against the relative merits of a diplomatic edition, may best be examined and evaluated by means of some of the highly melismatic cadential extensions of the Magliabechiano codex, for in his version these take on the appearance of *bel canto fiorature* reminiscent of the art of the *castrati* (Example 8, Pts. A and B).

Example 8

A. *Lauda* No. 34, fol. 49ʳ (Liuzzi, II, 137)

Cadential extension:

B. *Lauda* No. 79, fol. 38ʳ (Liuzzi, II, 106)

Rhythmic irregularities such as those in Example 9 tend to obscure the similarity of melodic patterns and sequential figures so important to the structural analysis of this music. Often an internal repetition is distorted by the constriction of an otherwise identical melodic fragment into a rhythmic configuration that masks the similarity of the patterns. Such melodic manipulation may be observed in the second of the *laude* honoring St. Dominic, here given in Liuzzi's transcription and in a diplomatic transcription for comparison (Example

Example 9

Lauda No. 86, fols. 117ᵛ-118ʳ
(Liuzzi, II, 351-52, and diplomatic transcription)

Refrain

Al-le – gro   canto popul cri-sti – a-no

Del gran-de   San Do-men-i – co

Di tan-ti val-o-ro – so ca   –   pi-ta   –   no.

Strophe

Ca–pi — — ta–no di mol–ti   ca – va–lie – ri

Fu   san – cto pre – ti – o –so.

Che   do – po Cris–to l'an–no se – — —

gui – ta–to.

E fu   de li mig–lior gon – fa–lo – nie–ri

Quel   fiu–me gra – ti – o–so,

Che   do–po Cris–to sia sta – to

tro – va–to;

9). Like many of the other items from the sanctoral cycle, the *lauda* contains no additional stanzas beyond that for which music is provided, and the poetry contains verses of differing lengths. The end rhyme of the refrain is preserved in the end of the stanza, and the music of the refrain likewise returns with only minor differences. But the coincidence of strong pulse with word accent and the consequent constricting of ligatures in the remaining intervals of duration result in a much less intelligible repetition of material than in the diplomatic version.

The abbreviated texts, intonations of second stanzas, and rich illuminations combine to raise some difficult questions concerning the origin and purpose of assembling such a collection as the Magliabechiano manuscript. While the profusion of

illuminations might suggest origin within a wealthy confraternity or a donation by an affluent patron who intended it as a
votive offering, there is no documentation to support such
hypotheses. If indeed it was a votive offering, then Moleta's
opinion, noted above, concerning the disposition of the text,
music, and illuminations would be quite appropriate. Bettarini
has proposed yet another theory, which suggests that the
Magliabechiano manuscript is a transcription from pre-existing
sources compiled with the intent of creating a treasury of
music--hence the emphasis on music rather than text.[32]

The lack of music for some of the *laude* of the Magliabechiano codex led Moleta to believe that "most *laudari* were
recited, or at most chanted, not sung."[33] To be sure, some
fourteenth-century manuscripts, in particular those of the
disciplinati societies, do allude to "saying" the *laude*. However, these same manuscripts clearly differentiate between
those times when the *laude* were said and those when they were
sung, employing both the verbs *dire* and *cantare*.[34] Especially
in the instance of the *laudesi*, however, Moleta's view fails to
take into account the fact that the singing of the *laude* was one
of their reasons for existence. To subscribe to the idea that
these items were merely recited is to underestimate the vitality
of oral tradition which obviates the need for written record.

On the basis of purely musical considerations, the *laude* in
the Magliabechiano manuscript, if sung as notated with their
often extremely florid passages, would not likely have been
employed in group performance. While most melismatic
passages occur within the *piedi* and *volta* which would normally be sung by a soloist or small *schola* (probably of paid
singers), the presence of luxuriant *fiorature* in cadential
elaborations of the refrain, which we would expect to be sung
by the group, poses a more serious problem. The notion of
fidelity to score in a note-accurate performance is a modern
concept, and in view of the fact that the entire company of
laudesi assembled for prayer would not even be able to see the
manuscript at the same time (nor can we expect that all would

be able to read musical notation), it is most probable that these melodies were sung by hired singers--soloists who had taken over the singing entirely.

Magliabechiano II I 212 (Banco Rari 19) (Mgl[2]). Although it contains no musical notation, this sister manuscript of Mgl[1] invites comparison with the *laudario* of Santo Spirito. The manuscript is also Florentine (more than half of its 105 texts also appear in Mgl[1]), but it is a somewhat later compilation probably dating from c.1360-80.[35] As in Mgl[1], there are signs here of close collaboration of scribe and illuminator. The *laude* are arranged in a sequence similar to that of Mgl[1], but not all of the illuminations have been painted. Six large framed miniatures were planned, though only three were in fact executed--i.e., those illustrating the opening *lauda*, the first of the two honoring the patron of the company, and the last on death.[36] A set of Latin sequences with musical notation occupies folios 70-98, but the *laude*, as in several other collections from the period, have only the carefully traced staves intended for the music which was unfortunately never entered.[37]

The fine quality of the illuminations reflects the status of the Compagnia di San Gilio (Egidio) which owned it. This company was a large civic institution that maintained the Ospedale di Santa Maria Nuova. Its rule of 1284, one of the oldest in the vernacular, is preserved in the Biblioteca Nazionale Centrale, Florence (B. R. 336; ex Palatino 1172).[38]

Miscellaneous Fragments. In addition to the two complete manuscripts containing monophonic *laude*, there are also some fragments which have survived the unscrupulous practice of dismembering volumes and peddling them page by page. Liuzzi notes several examples of miniatures which have found their way into widely scattered libraries in Europe and the United States. These include: (1) a single leaf representing Christ in Majesty, now in the Pierpont Morgan Library, New York[39] (fig. 11); (2) St. Michael slaying the dragon, now in the

British Library;[40] (3) the Resurrection and holy women at the tomb, in the Fitzwilliam Museum, Cambridge;[41] and (4) the Ascension, formerly of the Lehman Collection, Metropolitan Museum, New York.[42] A fifth, identified by Offner as a sister miniature of Nos. 1 and 2 in Mgl[1], is the painting of Christ in Majesty surrounded by the twelve apostles, in the Rosenwald Collection of the National Gallery of Art, Washington, D.C.[43] (fig. 12). This item is connected by Offner with the others on the basis of dimension of leaf and miniature, layout, and figure drawing, and he assigns it to the workshop of Pacino di Bonaguida. Two other illuminated *lauda* folios from the Rosenwald Collection are attributed to the Master of the Dominican Effigies--the Nativity with the Annunciation to the Shepherds[44] and Christ and the Virgin enthroned with forty saints[45] (fig. 13).

These surviving leaves and also others have been studied by Agostino Ziino, who has located fourteen folios of *trecento* Tuscan origin. These extant fragments demonstrate that *laude* exhibited considerably greater diversity than might be assumed from the comparison of only Cortona 91 and the Magliabechiano manuscript (Mgl[1]).[46] Several of the melodies seem to be *unica*; others present notably variant readings of *laude* also contained in the two complete collections which have been under examination in this study. All of the folios are illuminated, and the majority of them have received previous notice by art historians.[47]

The iconography of the miniatures has proven to be important in the attempt to establish the extent of instrumental accompaniment in the performance of the *laude*. Ziino, for example, discusses the representations of angel musicans playing and holding instruments--e.g., psaltery, vielle, lute, trumpet. Liuzzi had, to be sure, already observed the instruments in some of the miniatures that had been noted by Offner, and he had ventured to suggest on the basis of the musical iconography that these indicated instrumental accompaniment in the performance of *laude*. However, as a crucial point in his argument he had pointed to an angel playing a trumpet in *A voi gente facciam prego* (Mgl[1], No. 4),[48] a poem that deals with the Last Judgment. The illumination in this case, however, is an illustration of the text from the Apocalypse--a text which identifies angel trumpeters who summon the dead at the end of time.[49] However tenuous Liuzzi's claim for instruments in the performance of *laude* was in 1935, more recent archival research has shown incontrovertibly that instruments were used in Florence in the fourteenth and fifteenth centuries.[50]

Ziino's work is thus particularly significant since he has brought together research from different disciplines. To evidence gleaned from art history research and archival findings, he has added his own considerable experience in the critical study of this repertory and in so doing has been able to argue convincingly that some of the folios originate from the same *laudario*.[51] Foliation, style, and relative position of *laude* within a manuscript may all function as clues to origin. Apparently the more common practice in Tuscany was to follow a hierarchical scheme in arrangement of *laude* within a collection, whereas Umbrian codices which lack music are generally ordered according to the cycle of the Church year, as are liturgical books which combine the Temporal and Sanctoral Cycles.[52] Iconographical and hagiographical evidence also may permit identification of figures and symbols in the miniatures, which in turn are useful in ascertaining provenance.[53] For example, the prominent figures at either side of the cross in the Washington folio (fig. 13) are depicted as bearded and bald old men holding large scrolls. The fact that they are wearing the Carmelite habit strongly suggests origin in a Carmelite church in Florence. Their resemblance to the Lorenzetti panel paintings of Elias, the founder of the Carmelite Order, and Eliseus, his immediate successor, is striking.[54] St. Agnes' appearance in the second roundel from the top in the left-hand margin in the same illumination may also be significant, for the *laudesi* company in Maria del Carmine, Florence, was known by its popular title of the

Laudesi di Sant'Agnes--i.e., the company responsible for the Ascension plays produced throughout the *quattrocento*.

Another Florentine fragment, which almost certainly came from the same *laudesi* company in the Carmine, contains a depiction of St. Agnes in Glory (fig. 14). This fragment, now in the British Library, is especially significant since *laudari* of this period generally do not contain such large and sumptuous illuminations of a saint. (Most illuminations of this quality and size are reserved for representations of Christ and the Virgin or occasionally for a figure derived from Scripture such as the St. Michael in the fragment in the British Library.) Such honor to a saint suggests that he or she was the patron of the company or of the church to which it was attached. Ziino's theory that these fragments, as well as certain other related fragments, are from a presumed *laudario* belonging to the company of St. Agnes[55] is now reinforced by the inventory of the Compagnia di Sant'Agnes compiled by the artist Neri di Bicci in 1467 when he assumed his duties as *sindaco* of the company. Among the books inventoried by Neri are several collections of *laude* which are identified as illuminated manuscripts containing musical notation.[56] However, the evidence presented by Ziino and by this inventory is valuable but doleful testimony to the number of manuscripts to fall victim to unscrupulous mutilation. One of the most regrettable of these losses is the fourteenth-century *laudario* with musical notation which is described in the catalogue of the Biblioteca Nazionale Centrale, Florence, as Mgl XXXVI (ex Gaddiano 44). According to the inventory, it contained 160 *laude* with musical notation as well as a litany of the saints. A copy of the dedication, preserved in the manuscript division of the library, is interesting in itself:

> In the name of God. Amen. This book belongs to the Company of the *Laude* who sing in the church of the brothers of All Saints in Florence. The said company was ordained and begun by the will and authority of Mssr. Frate

Guglielmo, Master General of the above mentioned Order of
the *Umiliati* in 1336, on the eleventh day of the month of
November, in honor of the Lord God and his Holy Mother,
the Virgin Mary, and of St. Benedict, St. Vernando, St.
Lucy, and of all the saints and blessed in Paradise. . . .
These are the *laude* which were written and published, and
ordained for the use of the noble and holy brothers of the
Company of All Saints in Florence, according to the table
contained here. In the first place, a *lauda* to the Trinity.[57]

Curiously, in his discussion of the provenance of Mgl[1], Liuzzi
claims that the codex belonged first to the Company of Santo
Spirito and then to the *Umiliati* of Ognissanti.[58] Not noticing
the difference in description and the vast discrepancy in the
size of the collection, he obviously seems to have confused the
missing manuscript with Mgl[1]. In her modern edition of the
Catalogue of the Biblioteca Nazionale Centrale, Florence,
Becherini notes that the *Umiliati* manuscript has been missing
from the collection since 1883.[59] This codex is surely the one
that had been seen by Charles Burney, who reported examining
it during his visit to Italy in 1770:

Some of the companies of laudisti in Florence have subsisted
over five hundred years. I found a folio of manuscript of
laudi spirituali with notes in the Magliabechi Library,
composed for a company of friars of the Order of the
Umiliati and sung by them in the chapel of All Saints,
Florence, 1336.[60]

While the loss or dismemberment of such treasures as the
Umilati manuscript is to be lamented, at the same time their
loss serves to emphasize all the more the great value of the two
complete manuscripts with musical notation which have
survived intact. As damaging as the consignment to the coal
bin was for Cortona 91, perhaps that fate may have saved this
oldest *laudario* from a worse fate. That the Magliabechiano
codex (Mgl[1]) with its elegant illuminations has survived is all
the more remarkable.

5

The Marginal Liturgy of the *Disciplinati*: The Popular Office of *Tenebrae*

While the dramatic *laude* of Umbria sometimes tended toward a course leading from *devozione* to *rappresentazione*--from pentitential ritual to actual theatricalized presentations--it must nevertheless be pointed out that the same *devozione* was also the source of other developments which, although perhaps less spectacular, are nonetheless significant. Such developments include the traversing of the distance between *devozione* and *ufficio*--from private devotional observances to popular ceremony fashioned to a greater or lesser degree upon the Divine Office.

As demonstrated above, the appearance of new elements in the *laude* themselves and in their function within the popular ritual often proves to be an index of alterations in the nature of the confraternities singing them. One of the most striking of these new developments is evidenced in the later-fourteenth-century records of certain *disciplinati* whose *laudari* and other documents begin to indicate a more strictly regulated manner of taking the discipline. The description contained in the Ordo of San Stefano[1] (and paralleled almost verbatim in numerous other *disciplinati* statutes) thus leaves little opportunity for improvisation and also stresses the importance of ritual in their observances.

As the documents show, therefore, the *devozione* practiced by the *disciplinati* in the privacy of their oratories developed into the popular offices to which reference is frequently made in statutes of the *trecento* and *quattrocento*. The persistent recurrence of such references to an *ufficio* inevitably raises the question of the nature of this Office. We can with certainty say, however, that the term *ufficio* cannot be invested with an unequivocal meaning in this context. Even a cursory examination of the records reveals a wide range of practice, the least complicated being the simple recitation of familiar prayers in the manner of the Office at specified times of the day. The Statuti della Confraternita di San Rufino in Assisi, for example, required that "anyone is bound to say daily eight Our Fathers with Hail Marys for the hours of Matins and Vespers. For the other hours--that is, Prime, Terce, Sext, None, and Compline--five of the above are said."[2]

Not surprisingly, therefore, the ambiguity of the numerous references to an *ufficio* in Florentine confraternity documents suggests that the content of the rite could have been considerably different in the various instances where the term appears. Statutes and ordos of the period are threaded with statements such as "In Lent the *devozione* and discipline are made after the Office,"[3] "Every fourth Friday the first nocturn [of Matins] of the dead is sung and the discipline is taken,"[4] and "At all morning meetings the Matins of Our Lady is sung with Lauds."[5] While the exact interpretation of such references thus remains obscure, some conclusions may nevertheless be drawn in order to create an index of those events in the life of the *disciplinati* which seemed to occasion the saying of an office of some sort. Among these the *devozione*, or the exercise in which the discipline was taken, assumes a place of primacy not only for the frequency with which it appears in various documents but even more importantly for its position in the gradual development of dramatic elements that in time became a connecting link with the *rappresentazione*. Other occasions which invariably imply an *ufficio* are the ceremonies of Holy Week and the funeral services of the *fratelli*. Furthermore, in addition to the actual exequies, many statutes speak of a commemorative *ufficio delle morte generali* (General Office of the Dead) as well. Further allusions to *lauda*-singing, the act of self-inflicted scourging, and the incorporation of certain liturgical prayers in the offices produces a strange mélange of popular elements along with vestiges of liturgical usage which can perhaps only be properly understood if an Office could be completely reconstructed.

Most statutes do not, of course, include the text of the Office to which they make reference, but a few examples of such texts do exist. Two extant texts will be the focus of my analysis in this chapter. Both are remarkably well developed in form, complete in their redaction, and enriched by copious rubrics which contain the directions necessary to clarify the ceremonial and ritual movement. These examples, which are of approximately the same date, are both intended for the Office of Matins for Holy Thursday, and contain the discipline along with *lauda*-singing. Nevertheless, they are distinctly different in form.

The first example is the Office of the Florentine Compagnia della Disciplina in Sancta Maria del Carmine, also known as the Compagnia di San Niccolò di Bari (CRS 439). The inventory of the archives lists only the rule contained in this document and fails to note that bound with it is the actual text of the *disciplinati* Office of Matins and Lauds for the last three days of Holy Week, the Office of *Tenebrae*. The Latin text contains in addition rubrics in Italian. The manuscript is beautifully preserved (figs. 1, 15-16).

The second source to be subjected to analysis is the Office of the Compagnia della Madonna Santa Maria dal Baraccano in Bologna, preserved in that city's Biblioteca Archiginnasio, MS. Fondo Ospedale 35 (fig. 2). Like the Florentine example, it is also bound with the statutes of the confraternity. Although it is undated, the document can clearly be established as originating in the early fifteenth century both on paleographic evidence and by means of historical documentation. The church of Maria dal Baraccano was not built until the first decade of the fifteenth century, and clearly the Office belonged to a penitent group from that parish, for it begins with reference to this location: "This is the copy which was made for the brothers of the congregation of Maria del Barracane [sic]. The night of Holy Thursday, in commemoration of the Passion of Our Lord Jesus Christ."[6]

The ceremony of the *mandato,* to which reference has been made above in a previous chapter, was common to a number of *disciplinati* companies of the *trecento* and is specifically mentioned in several important manuscripts of Umbrian origin. Among these the statutes of the confraternities of San Rufino and San Lorenzo in Assisi make reference to the symbolic washing of the feet of the *fratelli* by the prior. In addition, the *lauda* for the occasion, *Venne Cristo humiliato,* is preserved in no fewer than three collections where it is identified by the rubric *La lauda per lo di de Iovedi sancto.*[7] We also know that the Umbrian *laude* tend to be more dramatic in character than the Tuscan. Yet none of the Umbrian examples provides more than a mere mention of the actual ceremony. For that reason the records from the North will necessarily be consulted, and the two examples which have been isolated for study in this chapter may be regarded as significant not only by their completeness but also by their exceptional length and the clarity of the description of the Office in the accompanying statutes. Thus the task of reconstructing the ceremony seems best begun through the initial examination of the respective statutes in order to ascertain how they correspond to and illuminate the Office texts.

Maria del Carmine. A careful reading of the *capitoli* of the *disciplinati* of the Carmine will reveal very precise information concerning the Office. For example, Chapter XIII, entitled *De Cantori,* demonstrates quite clearly that the Office was an exercise recited in choir:

> We ordain that each *correctore*, at the beginning of his term
> of office, should select two cantors whose duty it is to begin

the Office and to intone the lessons. And no one may interrupt them for any reason unless he is permitted to do so, so that the Office proceeds in an orderly and devout manner and without scandal. And each one is admonished to obey this rule.[8]

The first clear description of the Office, however, is encountered in Chapter XIV, entitled *Del'ordine delle oficio e oratione.* It is a lengthy and unusually detailed tracing of the service of evening prayer, the counterpart of the Divine Office of Compline.

> We ordain that our *correctore* is obliged to begin evening prayer at the hour and in the manner that seems best to him--that is, to bring the *fratelli* together in the oratory, to kneel in silence and pray with a devout heart to God for the remission of their sins. And all remain recollected, being either without support or prostrate. Having remained so for the short space of one Our Father and Hail Mary, the one who has been appointed devoutly says, *Giube Donne benedicere.* And the *correctore* answers thus: *Notte quieta, fine perfetta sono pacis conciedat nobis onipotens Dominus.* The brothers answer, *Amen.* And then he says a lesson such as this: *Fratres, sobrie estote e vigilate in orationibus.*[9] And then, persevering in prayer, they remain for the space of one-third of an hour, and, when the twenty minutes have passed, the *correctore* says, "Praised be Jesus Christ," in a manner that is heard by all. And all the others respond by rising to their feet and remaining in prayer for a space of a quarter of an hour. And having spent fifteen minutes thus, they remain kneeling so that they may say seven Our Fathers and Hail Marys more, if it pleases the *correctore.* And then this oration is said: *Vicita quesumus Domine, abitatione ista.*[10] And then in the name of God they again sit down, being reverently silent and devout of heart. And immediately two candles are lit out of reverence for God and the Virgin Mary, and two brothers who are appointed to do so kneel and begin to sing the *Ave Maria* and then a beautiful *lauda.* And the others who are sitting must stand and respond with devout hearts and joyful spirits. And at the

conclusion of the *lauda* those who are responsible begin to say the seven Penitential Psalms, with the *Gloria Patri et Filio*. Having said the psalms in chorus, all kneel, and the antiphon *Ne reminiscaris Domine* is said with the litany, versicle, and oration following. When the psalms have been completed, everyone is seated in silence and remains thus while two [brothers] who have been given the responsibility begin reverently to sing that devout song *Crocifisso in carne laudemus*, and the others respond with *Alleluia, alleluia, alleluia* and make the required genuflection. And then the oration of the cross is said: *Deus qui pro nobis filium tuum crucis patibulum*. This must be said only in paschaltide--that is, from Easter to Pentecost. And then is sung that noble canticle of the glorious Virgin, the *Magnificat*.[11]

There follows a series of numerous orations, but the chapter also contains further description of the service:

And then the brothers sit, and one who is appointed reads a sermon of St. Augustine, and seven *Paters* and *Aves* are said in honor of the Seven Gifts of the Holy Spirit. The oration of the Holy Ghost is said, . . . and then, while seated, the *correctore* chastises the brothers for their transgressions of the rule. The *camerlingo* then seats himself and calls each by name. Each brother is required to take to the treasurer an offering of money to help defray expenses of the confraternity. And he who is not able to do so is appointed to pay at the next meeting. This done, the *correctore* rises, goes to the altar, and begins the *Miserere mei* and the *De profundis*. The brothers follow him to the altar where, on their knees, they say three orations for the dead, and then, with the grace of God, they go to bed in silence.[12]

Several notable, though somewhat disparate, elements emerge quite clearly from this lengthy discourse in the rule. Perhaps the most obvious feature of the Office is its great length, which at once seems to suggest that it was not a daily occurrence but perhaps was reserved for the days of the *tornata* discussed in Chapter IV of the rule. Such meetings were scheduled on nearly forty days annually, with provision for scheduling more at the discretion of the *correctore*.[13] With regard to the structure of the ceremony itself, the most significant feature may be the incorporation in the description of complete Latin incipits, here rendered in a corrupt form, from the Divine Office. To continue the analogy with Compline, which properly ends with a Marian antiphon, the *disciplinati* insert the *Ave Maria*. The later interpolation of the *Magnificat*, however, creates a strange hybrid form suggesting the combination in the devotion of elements of Vespers as well as Compline.

Some information concerning the manner of execution is included in the documents. For example, the psalms appear to have been recited. However, at certain points it is clearly indicated that there is singing: "Comincino . . . a chantare l'Ave Maria e poi una bella lalda." And after the psalms is the indication: "Chomincino devotamente a chantare . . . *Crocifisso in carne laudemus*." This incipit is found in several other sources, most importantly in the late-fifteenth-century *Processionale* for Holy Week in Florence, Opera del Duomo, MS. 21, where it appears in a three-part setting.[14] The text is also found in Serafino Razzi's *Libro Primo dell Laudi*.[15] Unfortunately, no other incipits designating *laude* are included in the rule.

There is also a description, though less lengthy, of the morning office in Chapter XV, entitled *Del chiamare la mattina a matutino*:

> We ordain that the *correctore* and the *camerlingo* should arrange to call, or have called, the brothers [to prayer] at the proper hour of the morning. All gathered together, they begin Matins of the Virgin Mary in chorus, devoutly and slowly. The hymn is sung, that is, *Quem terra pontus*.[16] After the office of Matins has been said, everyone must sit down. The treasurer takes the scourges and passes them out, first to the *correctore* and then to the other brothers. The *camerlingo* immediately extinguishes the lights, and the

discipline is taken during the space of five Our Fathers and Hail Marys. Then one who is appointed says five stanzas of a *lauda* of the Passion, and the one in charge says the recommendations along with the *Miserere* and the *De profundis* and a prayer for the dead. When this is done, the *correctore* says a prayer for the Holy Church [and for the Archbishop of Florence][17] and for the city. Then for the deceased of the company and every other intention. At the conclusion he says devoutly, *Salutate la Vergine Maria*, and each one vests himself. The *camerlingo* again lights the candles, and the two who are appointed say the *Credo in unum Deum* while standing. And when the *et homo factus est* is said, each one kneels down and remains so until the *resurrexit tertia die*, and then each rises. When the *Credo* has been said, two chapters [of the rule] are read, and seven *Paters* and *Aves* are prayed along with the oration of the Holy Spirit. And if, in the said office, there should be anyone weak who cannot remain kneeling like the others, he has the right to ask permission to stay as best he can at the praises of God, always with devotion. And this [permission] must be given him. The *correctore* is obliged to have the Office said in the aforesaid way, allowing him, however, to permit of certain arrangements according to the time and his discretion.[18]

While less detailed than the evening Office, this particular exercise is nevertheless important for the taking of the discipline incorporated into it. The *devozione* took place in the dark and partially disrobed, for the passage speaks of "vesting again." There is once more no indication of how often the service was held, but the inclusion of the act of scourging would indicate that it was not a daily occurrence, for nearly all the penitent groups limited the *devozione* to one or two times weekly at most. Instead, as an earlier reference in Chapter V of the rule seems to indicate in its prescription that immediately upon rising the *fratelli* should go to the church to "give thanks to God and the saints," this would appear to have been a daily private devotion. The lengthy morning Office thus would have been reserved for certain specified days, perhaps the *tornate* noted in Chapter IV of the rule.

Directives related to the Office appear also in two other chapters of the statutes, but these are vague and offer little information concerning either music or ceremonial. In Chapters XVIII (*Dello uficio dei morti quando passa di questa vita*) and XIX (*Dello uficio dei morti generale*) there is in each case nothing more than an injunction to pray for the dead. Nor is there, unfortunately, an extant text for the Office of the Dead. No further commentary related to the music or ceremonial is contained in the rule itself.

However, as noted above, the manuscript which contains the rule also has bound with it the actual text of the Office of *Tenebrae*. This rare example of the marginal liturgy of the *disciplinati* in possibly its highest form of organization seems to be later in date than the rule itself, since the rule nowhere makes any mention of an Office for Holy Week. The *ufficio* contains only the hours of Matins and Lauds, and begins with Wednesday of Holy Week, which corresponds to the Divine Office of Maundy Thursday. The *disciplinati ufficio* for Thursday and Good Friday likewise is comparable to the Divine Office of Friday and of Saturday respectively. This seeming disparity is explained by the fact that the *disciplinati* services were held at night as a vigil.

The basic structure of the *disciplinati Tenebrae* from the Carmine is the same as that of the Divine Office--that is, Matins (consisting of three nocturns, each having three antiphons and psalms, a versicle and response, as well as three lessons, each followed by a responsory) and Lauds (consisting of five antiphons and psalms, a versicle and response, the Benedictus and antiphon, and a Collect). The differences reside in the interpolations of a more popular nature: the singing of *laude,* the taking of the discipline, and the re-enacting of the *mandato* or washing of the feet.

The dependence of the popular Office on the liturgical Office involves not only structure, however, but also the selection of the texts and chants. The same antiphons are used in both rites, and of the responsories only the ninth, in the third nocturn for Wednesday Matins, differs from the Divine Office.[19] In general the lessons at Matins are also drawn from the same sources as the liturgical model, but they are almost always abbreviated in length. The entire Office of *Tenebrae* for the designated three days includes forty-two psalms; however, while a tabulation of those used in the Divine Office reveals that there are thirty-eight different texts, the *disciplinati* Office employs only twelve--the seven Penitential Psalms and five others--which are simply repeated to reach the required total of forty-two.[20] Most likely the *disciplinati*, not possessing breviaries (and in any case more than likely not able to read), necessarily committed their psalms to memory. Nevertheless, the similarities between the Divine Office and this popular rite can only point to strong clerical influence.

The rubrics, written in the vernacular, describe the ceremonial and establish where the *laude* and hymns were sung. They also usefully indicate some aspects of performance practice. At the head of the Office stands the following rubric concerning its proper recitation:

> On the evening of Wednesday in Holy Week, at *tenebrae,* the first lessons are from the Lamentations of Jerimias. They are said by two *fratelli* in separate places, and the responses are made by the prior. The other six lessons are said by one [*fratello*] as at other times, and so also the responses. The brother who says the antiphons begins, and he who has said the lesson answers. The *Gloria Patri* is not said at the end of the psalms, but they are concluded *in voce di passione* [that is, in silence]. The bell is not rung, but a signal of the hand is made instead. The antiphons are said double. Fifteen candles are lighted, one of which is extinguished at the conclusion of each psalm, except the last [which is extinguished] at the *Benedictus.* In place of the usual psalms, the first six are taken from the *salmi graduali* and the other three from the Penitential Psalms. For Lauds the other four Penitential Psalms are used along with the *Laudate Dominum de celis* and the *Benedictus.* And thus

prescribed, the prior bows and begins in choir to say *Pater noster.*[21]

Certain portions of the Office were done in responsorial manner, the *cantori* alternating with the *fratelli*, as the rubric preceding the *Benedictus* indicates. Presumably here the word *tenebrae* is used to indicate the darkness at the extinguishing of the last candle and the customary noise made at that moment.

> The fourteen candles are extinguished, and the *governatore* says the antiphon of the *Benedictus* at the conclusion of which the fifteenth candle is extinguished, and for the first time the *tenebrae* is made. Then the *Benedictus* is sung by two or three *fratelli.* They sing the first half of the verse, and the chorus sings the other half. When it is concluded, the *tenebrae* is made for the second time. . . . [T]he *governatore* repeats the antiphon, and the *tenebrae* is made for the third time.[22]

Rubrics for Holy Thursday are even more abundant since they detail the manner of carrying out the *mandato.* Preceding the office of Matins for that day, for example, is a rubric with many references to singing:

> The sermon or *devozione* should be more fervent than usual. There are no recommendations on these three evenings of tears. . . . In addition to the aforesaid order, on Thursday night the washing of the feet is held, and a supper is prepared. and it is prescribed
>> Who should sing the Lamentations
>> Who should answer the antiphons with responses
>> Who intones the psalms
>> Who gives the sermon
>> Who sings the *mandato*
>> Who sings the *Ubi caritas*
>> Who sings the lessons
>> Who sings the *Benedictus.*[23]

The description of the actual manner of performing the *mandato* follows the responsory of the ninth lesson of Matins, and there is here also a clear indication of the location of hymns and *laude* in the rite:

> Lauds and *tenebrae* follow the washing of the feet. A place to sit is prepared for the washing, and the brother to whom the task is committed begins the *mandato*. At the words *surgit ad cenam* he stands, at *posuit vestimenta* he removes his mantle, and when *cum accepisset linteum* is said he takes the towel, and, doing in like manner, he begins to wash the feet. Helping him is the counselor. And if the one who reads the [Gospel account of the] *mandato* stops at the words *postquem ergo*,[24] in the meantime they must sing *Ubi caritas*. The reading is completed up to this point, and the rest is deferred until after the washing of the feet has been finished. In the meantime, that brother sits down, and two others elected for this purpose must sing at the same lectern:

> *Ubi caritas*

> If the washing of the feet has not yet been completed, all of the brothers then sing:

> *Dulcis Yhus memoria*

> And now, having washed the feet and tidied up the disorder, the brother who stopped at *postquam* must continue the ceremony in like manner. And while he does so, they prepare a simple supper, without superfluity, only symbolic as is fitting for such a day.

> *Postquam*

> At the end of the *mandato*, a sermon on a related subject is given by the prior or someone else more fit. Next, the prior, on his knees, begins embracing [the brothers] as God inspires him, and asking pardon and reconciliation. The other brothers follow, each one in turn exchanging the kiss of peace with the next as an act of humble charity. In choir

there follows the remainder of the office of Matins. The
governatore, bowing, begins in silence the *Pater Noster* and
then the antiphon for Lauds.[25]

The office of Lauds follows without interruption until the
Benedictus and *tenebrae* previously described. The *Miserere*
is recited, with rubrics indicating responsorial performance,
alternating between the *governatore* and the *fratelli*. At this
point, "the *devozione* should be made here as on other nights,
but with extraordinary fervor." The text of the previous day's
office supplies a brief rubrical description of the service.
After the *respice quesmus* and *Pater Noster*, the *devozione*
should take place in the dark. Then "two *fratelli* sing, while
the chorus joins in the refrain *Stabat Mater dolorosa*. At the
conclusion of this *lauda* with *ritornello*, the chorus answers,
Amen."[26] So ends the Office of Holy Thursday as observed by
the Compagnia della Disciplina di Maria del Carmine in
Florence.

Maria dal Baraccano. Juxtaposition of the document
examined above with the Office of the Compagnia della
Madonna dal Baraccano presents some significant points of
comparison. As the Florentine company was governed by a
correctore whose identity as either lay or religious is never
exactly made clear, the Bolognese confraternity was ruled by a
Padre Ordinario who, according to the statutes, was obviously
a layman elected from the ranks.[27] In addition, Chapter II of
the statutes prescribes the election of a *Padre Spirituali*, a
priest who served as confessor and spiritual director of the
group.[28] Like the rule of the *disciplinati* of the Carmine, the
statutes of Maria del Baraccano contain more lengthy and
more explicit remarks on the recitation of the Office than is
normally the case among similar documents of the period, for
two entire chapters in the manuscript are devoted entirely to a
discussion of the Office. Several curious and noteworthy
elements present themselves in Chapter VII, which is entitled

Del modo de dire l'offitio.

Dearest brothers, those who say the Office, before they begin, must say one *Pater* and *Ave* in silence. Then, kneeling before the altar, the *lauda Desedate, o peccadore* is said. At the end of the *lauda*, the P[adre] O[rdinario] says the *Confiteor*, and then the *fratelli* answer as at Mass with the proper oration. And those who say the Office then begin the Invitatory of Our Lady. After this, the seven Penitential Psalms are said by the *fratelli* who are in the usual places. At the end of the psalms, those who say the Office read a lesson of Our Lady, then the litany with some prayers as are contained in the book of the Office. And having completed this Office, the sacristans extinguish the lights. The discipline is taken devoutly on the bare flesh, or otherwise according to the discretion and with the consent and permission of our P[adre] S[pirituali], and with great fear of God. The P[adre] O[rdinario] first says, *Fratres, apprendite disciplina cum timore de peccato vestro.* Then those who say the Office begin *Gesù Cristo, Filij.* . . . The *fratelli* answer humbly, *miserere nobis.* Then the *Miserere mei* is said along with an oration for the souls of the deceased *fratelli.* Then a *lauda* of the Passion of Christ is said by one of the *fratelli* appointed by the *Padre Ordinario* to do so. It is followed by an oration for the Holy Father, the Lord Cardinals, the Archbishops and Bishops and prelates of the Holy Mother Church, and then for the Royal Emperor and all of the noble Christian lords and for this, our city, and for all of our spiritual fathers and all of the *fratelli* of this company, for each other and for widows, wards, the sick, travelers, those at sea, prisoners, pilgrims, and other persons in affliction. Then, while taking the discipline, five more Our Fathers and Hail Marys are said in honor of the five wounds of Jesus Christ. And this recommendation is said by one of the other *fratelli* appointed by the P[adre] O[rdinario]. At the conclusion of this, the P[adre] O[rdinario] says the special orations for the congregation, which does not participate in the Office, and then for the *Padre Spirituali*, for our brothers who have passed from this life and other intentions according to the needs of the time. . . . [Then] one *Pater* and one

144

Ave are said in silence, and then the *Salve Regina*[29] with its oration, while taking the discipline. Then each one again vests with the blessing of the Lord, and each prays silently in his heart until the lights on the altar are again lit. After this, the Creed is sung, with an oration, and the *Magnificat* with its oration, and the *Salve Regina* with its oration, all as contained in the book of the Office. This ends the said Office in praise of Jesus Christ. And when all these things have been done, an offering is made at the altar by whoever can do so.[30]

Although somewhat less clearly defined than its Florentine counterpart, this service appears nevertheless not to be as indebted to the Divine Office in spite of the fact that it employs the Invitatory of Our Lady and the seven Penitential Psalms. Twice curious allusions are made to anthems and orations "as contained in the book of the Office," which would appear to have been either another manuscript containing the Office text or, possibly more likely, the use of the liturgical books, reserved in the sacristy of the church, that would supply the items specified. Like the Office from the Carmine, this service includes the *devozione* taken in the dark. References to *laude* appear twice, and in the first instance the incipit is given: *Desedate o peccadore.*

Chapter VIII, *L'ordine del offitio del Viegnere Sancto* [sic], or *On the Order of the Office for the Good Friday*,[31] contains little more than the directive charging that the Office be celebrated annually and with unusual reverence befitting this day. It specifies that the service be held at midnight on Holy Thursday, and in addition reminds the *fratelli* that visitors may not be brought to the Office without the permission of the *Padre Ordinario* and the consent of a majority of the brothers. Anyone not present for the Office, even for a legitimate reason, must previously have excused himself.

Fortunately, the manner of celebrating this important feast, intended to be marked with special solemnity, is made much more explicit because of the inclusion of the text of the entire Office in the manuscript. The redaction is surprisingly complete, containing rubrics, clear indication of which psalms and orations are to be used, and even entire texts of the sermons to be presented at specified intervals in the Office. *Laude* play an important role in the service, and several incipits for these are indicated. The Office indeed opens with a *lauda*, followed by a Gospel reading and a sermon, all of which precede the washing of feet. After the *mandato* the seven Penitential Psalms are said with the antiphon *Ne reminiscaris*. Following are the discipline and a collection of readings and prayers interspersed with *lauda*-singing. The segment describing the *mandato* merits comparison with the Florentine version of this ceremony.

> Following the above sermon the lector reads the Passion as far as the place where Our Lord washes the feet of his disciples. Here he stops. Here begins the second sermon which our Lord made before washing the feet of the disciples.
>
> . . .
>
> After reading the aforesaid sermon, the *P[adre] O[rdinario]* commands the *fratelli* to remove their right shoe and stocking, and then the servants who are appointed bring in the hot water and other things necessary for the *P[adre] O[rdinario]* who is in office at that time, so that out of humility he can wash the feet of the brothers. And the lector continues reading the Passion up to the completion of the washing of the feet of all the *fratelli*, who are to remain attentive to the Passion of Our Lord. When the washing is completed and the *fratelli* have put on their shoes and stockings again, he stops reading, and the *P[adre] O[rdinario]* gives a sign that each should kneel at the bench in the usual manner. And, kneeling there, the *Padre Ordinario* commands the sacristan to take those thirteen candles which have been placed in the candelabrum for the *mandato* and to put them upon the altar.[32]

The *mandato* seems definitely to have been considered an

interpolation, for the description goes on to direct that "after the lighting of the candles on the altar, the Office is begun by the one whom the *P[adre] O[rdinario]* will have appointed, in this manner--that is, standing directly before the high altar and prior to beginning the psalms, he says, 'Brothers, be sober and watchful, for your adversary the devil goes about like a raging lion seeking someone to devour. Resist him steadfast in the faith. But you, O Lord, have mercy on us, thanks be to God'."[33]

The discipline follows in the manner common to that described in most *disciplinati* rules of the time--i.e., in the dark and accompanied by prayers and the singing of *laude.* Unlike the *mandato,* however, the discipline is seen as an integral part of the Office, for the document specifies:

> the two who have been appointed by the *Padre Ordinario* go before the altar and kneel, and in like manner all of the *fratelli* [do likewise]. And they then begin the Office, which must be done in the dark. And they take the discipline with great fear and reverence. The sacristan then lights all the lamps. When they are lighted, those two before the altar begin to sing: *Benedictus, Dominus Deus Israel quia visitavit et fecit redemptionem plebis sue.*[34] And all the other *fratelli* must respond by taking the discipline at the end of each successive verse. And this is done in reparation for scandal. When the psalm is completed, the discipline is again begun with great reverence and the fear of God as soon as the *P[adre] O[rdinario]* begins to say *Fratres, dillectissimi apprendite disciplina cum dolore de peccato vestro.*[35]

The manuscript significantly identifies three specific *laude* and quotes not merely the incipit but also the entire first two lines of each as they are interspersed with prayers and lessons. The quoted lines are:

> Quando Pilato intexe el populo ludo
> Fe a Christo spugliare la vestimento

(When Pilate understood the wishes of the Jewish people, he had Christ stripped of his garments)

Per satisfare alle gente feroce
Aspero crudele, rubesta ed acerba
(In order to satisfy these fierce, harsh, cruel, and bitter people)

Maria dicendo nel so pianto pio
Rendime, croce, el dolce figliol mio.[36]
(In her holy lament Mary said, "Give me the cross, my sweet Son.")

Unfortunately, the music for these *laude* seems to be lost, but two texts nevertheless survive in their entirety in other manuscript sources, which additionally preserve another *lauda* used in this rite. Long vernacular translations of the Gospel account of the Passion, known as *passio volgarizzato*, seem to have been popular in the fourteenth and fifteenth centuries. These are sometimes punctuated by sections in verse which are generally assigned to specific characters in the Passion story, perhaps in imitation of the quasi-dramatic rendition of the Passion from the Gospel of St. John in the liturgy on Good Friday. *Quando Pilato* and *Per satisfare* are found in the Passion setting of Nicolò di Mino Cicerchia, based on the manuscripts found at Siena in the Biblioteca Comunale degl'Intronati.[37] The *laude* mentioned in the statutes, *Desedate o peccadore*, is also preserved in a *laudario* (Rome, Biblioteca Nazionale, MS. V. E. 350) believed to have belonged to a confraternity from Siena.[38]

After the singing of the last *lauda,* the brothers vest. Another sermon is prescribed, in this instance by the *Padre Spirituali.* The *fratelli* are admonished to confess their faults but only after all visitors have been dismissed from the oratory. The *ufficio* is then brought to a close with the kiss of peace and a blessing.

The Bolognese Office is thus considerably more popular

in form than is the Florentine example. In the former, however, a curious phrase recurs: *per quello che dire l'uffitio* ("for those who say the Office"). Its signification is unclear, though it could possibly be understood to imply the setting apart of cantors (or at least a group who "say" the Office) as opposed to those who merely respond. Or the phrase might also suggest that not all of the *fratelli* were able to participate fully for other reasons, including the illiteracy of some of the faithful brothers. A provision of the rule concerning the election of the *Padre Ordinario* seems to imply such a problem, for it allows that those brothers who were not able to write were permitted to tell the names of their chosen candidates to the *Padre Spirituali* who then wrote them down.[39] While the text of the *disciplinati* Office of Maria dal Baraccano does in fact include psalms and a few phrases from the Divine Office, there is little evidence of specific imitation of the standard liturgical model, and the word *tenebrae* is not even used.

These statutes and other documents demonstrate that both confraternities placed an extremely high priority on the recitation of the Office. Because of the detail with which these rites are described in the rule, it would appear that the morning and evening Offices held a place of particular importance and that they were said with some degree of frequency, perhaps an average of once each week in the case of the *disciplinati* of the Carmine. Furthermore, both rules allude to recitation in choir, and the specific employment of the verb *cantare* makes it clear that singing played an important part in the service. *Laude* are the mainstay of the musical repertoire of the Office, while the description of the ceremonial contained in both sets of statutes provides some insight into the simple ritual which was involved. But when amplified by the actual Office texts, many details of ritual and performance practice are clarified. For example, it is established that parts of the Office were performed in antiphonal style, while at other times portions of the rite were responsorial. Certain

149

individuals functioned as cantors, while the *Padre Ordinario* or *correctore* fulfilled the role of liturgical leader or celebrant.

In the case of the *mandato*, both examples simply follow the Gospel text in re-enacting the story much like the *mandatum* of the Mass for Maundy Thursday. In no way can the re-enactment be considered a true dramatic representation in the same sense as, for example, the Office of the *disciplinati* of Gubbio. There are simply no indications of staging and costumes such as those contained in the elaborate inventories of some of the Umbrian confraternities.[40] And all action would seem rather to be simple ceremonial movement similar to that of the liturgy. Consequently, such an Office should properly be viewed as a culmination in itself, and no attempt ought to be made to speculate upon its possible role in anything so specious as an evolution into the *sacre rappresentazione*. Yet such popular offices as these are undeniably tributary branches from the same matrix that produced the dramatic representations. As such they constitute yet another and continuous tradition among the *lauda*-singing confraternities of that intense religious awareness of the anonymous *popolo bordone*--a monument of lay Christianity immortalized in the marginal liturgy of the late Middle Ages.

Notes

Abbreviations
Archival and Library References

F/ France
      Pa   Paris, Bibliothèque de l'Arsenal
GB/ Great Britain
      Lbm   London, British Library (formerly British Museum)
      Cfm   Cambridge, Fitzwilliam Museum
I/ Italy
      Ac   Assisi, Biblioteca Comunale
      Ad   Assisi, Duomo, of San Rufino (Cathedral)
      Ar   Arezzo, Biblioteca Comunale
      Bca   Bologna, Biblioteca Comunale dell'Archiginnasio
      Ct   Cortona, Biblioteca Comunale e dell'Accademica Etrusca
      Fas   Florence, Archivio di Stato
      Fm   Florence, Biblioteca Marucelliana
      Fn   Florence, Biblioteca Nazionale Centrale
      Fr   Florence, Biblioteca Riccardiana
      PEc   Perugia, Biblioteca Comunale Augusta
      PEbf   Perugia, Archivio del Pio Sodalizio Braccio Fortebracci
      Rn   Rome, Biblioteca Nazionale Centrale Vittorio Emanuele II
      Rv   Rome, Biblioteca Vallicelliana
      Rvat   Rome, Biblioteca Apostolica Vaticana
      Sc   Siena, Biblioteca comunale degli Intronati
US/ United States
      NYpm New York, Pierpont Morgan Library
      Wng   Washington, D.C., National Gallery of Art

Introduction

[1]John Henderson, "Piety and Charity in Late Medieval Florence: Religious Confraternities from the Middle of the Thirteenth to the Late Fifteenth Century," diss. (Univ. of London, 1983), p. 2.

²Ludovico Muratori, *Antiquitates Italicae Medii Aevi sive Dissertationes*, 2nd ed. (Arezzo: Belloti, 1773-80), p. 16, col. 41.

³Johannes Villani, *Historia universalis a condita Florentia*, in *Rerum Italicarum Scriptores*, XIII (Milan: Tipographia Societatis Palatinae in Regia Curia, 1728), p. 342.

⁴Following the chronology of Omer Engelbert, *Vita di San Francesco d'Assisi*, trans. Gino Rampani (1958; rpt. Milan: Mursia, 1976), p. 338.

⁵Although some works of the Sicilian school pre-date the *Cantico del sole*, that school was greatly affected by foreign influence.

⁶See chap. 3, p. 71.

⁷Ronald F. E. Weissman, *Ritual Brotherhood in Renaissance Florence* (New York: Academic Press, 1982), p. 54.

⁸On the geographical diffusion of the flagellants, see Pier Lorenzo Meloni, "Topografia, diffuzione e aspetti delle confraternite," in *Risultati e prospettive della ricerca sul movimento dei disciplinati* (Perugia: Bolletino della R. Deputazione di Storia Patria per l'Umbria, 1972), pp. 15-63. On Raniero, see Raffaelo Morghen, "Raniero Fasani e il movimento dei disciplinati del 1260," in *Il movimento dei disciplinati nel settimo centenario del suo inizio* (Perugia: Bottelino della R. Deputazione di Storia Patria per l'Umbria, 1960), pp. 29-42.

⁹Devotions to the *presepio* as well as to the sufferings of Christ are common in the *Meditations* formerly attributed to St. Bonaventure. See *Meditations on the Life of the Christ: An Illustrated Manuscript of the Fourteenth Century*, trans. Isa Ragusa and Rosalie B. Green (Princeton: Princeton Univ. Press, 1961). On the theory of relationship between this affective type of devotion disseminated by the Friars Minor and the affective quality found more prominently in painting of the time, see Émile Mâle, *L'Art religieux de la fin du moyen âge en France* (Paris: Armand Colin, 1925), p. 34.

¹⁰Henderson, "Piety and Charity," p. 77.

¹¹Monachi Patavini, *Chronicon de Rebus Gestis in Lombardia*

Praecipue et Marchia Tarvisina, in *Rerum Italicarum Scriptores*, VIII (Milan: Tipographia Societas Palatinae in Regia Curia, 1726), col. 699.

[12]For extensive treatment of Joachim's life and influence in the Middle Ages, see Marjorie Reeves' *Influence of Prophecy in the Later Middle Ages* (Oxford: Clarendon Press, 1969) and her *Joachim of Fiore and the Prophetic Future* (London: SPCK, 1976); see also Marjorie Reeves and Beatrice Hirsch-Reich, *The Figure of Joachim of Fiore* (Oxford: Clarendon Press, 1972).

[13]Reeves, *Influence of Prophecy*, p. 3.

[14]*Acta Sanctorum*, May, VII, 87-144.

[15]On Joachim's influence on the Franciscan Order, see Angelo Messini, "Profetismo e profezia ritmiche italiane d'ispirazione gioachimito-francescana nei secoli XIII, XIV, e XV," *Miscellanea Francescana, 41* (1941), 50-73, and "San Francesco e i francescani nella letteratura profetica gioachimita," *Miscellanea Francescana*, 45 (1946), 232-42.

[16]On Joachim's number theory see Reeves, *Influence of Prophecy*, chap. 1, and Raoul Manselli, "L'anno 1260 fu anno Gioachimitico?" *Il movimento*, pp. 99-108.

[17]Reeves, *Influence of Prophecy*, p. 34.

[18]Henderson, "The Flagellant Movement and Flagellant Confraternities in Central Italy, 1260-1400," *Studies in Church History*, 15 (1978), 51.

[19]Ibid., p. 152; see also Reeves, *Influence of Prophecy*, pp. 32ff.

[20]Henderson, "The Flagellant Movement and Flagellant Confraternities," p. 51.

[21]For further information about Raniero's identity and preaching, see Emilio Ardu, "Frater Raynerius Faxanus de Perusio," *Il movimento*, pp. 84-92.

[22]Henderson, "The Flagellant Movement and Flagellant Confraternities," p. 153.

[23]On the difficulty of distinguishing betwen the two, see Weissman, p. 58.

[24]See chap. 2.

[25]For an example of an altered text, see chap. 1, pp. 15-16.

Chapter 1
Non-Musical Documents: *Laudesi*

[1]Since this study treats only the monophonic *lauda*, no attempt will be made here to examine the various manuscript sources which contain polyphonic *laude*. For discussion of these the reader is referred to Knud Jeppesen, *Die mehrstimmige italienische Laude um 1500* (Leipzig: Breitkopf und Härtel, 1936); Piero Damilano, "Fonti musicali della laude polifonica intorno all metà del secolo XV," *Collectanea historia musicae*, 3 (1963), 59-90; and Giullo Cattin, "Nuova fonte italiana della polifonia intorno al 1500 (MS Cape Town, Grey 3.b.12)," *Acta Musicologica*, 44 (1973), 165-221.

[2]Gennaro Maria Monti, *Le confraternite medievali dell'alta e media Italia* (Venice: La Nuova Italia, 1927), I, 259.

[3]Fas, CRS *Santa Maria del Carmine*, 113, Vol. LXXXII, fol. 71[r]: "La compagnia delle laude ci debbono fare tre pitanze perpetualmente l'una pella festa della concezzione, l'altra per Santo Nicholao e l'altro pella anuntiatione. Debbono spendere per tutte tre queste feste. L. 34."

[4]Pietro Ridolfini, *Historia di Cortona di Iacomo Lauro Romano* (1633; rpt. Rome: Lodovico Grignan, 1639), p. 15[v].

[5]Fas, CRS A VIII, 1, fol. 3[v]. *Statuti della Compagnia di Sant'Agostino*, 1382: "Ordeniamo che la nostra compagnia . . . abbi sempre uno padre governatore due consiglieri uno proveditore uno apuntatore uno scrivano uno camarlingho tre maestri di novitii tre infermieri tre proveditore d'infermi . . . e un medico." See also Fr, MS. 2382, *Statuti della Compagnia di San Girolamo in Sancta Maria sopra Arno*, fols. 1[v]-4[v], which outline the functions of the various elected officers. See also Fas, CRS 439, *Santissina Regola della Compagnia della disciplina in Santa Maria del*

Carmine, on elections, fol. 1ᵛ; and Fr, MS. 2567, *Capitoli della Compagnia dell'Annunziata al Borghetto*, fol. 1ᵛ. For further discussion of officers and their obligations, see also Weissman, pp. 130ff.

⁶Fr, MS. 2567, fol. 5ᵛ, and Fas, CRS A VIII, 1, fol. 3ᵛ. Cf. Weissman, p. 30.

⁷For example, Fas, CRS, Z 1, 1427, fol. 4ʳ. *Statuti della Compagnia di San Zenobi*: "I capitani et consiglieri che sono faranno per tempi che provegino di certi laudesi et sonatori a cantare le dette laude." The words *et sonatori* have been canceled in the manuscript.

⁸Henderson, "Piety and Charity," p. 9.

⁹Weissman, pp. 74ff.

¹⁰Ibid., p. 75.

¹¹Quoted in Domenico Maria Manni, ed., *Chronichetti antiche di varj scrittori* (Florence, 1733), p. 211. See also Richard C. Trexler, *The Spiritual Power: Republican Florence under Interdict* (Leiden: Brill, 1974), esp. pp. 128ff.

¹²Notably those of Rodolfo Renier, Guido Mazzoni, and Enrico Bettazzi. See chap. 3, nn. 44-46 (below).

¹³*Miscellanea Francescana*, 4 (1889), 48-55.

¹⁴Henderson, "Piety and Charity," p. 28, establishes that of the Florentine companies originating in the last sixty years of the thirteenth century, fifty-nine percent were *laudesi* compared to eighteen percent flagellant and eighteen percent charitable. However, in the fifty years after the Black Death, *disciplinati* companies constituted more than sixty-two percent of new foundations.

¹⁵On mendicant influence, see Henderson, "Piety and Charity," pp. 23-25, and Weissman, pp. 43-45.

¹⁶Gilles Gerard Meersseman, *Ordo Fraternitatis Confraternite e pietà dei laici nel medioevo* (Rome: Herder, 1977), II, 975.

[17]Ibid., II, 977. See also Robert Davidsohn, *Forschungen zur Geschichte von Florenz* (Berlin: Mittler, 1908), II, 405, 430, and Monti, I, 157ff.

[18]Meersseman, *Ordo*, II, 977; Davidsohn, II, 431; Monti, I, 164.

[19]Meersseman, *Ordo*, II, 977; Davidsohn, II, 431; Monti, I, 155-57. For the statutes and commentary, see also Monti, I, 143-58.

[20]The primitive ordinances may be found in Giulio Piccini, *Libro degli ordinamenti de la compagnia di santa Maria del Carmino, scritto nel 1280* (Bologna: Romagnola, 1867). See also Davidsohn, II, 482, and Monti, I, 160.

[21]Davidsohn, II, 440.

[22]Meersseman, *Ordo*, II, 977.

[23]Davidsohn, II, 435-49; Monti, I, 166-76. Also see Fr, MS. 391, fol. 2ᵛ. Throughout his study of the Florentine confraternities, Henderson rightly identifies the company of Orsanmichele as a charitable society. However, in the present study that company is treated under the heading of *laudesi* by virtue of the fact that its members regularly engaged in singing *laude*, although that practice was not its primary reason for existence. The company was first and foremost an agency for poor relief.

[24]Meersseman, *Ordo*, II, 954ff; for the complete letter, see ibid., II, 1938.

[25]Ibid., II, 974ff.

[26]Quoted in Fernando Liuzzi, *La lauda e i primordi della melodia italiana* (Rome: Librerio dello stato, 1935), I, 246.

[27]Meersseman, *Ordo*, II, 968.

[28]Trexler, p. 128.

[29]Fas, CRS Z 4, fol. 20ᵛ: "due libri la dove sono scritte tutti gli uomini e femine de la compagnia."

[30]Fr, MS. 2567, fol. 15[r]: "gli huomini paghino soldi 5 le donne tre e i fanciulli minori di quindici anni soldi uno."

[31]Fr, MS. 1329, fol. 5[v]: "e ogni persona di compagnia maschio o femina si debba confessare spesso e comunicare almeno una volta l'anno." See also Trexler, p. 131, and, on the participation of women, Weissman, pp. 212ff.

[32]Fr, MS. 391, fol. 6[v]: "ssi debbia fare luminaria la sera alla lauda con candelotti accesi in mano dinanzi alla ymagine de la vergine Maria a le spese della compagnia." On the importance of images and the *laudesi* oratories, see Henderson, "Piety and Charity," p. 48.

[33]Fn, Banco rari 336 (già Palatino 1172), fols. 10[v]-11[r]: "Anche ordiniamo che ciascuno de la compagnia quando vede la sera acciese le candele ne la chiesa di san gilio a cantare le laude debbia intrare ne la detta chiesa et in cantando et rispondendo debbia ubidire i suo capitani."

[34]Ibid., fol. 22[v]: "I camarlinghi di questa Compagnia siano solliciti di venire ogni sera a la chiesa di san gilio et apparecchiare lo leggio e lo libro de le laude et l altre cose ch e stato usato per cantare le laude pognendo due candele accese sopra due candellieri dinanzi agli altari e una chon candelliere dinanzi al gonfalone quando . . . si cantano le laude."

[35]Ibid., fol. 6[v]: "Tutti quanti quelli che sono de la Compagnia debbiano la sera venire a santo gilio a cantare le laudi se possono e chi non puote dica per la sera che non vi viene tre pater nostri con ave maria." Also, San Zenobi, Vol. 2170, fasc. 1, *Statuti*, 1326-1490, fol. 2[v], and Meersseman, *Ordo*, II, 960, 1056, document 44, chap. 4.

[36]Piccini, ed., *Libro degli ordinamenti de la Compagnia di Santa Maria del Carmino scritte nel 1280*, p. 26.

[37]For example, Fas, CRS Z 4, fol. 74[r]: "un libricciolo piccolino coperto di quoio vermaglia dove sono scritte laude insegnare a fanciulli."

[38]Fr, MS. 391, fol. 2[v]: "Lofficio de governatori delle laude sia da ssettare e di ordinare come si cantino ogni sera le laude dinanza all ymagine della nostra donna al pilastro sotto la loggia e in fare la scuola le domeniche per imparare e per che simparino a cantare le laude . . . nella casa o bottega della compagnia. . . ." Similar provisions for teaching the *laude* are found

also in Fas, SZ I, fol. 6[r]: "Anche ordiniamo e fermiamo che lli regitori abbiano et debbiano avere studio che ne di domenicali facciano insegnare cantare le laude a quelli della compagnia i quali non le sapessero. Et pero abbiano piena podestade di comandare a cui loro piacie et quanti della compagnia che la domenica si debbiano raunare nella predecta chiesa a cantare quelli che sanno per insegnare et quelli che non sanno per apparare."

[39]Piccini, p. 28.

[40]Meersseman, *Ordo*, II, 1057, document 44, chap. 9.

[41]Henderson, "Piety and Charity," p. 45.

[42]Meersseman, *Ordo*, II, 977.

[43]Ibid., II, 937-42. See documents 33, p. 1042, and 39, p. 1047, for texts of letters of indulgence.

[44]Henderson, "Piety and Charity," p. 51.

[45]See ibid. for the opinion that these were large illuminated star-shaped frames with an image of the Madonna at the center accompanied by painted cherubim and seraphim. See also ibid., p. 71, nn. 42-45, for related inventory entries, and, for corroboration, the description in n. 47 below.

[46]Ibid., pp. 52ff. This emphasis upon pageantry is reflected in the tendency to refer to *laudesi* by the term *di stendardo*, which in fact was the more common usage in the fifteenth century; obviously the reference was to the banners (*stendardi*) which were carried in procession.

[47]Fas, SZ 154: "con lumi et con li angeli pendenti della stella secondo el modo consueto et . . . con li organi e trombetti come e di anticho costume" (fol. 29[r]).

[48]Henderson, "Piety and Charity," pp. 49-50.

[49]Meersseman, *Ordo*, II, 950.

[50]Ibid., II, 943.

[51]Ibid.

[52]Ibid., II, 1052, document 42, chap. 6.

[53]See Frank D'Accone, "Le compagnie dei laudesi in Firenze durante l'ars nova," *L'ars nova italiana del trecento*, 3 (1970), 253-82, "Alcune note sulle compagnie fiorentine dei laudesi durante il quattrocento," *Rivista italiana di musicologia*, 10 (1975), 86-114, and "Music and Musicians at the Florentine Monastery of Santa Trinita, 1360-1363," in *Memorie e contribute alla musica dal medioevo all'età moderna offerti a Federico Ghisi nel settantesimo compleanno, 1900-1971* (Bologna: A.M.I.S., 1973), pp. 131-51.

[54]D'Accone, "Le compagnie dei laudesi," p. 256.

[55]Ibid., p. 264.

[56]D'Accone, "Alcune note sulle compagnie fiorentine," p. 92.

[57]Quoted in ibid.

[58]On Chellino, see D'Accone, "Le compagnie dei laudesi," pp. 264-65, 271; on Squarcialupi, see D'Accone, "Alcune note sulle compagnie fiorentine," pp. 103-04.

[59]See n. 85, below.

[60]D'Accone, "Alcune note sulle compagnie fiorentine," p. 102, points out that even the wealthy company of Orsanmichele experienced financial pressures during the time of the construction of its oratory.

[61]Ibid., pp. 99-100, referring to San Zenobi.

[62]D'Accone, "Le compagnie dei laudesi," p. 273.

[63]Ibid., p. 278.

[64]Ibid., pp. 279-80. On Gherardello's relationship with the monks at Santa Trinita, see D'Accone, "Music and Musicians," pp. 142ff.

[65]Quoted in Piero Damilano, "Fonti musicali della lauda polifonica

intorna alla metà del secolo XV," *Collectanea Historica Musicae*, 3 (1963), 60. See also Bonaccorsi, "Andrea Stefani musicista della 'ars nova'," *Rivista musicale italiana*, 21 (1948), 103-05, and Nino Pirrotta, Preface to *The Music of Fourteenth Century Italy*, Corpus mensurabilis musicae, 8, Pt. 5 (1964), p. iii.

[66]Frank D'Accone, "Alcune note sulle compagnie fiorentine," p. 101.

[67]Quoted in D'Accone, "The Musical Chapels of the Florentine Cathedral and Baptistry During the First Half of the Sixteenth Century," *Journal of the American Musicological Society*, 24 (1971), 3, 37.

[68]D'Accone, "Alcune note sulle compagnie fiorentine," p. 100.

[69]Ibid., p. 92.

[70]Fas, CRS 4, *Libro di Partiti A. delle Compagnia di Sant'Agnese, 1438-1509*, fol. 3[v].

[71]Ibid., fol. 114[r].

[72]Ibid., fol. 116[v].

[73]D'Accone, "Alcune note sulle compagnie fiorentine," p. 89.

[74]Ibid., p. 94.

[75]Ibid., p. 103.

[76]Ibid., p. 188.

[77]Fas, CRS 4, fol. 52[v]: "in luogo parte di remuneratione e parte per limosine perche e povero."

[78]Ibid.: "essendogli miglioratogli la boce assai e cantar meglio."

[79]Ibid. Also, Fas, CRS, 125, *Entrate e uscite della Compagnia di Sant'Agnese, 1471-1502*, fol. 67[v], cites some monthly payments.

[80]Fas, Reg. 102, fol. 90[r].

[81]Meersseman, *Ordo*, II, 997-98.

[82]Ibid.

[83]See Example 7 (pp. 113-14 above).

[84]Several of the Medici family were actually members of various confraternities. Lorenzo himself belonged to a number of companies in Florence and held office in the *Disciplinati* of San Paolo several times. See Weissman, p. 117n. In addition, Fas, CRS 4, the *Libro di Partiti A* of the Company of Sant'Agnese, is rich in references to the association of the Medici family with that company. Fol. 15^r: on 1 January 1488, Lorenzo was appointed one of the councilors; fol. 17^r: on 13 January 1488, Piero di Lorenzo de'Medici was allowed by the captains to be elected to any office, notwithstanding the fact that he had not yet reached the required age; fol. 19^v: Piero was elected captain for six months beginning 1 July 1488; fol. 27^v: a privilege was granted to Piero allowing him (by virtue of his benefices to the company) to use belongings of the company to celebrate the feast of the Holy Spirit and every other feast which he may wish, as it pleases him; fol. 29^r: Lorenzo di Piero di Cosimo de'Medici was captain for six months beginning the calends of January 1492; fol. 48^v: the company held funeral services for Lorenzo; fol. 51^r: Monsignore (Giovanni?) de'Medici became captain for six months beginning 1 July 1492; fol. 55^r: Giuliano di Lorenzo de'Medici entered the company as a novice, at the age of sixteen.

[85]Quoted in Götz Pochat, "Brunelleschi and the 'Ascension' of 1492," *Art Bulletin*, 60 (1978), 233.

[86]Quoted in Alessandro d'Ancona, *Origini del teatro italiano*, 2nd ed. (Turin: Loescher, 1981), pp. 251ff; cf. the somewhat different translation, derived from a German translation of the Russian text, in *The Staging of Religious Drama in Europe in the Later Middle Ages*, ed. Peter Meredith and John F. Tailby, Early Drama, Art, and Music, Monograph Series, 4 (Kalamazoo: Medieval Institute Publications, 1983), pp. 245-47. See also Cesare Molinari, *Spettacoli fiorentini del quattrocento* (Venice: Neri, 1969), pp. 47ff; Virginia Galante Garrone, *L'apparato scenico del dramma sacro in Italia* (Turin: Fondo di Studi Parini-Chirio, 1935), p. 81; *Il luogo teatrale a Firenze*, ed. Mario Fabbri *et al.* (Florence, 1975); and Arthur R. Blumenthal, "A Newly Identified Drawing of Brunelleschi's Stage Machinery," *Marsyas*, 13 (1966-67), 20-31. For analysis of the

Ascension Play in the Carmine, see Cyrilla Barr, "Music and Spectacle in Confraternity Drama of Fifteenth-Century Florence: The Reconstruction of a Theatrical Event," in *Christianity and the Renaissance* (Syracuse: Syracuse Univ. Press, forthcoming).

[87]Fas, CRS, Vol. 98, *Entrate e uscite della Compagnia di Santa Maria del Carmine, 1424-41*, fol. 18[v]. The payment is dated 8 July 1425, the same year that Felice Brancacci commissioned the artist to paint the frescoes of the family chapel in the Carmine. On the association of artists with the spectacles, see Martin Wackernagel, *The World of the Renaissance Artist*, trans. Alison Luchs (Princeton: Princeton Univ. Press, 1981), esp. pp. 193-204.

[88]Giorgio Vasari, *Lives of the Most Eminent Painters, Sculptors and Architects*, trans. William Gaunt (London: Dent, 1963), II, 55.

[89]Ibid., II, 56.

[90]Quoted in d'Ancona, *Origini*, p. 153. See also *Staging*, ed. Meredith and Tailby, pp. 243-47.

[91]Luigi Banfi, ed., *Sacre rappresentazioni del quattrocento* (Turin: Unione Tipographico-Editrice Torinese, 1968), pp. 84-85.

[92]Ibid., p. 425. Numerous examples of musical interpolations in *rappresentazioni* may be found in Bianca Becherini, "La musica nelle sacre rappresentazioni fiorentini," *Rivista musicale italiana*, 53 (1951), 193-241.

[93]Molinari, p. 36.

[94]Giuseppe Richa records the dimensions of the church in his *Notizie istoriche delle chiese fiorentine* (Florence: Viviani, 1762), X, 16-17: "the height is 50 braccia, the width 36 and the length 24." He quotes a source which he identifies only as "a manuscript belonging to the Fathers of the Oratory." Several other accounts of the dimensions are found, however, to contradict those of Richa, but all agree that the building was large and appropriate to accomodate the spectacle. See also the description of Abraham of Suzdal in d'Ancona, *Origini*, p. 251, and Ugo Procacci, "L'incendio della chiesa del Carmine de' 1771," *Rivista d'Arte*, 14 (1932), 140-242.

[95]See Henderson, "Piety and Charity," p. 55, for a graph representing expenditures (figures in *Lire di piccioli*) of the company of Sant'Agnese from 1425 to 1450.

[96]Expenses for 1438, the year preceding the Council, are quite extensive (Fas, CRS 98, *Entrate e uscite B, 1424-41*, esp. fols. 141r-143r) as are those of 1471, the year of the visit of the Duke of Milan (Fas, CRS 125, *Entrate e uscite B, 1471-1502*, esp. fols. 51v ff). Henderson ("Piety and Charity," pp. 56, 72n) cites a payment in Fas, CRS 1, 4, fol. 10r, for things for the Feast of the Assumption in the amount of 100 lire specified in the account as occurring during a visit of the Ambassador of the King of Spain in 1486.

[97]Even after the expulsion of the Medici in 1494 the plays continued to be part of such special occasions as the visit of Margaret of Austria in 1533, the marriage of Joan of Austria to Francesco de'Medici in 1565, and the marriage of Virginia de'Medici to Cesare d'Este in 1586.

[98]Henderson, "Piety and Charity," p. 59.

[99]Meersseman, *Ordo*, II, 1001.

[100]Ibid.

[101]Meersseman notes (*Ordo*, II, 1002) that in some instances the companies met in the convents and disrupted the friars' recitation of the Office with drinking, with merry-making, and even with a band of instrumentalists.

[102]Fn, Palatino 173, fol. 94v. See also Cyrilla Barr, "The Ubiquitous Fra Serafino Razzi: Some Thoughts on his *travestimenti spirituali*," *The Musical Quarterly*, forthcoming.

[103]Published in Venice, but edited by Filippo Giunti of the famed Florentine family of printers and engravers. Filippo explains in his Preface that it was printed in Venice because the Florentine presses were not yet capable of printing music.

[104]*Corona di sacre canzoni*, published in 1675 with successive editions, each vastly enlarged, in 1689 and 1710. All three were published in Florence by del Rosso, Carlieri, and Bindi, respectively. A fourth volume under the title *Colletta di laudi spirituali* was also published in Florence by Bindi in 1706.

Chapter 2
Non-Musical Documents: *Disciplinati*

[1]The most comprehensive collection of writings on the *disciplinati* may be found in the papers of the Congress held in Perugia to commemorate the seven-hundredth anniversary of the movement of 1260; the proceedings of this Congress have been published: *Il movimento dei disciplinati nel settimo centenario del suo inizio* (Perugia: Bollettino della R. Deputazione di Storia Patria per l'Umbria, 1960); see also *Risultati e prospettive della ricerca sul movimento dei disciplinati*, published under the same auspices in 1972.

[2]Henderson, "Piety and Charity," pp. 81-82.

[3]Meersseman, *Ordo*, I, 468.

[4]Ibid., I, 469.

[5]Ibid., I, 463. Essentially the same treatment of the subject may be found in the author's "Disciplinati e penitenti nel duecento," in *Il movimento*, pp. 43-72.

[6]Meersseman, *Ordo*, I, 511ff, "Disciplinati e penitenti," p. 61, and *Dossier de l'Ordre de la Pénitence au XIIᵉ siècle* (Freiburg: Editions Universitaires, 1961), pp. 183-215. See also Pierre Mandonnet, "Les Origines de l'ordo des poenitents," *Compte rendu Congrès Scientifiques international* (Freiburg: 1903).

[7]Patavini, *Chronicon*, in *Rerum Italicarum Scriptores*, VIII, col. 713; Jacobus de Voragine, *Chronica de Civitate Jenuensi*, in *Rerum Italicarum Scriptores*, IX (Milan: Tipographia in Regia Curia, 1726), col. 49.
[8]Salimbene, *Cronica*, ed. Scalia, II, 675: "Componebant laudes divinas ad honorem Dei et b. Virginis quas cantabant dum se verberando incederent."

[9]Meersseman, *Ordo*, I, 504.

[10]Ricobaldi Ferrariensis, *Historia Imperatorum Romano Germanicorum*, in *Rerum Italicarum Scriptores*, IX, col. 134.

[11]Bartholomaeo, *Cronica di Bologna*, in *Rerum Italicarum Scriptores*, XVIII (Milan: Tipographia Societatis Palatinae in Regia Curia, 1731), col. 271.

[12]Caffari, *Annales Genuenses*, in *Rerum Italicarum Scriptores*, VI (Milan: Tipographia Societatis Palatinae in Regia Curia, 1725), col. 527.

[13]Fol. 8[v]: "Madonna santa Maria/ mercé de noi peccatore./ Faite prego al dolçe Cristo/ ke ne degia perdonare." See also Giorgio Varanini, *Laude Cortonesi* (Verona: Fiorini, 1974), I, 102n.

[14]Meersseman, *Ordo*, I, 499, and "Disciplinati e penitenti," pp. 46-53.

[15]Statutes of the Battuti di Cividale del Friuli, cited in Meersseman, *Ordo*, I, 500.

[16]On flagellation and its place in the early Church, see Jean Leclercq, "La Flagellazione volontaria nella tradizione spirituale dell'occidente," in *Il movimento*, pp. 73-83, and Henderson, "The Flagellant Movement," pp. 147-60.

[17]Meersseman, *Ordo*, I, 498.

[18]Henderson, "The Flagellant Movement," p. 154.

[19]Meersseman, *Ordo*, I, 500.

[20]Fas, CRS 345, *Capitoli della compagnia di San Giovanni Battista*, fol. 3[v]: "Ancho ordiniamo quando alcuno fosse recevuto se debia avere sua vesta e sua corda e sua disciplina . . ." ("We ordain that when anyone is received he must have his own tunic, his cord, and his discipline. . ." [Fas, CRS 544, fol. 17[v]]).

[21]Excellent illustrations are contained in the plates accompanying the two articles of Adriano Prandi, "Intorno all'iconografia dei disciplinati," in *Il movimento*, pp. 496-508, and "Arte figurativa per le confraternite dei disciplinati," in *Risultati*, pp. 166-85.

[22]Ad 76, fols. 4[r], 5[v], and CRS 345, fol. 3[v]. In addition, some companies made an annual offering of wax. See Fr 2382, *Statuti della*

Compagnia di San Girolamo, fol. 1^{v}.

[23]Fr 2567, fol. 23^{v}: "et perche le vesta e uno habito di religiose si prohibisce per questo presente capitolo che nessuno possa portasela a casa e questo si fa per levare la occasione delli scandoli che posson nascere in adoperarle o prestarle ad altri per far maschere o altre simil cose vietate da sacrisanti concili" ("[A]nd because the tunic is a religious habit it is prohibited in this present chapter that anyone should wear it at home, and this [rule] is made in order to avoid occasions of scandal which arise when using it or lending it to others for masquerades or similar things forbidden by most holy counsels"). Also Fr 2382, fol. 7^{v}; and Fas, CRS 544, *Capitoli della Compagnia del Gesù*, fol. 17^{v}.

[24]In the case of the company of Annunziata al Borghetto, for example, the novitiate appears to have been six months: "Circa le veste habbiamo ordinato che ogni volta che uno sara accetato nel numero di nostri fratelli . . . infra sei mese debbia farsi la vesta . . ." (fol. 2^{v}) ("Concerning the habit we have ordained that every time someone is accepted into the number of our brotherhood . . . within six months he must take the habit . . .").

[25]Ad 75, fol. 2^{r}; Fr 2382, fols. 7^{v}9^{v}; and Fas, CRS 354, fol. 3^{v}. The latter prescribes that a new member must be approved by a two-thirds vote of the company.

[26]*Laudario Oliveriana di Pesaro*, quoted in Arnaldo Fortini, *La Lauda in Assisi e le origini del teatro italiano* (Assisi: Società internazionale di studi francescani, 1961), p. 130. De Bartholomaeis believed the manuscript to have belonged to the Confraternita di Sant'Antonio in Assisi (see Fortini, p. 270n), but Angela Maria Terruggia has produced convincing arguments for Gubbian origin. See "In quale momento i disciplinati: hanno dato origine al loro teatro?" in *Il movimento*, p. 445n, and Terruggia's "Lo sviluppo del dramma sacro vista attraverso i codici di Assisi," *Annuario dell'Academia Etrusca di Cortona*, 11 (1960), 53. See also Giuseppe Mazzatinti, "Laudi dei disciplinati di Gubbio," *Il Propugnatore*, n.s. 2 (1889), 152. For description of the investiture service which includes references to singing, see Fr 2382, fols. 7^{v}-9^{v}.

[27]Henderson, "Piety and Charity," pp. 89-93. For a table showing the number of members expelled from the company of Gesù Pellegrino during the period 1341-63, including the reasons for expulsion, see ibid., p.

90. Unfortunately, in 56.2 percent of the cases no reason was given, though 20.5 percent were disciplined for non-attendance and 9.6 percent for disobedience. Other reasons included joining another company, usurious practices, playing dice, and frequenting taverns. For a table of punishments imposed in the same company in 1365-69, see ibid., p. 92. Out of a total of 204 penalties, the most commonly imposed were for reasons of non-attendance, missing confession, disobedience, failure to do punishments, and not paying subscriptions.

[28]Ibid., p. 93.

[29]On secrecy, see CRS 439, fol. 3^v, and also Monti, I, 45.

[30]Henderson, "The Flagellant Movement," p. 159n.

[31]Henderson, "Piety and Charity," p. 89.

[32]For examples of companies which held meetings twice weekly, see Ad 75, fol. 3^v, and CRS 554, fol. 26^r.

[33]Henderson, "Piety and Charity," p. 85.

[34]Fr 2566, fol. 7^v: "e a fare detta devozione si tenghi questo modo, che finito l uficio e sagrestani dieno con reverence le discipline a fratelli . . . lo ghovernatore dica alquante parole chonfortando i fratelli a penitencia della passione. E di poi se dica alquante parole sotto brevita exortando e fratelli a ben fare. Poi si tenghi silencio facendo la disciplina per spacio di due cinque Pater Nostri e Ave Maria. Poi si facino le prece e quelle facte si dicha el salmo *Miserere mei Deus* overo *Di Profundis clamavi* . . . o veramente si chanti psalmi laude o hymny secondo la volunta di che sara a chomandare."

[35]Ad 20, fol. 4^v, and Ad 21, fol. 4^r-4^v: "Et immediate surgat debens laudes vulgares cantare. Qui cantando illos ex devotionae moveat corda fratrum ad plantum et lacrimas intendentium magis ad verba quam ad voces.

"Laudes autem huiusmodi tali ordine disponantur quia diebus veneris vel aliis quibus de passione ageretur vel disponitis passioni cantentur laudes de passione salvatoris nostri iesus et mestissime matris eius. Sed diebus dominicalibus et festivis et quocumque alio tempore cantentur laudes diei vel festi si de festo agitur disciplina vel alias secundum diei devotionem vel sollempnitatis festi et temporis dispositionem. Et incantus cuiuslibet stantie seu versus si disciplina nunc agitur investibus facti. Finita stantia sive versu fiat disciplina set dum cantor cantaverit laudes. Ad sonum campanelle vel aliud signum surgens disciplina quiescat et hic prosequatur et fiat donec laudes predicte complete fuerint per cantorem laudabis."

[36]Work undertaken in the course of the present study indicates that to date no comprehensive investigation has as yet been made to determine the influence of liturgical practices of specific orders upon those confraternities under their supervision.

[37]For example, Fas, CRS 439, chap. 19, fol. 6[r].

[38]Conversely, a brother who did not meet these requirements might be denied such honors at his burial. Ibid., fol. 6[v], ordains that in the case of a brother who had not participated in the exercises of the company or who had not paid his dues within four months of the time of his death, the company was not obliged to do anything for him, "neither the Masses nor the Paters, nor the Office of the Dead." However, if a two-thirds vote of the company could demonstrate a legitimate reason for the brother's failure to participate in the activities of the company, then they were obliged to fulfill the usual obligations. A negative vote, however, exempted the company from all such duties--"non si faccia nulla per la sua anima." The rule did not apply to those who had belonged to the company for twenty years or more. "E questo non si intenda per niuno il qua fosse state nella compagnia anni venti o piu."

[39]Henderson, "Piety and Charity," p. 113.

[40]On funeral services of various Florentine companies, see ibid., pp. 112, 130n.

[41]Fas, CRS 345, fol. 4[r]: "se alcuno dela compagina al nostro Signor Cristo piacesse de chiamare a se si debbia essare vestito de la sua vesta de la corda e la suo disciplina en mano e scalco e scoperto."

[42]Ibid.: "Col li ceri e cum la croce e ciascheduno cum uno candelo in mano aceso quando se partino dala casa del morto enfine che lli enne sepellito . . . a la sepultura se debiano cantare quelli electione e laude che se confano a quello mestiero. . . ."

[43]Fr 3014, fol. 23[r]: "un sermone breve delle miseria et fragilita di nostra vita con una prece sola per l anima del fratello morto e di tutti quelli della nostra compagnia et rivestiti conveniente lauda cantando. . . ."

[44]Ct 120, fol. 11[r].

[45]Ct 91, *lauda* No. 36, fol. 88[v]. The text occurs (with different melody) in Fn Mgl[1], fols. 134[v]-135[v]; text only in: Fn Mgl[2]; Florence, Archivio della Curia Arcivescovile, MS. Fior.; Arezzo, Biblioteca Comunale, MS. 180 della Fraternità dei Laici (Aret.); and Paris, Bibliothèque de l'Arsenal, MS. 8521. See also Giorgio Varanini, *Laude Cortonesi*, I, 246.

[46]PEc 955 is a large collection containing 117 *laude* (both lyrical and dramatic), five of which are repeated to bring the total to 122. The manuscript contains only the texts of the *laude* and is arranged according to the liturgical cycle. Although the first section which contains the confraternity's statutes is dated 1374, there is good reason to believe that the *laude* were actually transcribed as early as 1350. See Anna Maria Vinti, "Precisazione sul movimento dei flagellanti e sui maggiori perugini," *Studi di filologia italiana*, 8 (1950), 316-19.

[47]Rv A26 is a very rich collection of 158 *laude*, five of which are repeated. The texts vary from short to long and are complex enough to be considered true *rappresentazione*. The latter often contain abundant Latin rubrics which may occur between verses. The manuscript is arranged in sections; the first, which is the liturgical cycle, contains fifty-one incipits; the second consists of fifty-one Lenten *laude*; the third is the sanctoral cycle containing forty-two texts; the fourth is made up of twelve *laude* for Sundays; and the last contains eleven *laude* for the dead. See Ernesto Monaci, "Uffizi drammatici dei disciplinati dell'Umbria," *Rivista di folologia romanza*, 1 (1874), 235-71; 2 (1875), 29-42.

[48]MS. 36/ii has been studied and edited by Arturo del Pozzo, "Contrasti spirituali in un codicetto Assisano del secolo XIV," *Giornale storico della letteratura italiana*, 86 (1925), 81-99.

[49]For discussion of the manuscript, see below.

[50]See n. 70, below.

[51]Jacobus de Voragine, *Chronica de Civitate Jenuensi*, in *Rerum*

Italicarum Scriptores, IX col. 49: "The fear of the Lord came over them to such a degree that nobles as well as plebians, old and young, even five-year-old children went in procession two by two through the squares of the cities, naked--with only their private parts covered--having laid away their shame."

[52]Ibid.

[53]Ibid., col. 50.

[54]Ibid.

[55]Caffari, *Annales Genuenses*, in *Rerum Italicarum Scriptores*, VI col. 527.

[56]Ibid., col. 704.

[57]Henderson, "The Flagellant Movement," p. 152.

[58]Ibid., p. 153.

[59]Monachi Patavini, *Chronicon de Rebus Gestis in Lombardia*, *Rerum Italicarum Scriptores*, VIII, col. 713.

[60]Henderson, "Piety and Charity," p. 86n.

[61]Pietro Ridolfini, *Historia di Cortona di Iacomo Lauro Romano* (Rome: Grignan, 1639), fol. 15v.

[62]Weissman, p. 50.

[63]For fuller discussion of two specific *mandato* services, see chap. 5. See also Cyrilla Barr, "Musical Activities of the Pious Lay Confraternities of quattrocento Italy: A Chronicle of Change," *Fifteenth Century Studies*, 8 (1983), 15-36.

[64]Henderson, "Piety and Charity," p. 87.

[65]Ad 76, fol. 17r-17v: "a celebrare con reverentia devota e profunda humilita alla quale la devina maesta a lavare i piede di pescadure e di serve sinchino mustrando a nuye exempio de humilita che come esso se signore e

maestro. Cosi nui con disciplina e in carita del servo e en umilita l uno al l altro faciamo cio e imaiure lavando i piede ai menure e comince el priore el sopriore e gl offitiagle a tucta i menure e piu povere fornito el mandato coloro che vorrono em qualla devotissima nocte predicta ello loco nostro stare acioche tucta quella nocte lagremosa a dolorosa expendano en lagreme sieno benedicte a Dio."

[66]Ac 705, fol. 11[v].

[67]For more detailed study of these dramatic *laude*, see Kathleen Falvey, "Scriptural Plays from Perugia," diss. (State University of New York at Stony Brook, 1974), and "The First Perugian Passion Plays: Aspects of Structure," *Comparative Drama*, 11 (1977), 127-38. I am grateful to Professor Falvey for permitting me to read and quote from other works in progress: "The Two Judgment Scenes from the 'Great' St. Andrew Advent Play," and "The Orvieto Creation Play in Context."

[68]Ad 80, quoted in Fortini, *La lauda in Assisi e le origini del teatro italiano*, p. 95.

[69]Ad 74 (Sant'Antonio), 75 (San Rufino), and 76 (San Lorenzo), for example. Ad 74 does not, however, include the phrase referring to the representation for the people.

[70]Ad 40, fol. 19[v].

[71]The codex (once owned by Emmanuele Illuminati) contains fourteen *laude*, Latin lessons, a ritual for the blessing of the habit, and other orations for use while taking the discipline. In addition to the Passiontide *laude* discussed here, the manuscript contains *laude* for Corpus Christi, No. 4; St. Francis, No. 5; Easter, Nos. 6 and 10; St. Stephen, No. 12, Holy Innocents, No. 13; and the dead, No. 14.

[72]All five are discussed in Michele Catalano, "Laudari ignoti di disciplinati Umbri," *Annuario Istituto Magistrale*, Assisi, 5 (1925), and "Laudari dei disciplinati assisiati," *Annuario Istitutio Magistrale*, 7 (1928-31), 29-33.

[73]Del Pozzo believes the arrangement of the manuscript presents the *laude* in chronology, actually representing the sequence of events thus: death, the funeral, the events after the burial.

[74]PEc 955, Rv A26, Ad 36/iv, and Rn 478.

[75]The work is in two sections, the first of which contains sixteen *laude*, seven of which are dramatic. These are followed by a section consisting of Latin orations and an Office of the Dead.

[76]Del Pozzo, pp. 87n, 88.

[77]These two manuscripts from the early fourteenth century contain many rubrics for the *disciplinati* ceremonial as well as prayers. The second of the two appears to be no more than a copy of the first but is executed in a finer hand.

[78]AD 78, fol. 7[r] (italics mine): "In hora autem prima omnes induti vestibus vadant ad Ecclesiam beati Francisci et Beatae Mariae Angelorum *lacrimosos laudes et cantus dolosos et amara lamenta Virginis Mariae proprio orbatae filio cum reverentia* popolo representent magis et lacrimas intendentes quam ad voces factus vero laudibus omnes ad locum nostrum insimul revertantur."

[79]Of the fourteen (or fifteen) *laude* contained in it, Nos. 1-3, 7-8, 11, and 15 are in honor of the Passion of Christ. The discrepancy in the number of *laude* results from the fact that although there appear to be fifteen texts, Nos. 7 and 11 are actually parts of the same one. The rubric of the former makes it clear that it was intended to be the conclusion of No. 11. Indeed, the same text as it appears in the Gubbian *laudario* Landau 39 combines the two, thus placing the events of the Passion in their proper chronology.

[80]It is contained also in MSS. Fn Landau 39, Rn 478, Oliveriano; portions of it appear also in Rv A26.

[81]Fol. 13[r]-13[v]. The reading in Fn Landau 39, which is unfoliated, differs only slightly:
> Levate li occhi e resguardate
> morto e Christo oggi per noie
> le mane e i piedi en croce chiavate
> aperto el lato O triste noie
> piangiamo e famo lamento
> e narriamo del suo tormento.

[82]Fol. 13[v]: Fn Landau 39 reads:
> O sorella della scura

or me date um manto nero
a quella che giamaio non cura
de bel drappo ne de velo
puoj ch io so abandanato
e dello mio filgliolo robbata.

[83]Fol. 13ᵛ. The Landau manuscript reads:
Oggi di de vedovanca
piena di pena e de dolore
morto e nostra speranca
christo nostro salvatore
ciascum faccia novo pianto
e a Maria dare esto manto.

[84]Ad 59, labelled *Libro di amministrazione dell'ospedale*, contains scattered entries of the *Inventario di sacrestia* on fols. 45ʳ-46ʳ. See also Ad 40, fasc. 2, fol. 17ᵛ.

[85] Ad 40, fol. 19ʳ.

[86]On the Gubbian companies, see Giuseppe Galli, "I Disciplinati dell'Umbria del 1260 e le loro laudi," *Giornale estorico della letteratura italiana*, 9 (1969), 107-08, and *Laude inedite dei disciplinati umbri scelte di sui codice più antiche* (Bergamo: Istituto italiano d'arte grafiche, 1910). See also Giuseppe Mazzatinti, "I disciplinati di Gubbio e i loro uffizi drammatici," *Giornale di filologia romanza*, 1 (1880), 80-109, and "Laudi dei disciplinati di Gubbio," *Il Propugnatore*, n.s. 2 (1889), 145-96; Guglielmo Padovan, "Gli Uffizi drammatici de' disciplinati di Gubbio," *Archivio storico per le Marche e per l'Umbria*, 1 (1884), 119.

[87]It is clear from other records of the Gubbian confraternities that more than one *laudario* must have existed. Mazzatinti cites records of payment to singers for singing *laude* for Christmas, for the feast of St. Ubaldo, and for the ascent of the famous hill of Santa Maria di Marco as well as for other feasts of the year. Landau 39 contains no such *laude*.

[88]Inventory quoted in Mazzatinti, "I disciplinati di Gubbio," p. 97.

[89]For the *laude* to San Tomasso, see Mazzatinti, "Laudi dei disciplinati di Gubbio," pp. 146-51.

[90]Clearly from an Office Book.

[91]Quoted in Padovan, p. 11.

[92]See ibid., pp. 66ff, for extensive account of activities of this company.

[93]For a manuscript of 1355 with frequent references to the same four brothers for carrying the cross on Palm Sunday as well as for many other services, see ibid., p. 9.

[94]Terruggia, "In quale momento," p. 444.

[95]Ad 20, fol. 4^v; Ad 21, fol. 4^r, col. 2, and 4^v.

[96]The cycle is actually truncated, omitting the period between Easter and Trinity Sunday.

[97]The *Laudario*, dated in 1405, was compiled by a certain Tramo di Lonardo who was a *disciplinato* of the company of San Francesco in Orvieto. The plays are contained in fols. 21-51, 58-64 (Falvey, "Creation").

[98]The liturgical cycle in PEc 955 begins with Christmas and ends with the Vigil of Christmas; Rn 527, from Advent up to the Assumption (15 August); Rv A26, from Advent through Lent, followed by the Sanctoral cycle.

[99]Falvey, "Advent."

[100]Ibid., p. 2. The collection could not have originated before 1333, for the *lauda Daie Giudere foi crocifisso* refers to the flood which devastated Florence on 4 November 1333.

[101]Ibid., p. 3.

[102]See Falvey, "The First Perugian Passion Play," pp. 129-32, for more detailed analysis of scriptural references. The following comments on *Signore scribe* are indebted to Professor Falvey's study of the text.

[103]Ibid., p. 130.

[104]Ibid.

[105]Ibid., p. 135.

[106]PEc 955, fol. 43ᵛ. The marginalia appear to be later additions.

[107]For further discussion of form, see Andrea and Giovanni Lazzarini, "Il canto passionale delle sacre rappresentazione," *Miscellanea francescana*, 54 (1954), 246-54, and Falvey, "The First Perugian Passion Play," pp. 127-28. On the question of recitation of the *lauda* as opposed to singing, Monti emphatically states that "le laude--ripeto--non erano dette ma cantate" (II, 116).

[108]Raoul Guêze, "Le Confraternite di Sant'Agostino, San Francesco e San Domenico in Perugia," in *Il movimento*, pp. 597-623.

[109]"Appunti per la storia del teatro italiano," *Rivista di filologia romanza*, 1 (1872), 257-60. Falvey notes ("The First Perugian Passion Play," p. 138n) that these inventories were destroyed in an anti-fascist uprising at the end of World War II.

[110]PEbf, C IV, 427, fol. 132ᵛ; cited in Terruggia, "In quale momento," p. 458.

[111]PEbf, A 440, fol. 2ᵛ:
1427 Queste sonno le cose quale prestammo alli homene della fraternita de Sancto Domenico. . . .
    IIII tonicelle verde gialle e azure e l altra roscia e azura
    1 cortina acura fregiata e acure pichole
    3 cortine listate roscie e acure pichole
    1 capello de levero atto da re
    1 corona d ottone da re
    1 palla ad oro con una bachetta atta da re
    V barbe et cinque capellature
    1 capello de seta aguzo con gillgli penti
    3 veglie de seta con capite belgle atte Marie
    1 vello bello de bambascio con capita
    1 barba lungha nera senca capellatura

[112]Ibid., fol. 8ʳ:
MCCCCXLI Quiste sonno le cose prestate a quilli de la frate< >neta de

Sancto Domenicho per la devotione ovvero rapresentatione de la morte. . . .

In prima   el mantello ⎫
           scorpiccio ⎬ de la morte
           cacioppola ⎪
           le mano   ⎭

E per la devotione de la passione
           4 tonecelle
           1 piovale giallo
           2 camiscie senca bende colli amitti
           10 capellature: cinque belle cinque mecane
           7 barbe
           1 veste encarnata colle calce
           1 altro pajo de calce encarnate di chuoio
           7 corone d angnoglie gialle

Falvey, "The First Perugian Passion Play," p. 133, notes that these garments of flesh-colored leather enabled the actor portraying Christ in the scourging scene to appear nude. This is borne out by the reference in the *lauda* text (PEc 955, *Signor Scribe*, l. 311) which stresses that Pilate had Christ stripped *nudo nudo* and by Magdalene's speech *O maestro mei cortese* (ll. 379-90) in which she laments the nudity of Christ.

This simulation of nudity is not uncommon and may be found in the medieval drama of other nations as well. See *The Staging of Religious Drama in Europe*, ed. Meredith and Tailby, p. 140.

[113]The exception is the Confraternita di Maria della misercordia o del mercato in Gubbio. See n. 92, above.

Chapter 3
The Musical Documents: Cortona 91

[1]See Vincenzo de Bartholomaeis, *Le Origini della poesia drammatica italiana* (Bologna: N. Zanichelli, 1924); Annibale Tenneroni, *Inizzi de antiche poesie italiane religiose e morali con prospetto dei codice che la contengono et introduzione alla laudi spirituali* (Florence: Olschki, 1909); and Lodovico Frati, "Giunte agli 'Inizii de antiche poesie italiane e religiose' a cura di Annibale Tenneroni," *Archivum Romanicum*, 2 (1918), 185-207, 325-43; 3 (1919), 62-94.

[2]Of the various studies of Cortona 91 the most complete is that of Fernando Liuzzi, *La Lauda e i primordi della melodia italiana* (Rome:

Librerio dello stato, 1935), 2 vols. A more recent and comprehensive effort is the projected four-volume work being prepared by Giorgio Varanini, Luigi Banfi, Anna Ceruti Burgio, and Giulio Cattin (*Laude cortonesi dal secolo XIII al XV* [1981-]). At this writing two volumes have appeared, the first of which, in two parts, deals with Cortona 91. The following are also by Giorgio Varanini: "Un terzo laudario cortonese," *Studi e Problemi di Critica testuale*, No. 6 (1973), pp. 69-71; "Il manoscritto trivulziano 535--Laude antiche di Cortona," *Studi e Problemi di Critica testuale*, No. 8 (1974), pp. 13-72; "Di una malnota testimonianza manoscritta di tre laudi cortonesi," *Annali della Facoltà di Economia e Commercio in Verona*, ser. 2, 1 (1966-67); and *Laude dugentesche* (Padua: Antinore, 1972), pp. 94-106. See also Agostino Ziino, *Strutture strofiche nel laudario di Cortona* (Palermo: Lo Monaco, 1968).

Performing editions of varying quality include: Antonio Canuto and N. Praglia, *Quarantadue laudi francescane del laudario Cortonesi. XIII secolo* (Rome: Edizione N. Praglia, 1957); Gilberto Brunacci, "Le laude del laudario cortonese secondo la trascrizione dell'acc. Can. Don Nicolo Garzi," *Secondo annuario accademica etrusca di Cortona* (1935), 13-84; Clemente Terni, "Per una edizione critica del Laudario di Cortona," *Chigiana*, n.s. 21 (1964), 111-29. Selected *laude* from the manuscript were published by Liuzzi in questionable modern arrangments with strings, woodwinds, harp, and organ under the title *La passione nella intonazioni del laudario 91 di Cortona* (Rome: A. di Santis, 1932).

Recordings of the Cortona *laudario* (either entire or in part) include the following: *Laudario di Cortona*, Società cameristica di Lugano, Nonesuch Records, H1086; *Storia della musica italiana*, a cura di Cesare Valabrega, Vol. I, RCA Italiana, ML 40000; *Poesia, prosa, teatro*, 42 divizione, Alfredo Bianchini, Voce del Padrone, QFLP 8065; *Trovatore-Laude*, trascrizione di Raffaello Monterosso, *Monumenta Italicae*, Philips, A 00773; and *Laudario di Cortona*, Quarteto polifonico italiano, Angelicum, STA 8976.

[3]The *laudario* belonged to the Compagnia di Santa Maria delle laude e dello Spirito Santo detta del Piccione. For discussion, see chap. 4.

[4]See chap. 4, Table 4, for titles. In every case the readings in Mgl[1] are significantly truncated.

[5]See Girolamo Mancini, "Laudi francescane dei disciplinati di Cortona," *Miscellanea Francescana*, 4 (1889), 48-55.

[6]Banfi believes that this portion of the manuscript which is written by several different scribes was done in successive additions over a period of years. The inferior quality of the vellum and the discrepancy in the size of the fascicles has led him to characterize it as *produzione casalinga*, perhaps for personal use (*Laude cortonesi*, I, Pt. 2, 318-20).

[7]Varanini, *Laude Cortonesi*, p. 63.

[8]Fresco cycles of both saints are found in the lower church at Assisi.

[9]See *Legenda aurea vulgo historia lombardica dicta*, ed. Thomas Graesse (Leipzig: Librariae Arnoldianiae, 1846), pp. 40-48, 789-97.

[10]Varanini, *Laude Cortonesi*, pp. 40-41, 64.

[11]Francis obtained verbal approval of his rule from Innocent III in 1210. The rule which is now called the First, or *non bollata*, was compiled by Caesarius of Speier in 1221, and the rule now referred to as the Second was confirmed by Pope Honorius III in 1223.

[12]*Acta Sanctorum*, June, III, 97.

[13]Francesco Salvatore Attal, *Frate Elia compagno di San Francesco* (Genoa: Società editrice internazionale, 1953), pp. 100ff.

[14]Edward Lempp, *Frère Elie di Cortone* (Paris: Fischbacher, 1901), p. 144.

[15]*Analecta Franciscana* (Florence: Quaracchi, 1951), III, 232. See also Lempp, pp. 113-14, n. 3.

[16]*Cronica Fratris Salimbene de Adam Ordinis Minorum*, in *Monumenta Germania Historia, Scriptores*, XXII (Hanover: Societas Aperiendis Fontibus Rerum Germanicorum Medii Aevi, 1905), 158; *Annales Minorum*, 3rd ed. (Fonseca, 1931), IV, 229. See also *Analecta franciscana*, III, 225, and *Acta Sanctorum*, Oct., II, 778.

[17]*Analecta Franciscana*, X, 619, and *Legenda Maior*, XIII, 8.

[18]*Cronica Fratris Salimbene de Adam Ordinis Minorum*, in *Monumenta Germania Historia, Scriptores*, XXII (Hanover: Societas

Aperiendis Fontibus Rerum Germanicorum Medii Aevi, 1905), pp. 181ff. It is recorded that Vita of Luccha was frequently called upon to sing for the bishops, cardinals, and even the Pope. See Heribert Holzapfel, *A History of the Franciscan Order*, trans. Antonin Tibesar and Gervase Brinkmann (Teutopolis, IL: St. Joseph Seminary, 1948), p. 237.

[19]Mancini, *Cortona nel medio evo* (Florence: Carnesecchi, 1897), pp. 106ff.

[20]The story of the relic is told in the *Speculum Vitae*, but a more complete version is contained in the *Vita* of Blessed Guido of Cortona (*Acta Sanctorum*, June, III, 98).

[21]Mancini, *Cortona nel medio evo*, p. 48.

[22]Ibid., p. 107.

[23]Ct, MS. 120.

[24]It is clear that the company practiced the discipline; see ibid., fol. 10[r]: "Ancho ordenamo quando alcuno passasse de la nostra conpagnia de questa misera vita debia avere ordenato de volere essare sepillito con quella cappa et disciplina con la quale esso andava a processione . . ." ("Also, we ordain that when one of our company passes from this miserable life he must be buried with that robe and scourge with which he went in procession").

[25]See Nino Pirrotta, "Ars Nova and Stil Novo," *Music and Culture in Italy from the Middle Ages to the Baroque* (Cambridge: Harvard Univ. Press, 1984), p. 36.

[26]See Varanini, *Laude Cortonesi*, pp. 42-50, for discussion of the theory.

[27]For example, Sc, MS. I II 4. See also Varanini, *Laude Cortonesi*, pp. 44-45. The *Proverbs* of Garzo appear in several modern editions: Guido Mazzoni, ed., *Laude Cortonesi del secolo XIII* (Gargani, 1890), pp. 114-38; *Poeti del duecento*, ed. Raffaello Mattioli, Pietro Pancrazi, and Alfredo Schiaffini, *La letteratura storia e teste*, 2 (Milan: Ricciardi, n.d.), pp. 295-313.

[28]See Holzapfel, pp. 138ff, and Jules Baudot, *The Roman Breviary: Its Sources and History* (St. Louis: Herder, 1909), pp. 112ff.

[29]Through the efforts of the Franciscans, the feast was extended to the universal Church in 1334 by Pope John XXII.

[30]For complete discussion of the authentic sources treating the life of the saint, see Raphael Huber, *St. Anthony of Padua: Doctor of the Church Universal* (Milwaukee: Bruce, 1949), esp. pp. 99-154.

[31]Ibid., p. 101.

[32]Ibid. Julian was trained in music and before entering the Order was *maestro di cappella* of Sainte Chapelle under the king St. Louis; see ibid., p. 115.

[33]Ibid., p. 103, and *Analecta Franciscana*, II, 46.

[34]Huber, *St. Anthony*, pp. 102, 129.

[35]Léon de Kerval, *Sanctii Antonii di Padua vitae duae quarum altera hucusque inedita* (Paris: Fischbacher, 1904), p. 42.

[36]*Acta Sanctorum*, III, 200.

[37]The enthusiasm of the Cortonesi for their two local saints is evidenced by the fact that for many years Guido was honored by two feasts annually, one commemorating the loss of the sarcophagus containing his body and the other celebrating the finding of his head. Margaret is still honored by two feasts, the liturgical commemoration on 22 February and a civic holiday on 10 May.

[38]*Acta Sanctorum*, III, 97.

[39]Mancini, *I manoscritti*, p. 51.

[40]Rodolfo Ranier, "Di antico codice di flagellanti nella biblioteca di Cortona," *Giornale storica della letteratura italiana*, 11 (1888), 109-24.

[41]Guido Mazzoni, "Laudi cortonesi del secolo XIII," *Il Propugnatore*, n.s. 2 (1889-90), 205-70; n.s. 3 (1889-90), 548. The work appeared

later as a monograph under the same title (Bologna: Gargani, 1890).

[42]Enrico Bettazzi, *Notizia di un laudario del secolo XIII* (Arezzo: Bellotti, 1890).

[43]De Bartholomaeis, *Le Origini della poesia drammatica*, p. 241.

[44]"Ballata e lauda all origini della lirica musicale italiana," *Annuario della R. Academia di Santa Cecilia* (1931), pp. 527-46; "Drammi musicali dei secoli XI-XIV," *Studi medievali*, n.s. 3 (1930), 46-57; "Jacopone da Todi: una lauda nell'intonazione del codice 91 di Cortona," *Solaria*, 6, No. 5 (1931), 56-62; "I Primi canti italiana per la nativita e l'infanzia di Cristo," *Illustrazione Vaticana*, 32 (1931), 84-96; and "Profilo musicali di Jacopone," *Nuova Antologia*, 279 (1931),171-92.

[45]"Melodie italiane inedite del duecento," *Archivum Romanicum*, 14 (1930), 527-60.

[46]Friedrich Ludwig, "Die geistliche nichtliturgische weltliche einstimmige und die mehrstimmige Musik des Mittelalters," in *Handbuch der Musikgeschichte*, ed. Guido Adler (Frankfurt: Frankfurter Verlag, 1924), pp. 127ff.

[47]For discussion of successive additions and possible *disciplinati* influence, see Banfi, pp. 330ff.

[48]Meersseman, *Ordo*, II, 954-55, discussed by Varanini, pp. 38ff.

[49]Pirrotta, p. 32.

[50]Richard Hoppin suggests that the forms of the *lauda* should not be regarded as deviations from or variants of the fixed form of the *ballata* but rather as a part of the developmental stage in the evolution of the so-called fixed forms of the *ballata* and *virelai* which are apparent even earlier in French song (*Medieval Music* [New York: Norton, 1978], p. 314). Other scholars, however, believe that the *lauda* was not influenced by the secular form of the *canzona a ballo* but may rather have come from the Arabic-Hispanic *zajal* form, probably by way of the Italian maritime cities of Pisa and Genoa. See Terni, "Per una edizione critica del Laudario di Cortona," pp. 111-29, and Aurelia Roncaglia, "Nella preistoria della lauda: *ballata* e strofa zagialesca," in *Il movimento*, pp. 231-34.

[51]Higinio Anglès, "The Notation and Rhythm of the Italian Laude," in *Essays in Musicology: A Birthday offering for Willi Apel*, ed. Hans Tischler (Bloomington: Indiana Univ. Press, 1968), p. 52.

Chapter 4
Historical Documents:
Magliabechiano II I 122 and Other Manuscripts

[1]Adolfo Bartoli, *I manoscritti italiani della Biblioteca Nazionale di Firenze* (Florence: Sansoni, 1879), p. 139; Robert Davidsohn, *Forschungen zur Geschichte von Florenz*, V, 440.

[2]Henry J. Grossi, "The Fourteenth-Century Florentine *Laudario* Magliabechiano II I 122 (B. R. 18): A Transcription and Study," diss. (The Catholic Univ. of America, 1979), p. 18.

[3]See Richard Offner, *Studies in Florentine Painting* (New York: F. F. Scherman, 1927), p. 311; Pietro d'Ancona, *La miniatura fiorentina* (Florence: Olschki, 1924), pp. 89-94; Mario Salmi, *Intorno al miniatore Neri da Rimini* (Florence, 1931), pp. 11-12; Valerio Mariani, "Beato Angelico e le laude del duecento italiano," *Illustazione Vaticana* (1931), pp. 21-25; and Paolo Toesca, *Monumenti e studi per la storia della miniatura* (Milan: Hoepli, 1930), p. 31.

[4]Liuzzi discusses them briefly, assigning them to c.1330-40, but he takes little notice of the scheme of arrangement: "La distibuzione della materia, nel nostro laudario, non offre particolare interesse"; see esp. pp. 79-81.

[5]Agostino Ziino, "Laudi e miniature fiorentine del primo trecento," *Studi musicali*, 7 (1978), 39-83; see esp. pp. 65-67.

[6]Vincent Moleta, "The Illuminated Laudari Mgl[1] and Mgl[2]," *Scriptorium*, 32 (1978), 29-50.

[7]Ibid., p. 31n.

[8]Grossi, p. 37.

[9]Moleta, p. 34.

[10]For example, No. 81, fol. 111^r, in honor of San Zenobio, and No. 91, fol. 125^v, in praise of Santa Reparata. One of the oldest and most important *laudesi* companies of the city was the Compagnia di San Zenobi, detta di Santa Reparta, which met in the crypt of the old cathedral. See Davidsohn, III, 189ff, and Monti, I, 152ff.

[11]Moleta, p. 33.

[12]Fol. 96^v.

[13]For discussion of "professional" singers in this context, see chap. 1.

[14]Cf. Ernst T. Ferand, "In Memoriam: Fernando Liuzzi," *The Musical Quarterly*, 28 (1942), 495.

[15]Ibid., pp. 496-97. Liuzzi was a prolific writer whose bibliography includes several books, over thirty articles, and numerous compositions (chamber music and works for the stage). Unfortunately, at the time when he was becoming recognized internationally he was discredited in his own country as a result of racial legislation enacted during the Mussolini regime. The same state that had financed the sumptuous printing of *La lauda* in 1935 only a few years later dismissed him and confiscated all remaining copies of the work. He had at the time nearly completed a huge study of Italian music in France from Venantius Fortunatis to Lully; although it was already in 500 galley proofs, it too was confiscated.

[16]Ibid., p. 500.

[17]*Music and Letters*, 20 (1939), 447.

[18]The trend towards diplomatic editions may even be observed in *Lo 'ntellecto divino*, in *The Oxford Anthology of Music*, ed. W. Thomas Marrocco and Nicholas Sandon (New York: Oxford Univ. Press, 1977), p. 76; and *Lauda novella sia cantata*, in *The Anthology of Medieval Music*, ed. Richard Hoppin (New York: Norton, 1978), p. 103.

[19]Heinrich Riemann, "Die geistliche nichtlurgische Musik des Mittelalters," in *Handbuch der Musikgeschichte*, ed. Adler, pp. 127-28.

[20]Heinrich Besseler, "Musik des Mittelalters und der Renaissance," in *Handbuch der Musikwissenschaft*, ed. Ernst Bucken (Widmark-Potsdam: Athenaion, 1931), p. 152.

[21]Friedrich Gennrich, *Grundriss einer Formenlehre des mittelaltischen Liedes als Grundlage einer musikalischen Formenlehre des Liedes* (Halle: Niemeyer, 1932), pp. 73-75.

[22]Liuzzi, *La lauda*, I, 192.

[23]For discussion of Rokseth's theories, see her "Le Laude e leur edition par M. Liuzzi," *Romania*, 65 (1939), 383-84.

[24]For a differing opinion on the accentual nature of French poetry, see Curt Sachs, *Rhythm and Tempo* (New York: Norton, 1953), p. 178.

[25]Rokseth, p. 388.

[26]Jacques Handschin, "Über die Laude (à propos d'un livre recent)," *Acta Musicologica*, 10 (1938), 14-31, esp. 22.

[27]Rafaello Monterosso, *Musica e ritmica trovatori* (Milan: Giuffre, 1956), p. 59. See also the same author's "Il linguaggio musicale della lauda dugentesca," in *Il movimento*, pp. 476-95.

[28]Monterosso, *Musica e ritmica*, p. 66.

[29]Higinio Anglès, *La Musica de las Cantigas de Santa Maria del Rey Alfonso el Sabio* (Barcelona: Diputacion Provincial de Barcelona, 1958), 3 vols. For discussion of the *lauda*, see III, Pt. 2, 483-516; for Anglès' charts for the transcription of ligatures for Cortona 91, see pp. 491-95, and pp. 495-500 for ligatures found in Mgl[1].

[30]Higinio Anglès, "Notation and Rhythm," p. 57.

[31]Grossi, p. 14.

[32]Rosanna Bettarini, "Notizia di un laudario," *Studi di filologia italiana*, 28 (1970), 59n.

[33]Moleta, pp. 29n, 36.

[34]See, for example, Fas, CRS 439, fols. 3r-4r: "e due i quali sara inposto comincio ginochione a chantare l'Ave maria e poi una bella lalde." Fol. 5r: "E poi a uno a chi sara inposto dicha una lalda della passione di cinque stante. . . ."

[35]For discussion of the decorative scheme of Fn Mgl[2], see Moleta, pp. 44-49.

[36]Ibid., p. 44.

[37]A notable example is the Pa 8521, the Pisan *laudario* now in Paris; see Erik Staff, *Le Laudarie di Pise du MS 8521 de la Bibliothèque National de l'Arsenal de Paris* (Uppsala: Almqvist & Wiksell, 1931). By the frequent moving of the clefs, the scribe has prepared a staff that never exceeds two or three lines, whereas Cortona 91 and Mgl[1] employ four-line staves.

[38]The statutes are published in Monti, II, 144ff.

[39]MS. M742. See Richard Offner, *A Critical and Historical Corpus of Florentine Painting* (New York: College of Fine Arts, 1930), Sec. 3, ii, Pt. 2, Pl. 8.

[40]Lbm, MS. Add. 35,254B; see Offner, *Corpus of Florentine Painting*, Pl. 9.

[41]MS. 194. Offner, *Corpus of Florentine Painting*, Pt. 1, Pl. 10.

[42]Ibid., Pl. 12. The illumination has now passed into the hands of an anonymous collector.

[43]Wng, MS. B-20,651, acquired in 1952. See *Medieval and Renaissance Miniatures from the National Gallery of Art*, ed. Gary Vikan (Washington, D. C.: National Gallery of Art, 1975), pp. 22-23.

[44]Wng B-15,393; see *Medieval and Renaissance Miniatures*, ed. Vikan, pp. 26-32. The Master of the Dominican Effigies, so called for his panel painting in Santa Maria Novella of Christ surrounded by Dominican saints, was active in Florence c.1336-45. For a different view of this attribution, see Ziino, pp. 64ff, for the conflicting opinion of Giulietta Chelazzi Dini.

[45]Wng B-22,128.

[46]See Ziino, pp. 65-67.

[47]See n. 3, above.

[48]Fols. 6^v-8^r.

[49]In Fn Mgl[1], ll. 17-18 of the text (fol. 7^v) are illegible but the same poem appears in Cortona 91, Fn Mgl[2], Pa 8521, and Fior., where it reads:
    ad un suono di corno
    seranno risurgent
The lines are undoubtedly inspired by St. Paul in *1 Cor.* 15.52: "the trumpet shall sound, and the dead shall rise again incorruptible" (Douay-Rheims).

[50]See D'Accone, "Le Compagnie dei laudesi in Firenze," pp. 253-82; "Alcune note sulle compagnie florentine," pp. 86-114; "Music and Musicians at the Florentine Monastery of Santa Trinita," pp. 131-51. See also my "Music and Spectacle in Confraternity Drama of Fifteenth-Century Florence," forthcoming.

[51]Ziino, pp. 66-67.

[52]For example, PEc 955, Rn A26, Ad 36/iv, discussed in chap. 2, above.

[53]Notably the Carmelite provenance of Christ and the Virgin Enthroned with Forty Saints (Wng B-22,128). For discussion of the Carmelite figures in the foreground at either side of the cross, see my "Music and Spectacle."

[54]See H. B. J. Maginnis, "Pietro Lorenzetti's Carmelite Madonna: A Reconstruction," *Pantheon*, 33 (1975), esp. 12, 14; and also Federico Zeri, "Pietro Lorenzetti: quattro pannelli dalla pala del 1329 al Carmine," *Arte illustrata*, 58 (1974), 146-56.

[55]Ziino, p. 62.

[56]Inventario, Neri di Bicci, Fas, CRS, Sant'Agnese 115, fol. 164^r. (1) Uno libro grande choverto d assi choperte di chuoio chompassi d otone e bullete grosse richamente fatto suvi iscritto molte laude cho molti begli

mini istoriato di charta pechora. (2) U libro choverte d assi e di chuoio di charta pechora suvv molte laude antiche dipintovi suso un crocifiso e piu altri mini. Adoperasi ogni di. (3) Uno libro di laude choverto d assi charta pechora miniato di mini grandi a penello e a penna. (4) Uno libro di laude choverto d assi chon bullette charte di pechora iscritovi suso molte laude zolfate e fighurate basso. (5) Uno libro di charta pecora choverto d asse imbulletato inscritovi suso laude. For more detailed discussion of the Inventory, see my "A Renaissance Artist in the Service of a Singing Confraternity," in *Life and Death in Fifteenth-Century Florence* (Durham: Duke Univ. Press), forthcoming.

[57]Bianca Becherini, ed., *Catologo dei manoscritti musicali della Biblioteca nazionale centrale di Firenze* (Kassel: Bärenreiter, 1959), pp. 89-90.

[58]Here Liuzzi is repeating the error of Ludwig, p. 176: "Die Compagnie bei den Augustinern von Ogni Santi auf die beide die grosste Musikhandschrift die alteren Laudi Epoche, Florenz, Naz. II I 122 zuruckgeht."

[59]Becherini, pp. 89-90.

[60]Charles Burney, *A General History of Music* (London, 1782), II, 327. A portion of the inscription is also preserved in the manuscript division of the Biblioteca Nazionale Centrale in Florence. See Ziino, p. 69n.

Chapter 5
The Marginal Liturgy of the Disciplinati:
The Popular Office of Tenebrae

[1]Ad 20, fol. 4^v, and Ad 21, fol. 4^r-4^v. The text is quoted above in chap. 2, n. 35.

[2]Ad 75, fol. 3^v: "Item quidlibet teneatur dicere qualibet die octo pater noster cum ave Maria singulis mattutinis et vesperis in alias vero horis silicet prima tertia sexta nona et completario dicat quinque ut supra."

[3]Fr 2382, fol. 5^v: "la quaresima di fare doppo l ufficio devozione et

discipline. . . ."

⁴Fr 3041, fol. 17^r: "Ogni quarto venerdi si canti el primo noctorno de morte e facciasi discipline."

⁵Ibid., fol. 17^v: "tucte le tornare da mactina si canti il mattutina di nostro Donna con le laude."

⁶Bca, MS. Fondo Ospedale 83 (35): "Questa sia la copia el quale si fa per li fradielli dela cumgregatione de Madona sancta Maria dal Baracane la nocte della Gnoba Sancta per comemoratione dela passione del nostro Signore Gesu Christo." This manuscript lacks folio numbers.

⁷The *lauda* is contained in Ac 705, fols. 11^v-12^v; Rn 478, fol. 17^r; and Fn Landau 39, fol. 5^v. See also chap. 2, above, for discussion of the Umbrian *mandato*.

⁸Fas, CRS 439, fol. 4^r: "Ordeniamo che ongni correttore nel principio del suo uficio elegha due cantori i quali comincino l oficio e inponghino le licione e neuno entri loro inançi per veruna cagione se no gli fosse inposto accio che l uficio vada ordinato e divoto e sança scandalo e ciascheduno sia preghato di cio ubidire."

⁹These corrupt Latin quotations come directly from the opening of the Divine Office of Compline.

¹⁰*Vicita quaesumus* is the beginning of the oration, immediately preceding the Marian antiphon, at the end of the Divine Office of Compline.

¹¹Ibid., fol. 4^r-4^v: "Ordiniamo che l nostro correttore sia tenuto di fare cominciare la sera l oratione a quella ora che a llui parra e in quello modo cioe inprima faccia porre ginochione tutti i fratelli nell oratorio stando in oratione e in silençio col quore divoto a dDio per remissione de suoi peccati. E tutti istieno sopra se sança apogiarsi o stare bochoni. Istati per pocho di spatio d uno Pater Nostro e una Ave Maria uno a chui sara inposto dicha divotamente *Giube Donne benedicere* e l correttore risponda chosi *notte quieta fine perfetta sono pacis conciedat nobis onipotens Dominus*. Rispondino i frateglli Amen. E poi dicha quello tale questa letione cioe *Fratres sobrie estote e vigilate in orationibus e reliqua*. E poi perseverando nella oratione estiene per ispatio d una terça ora e passata la terça ora il correttore si levi ritto dicendo Lodato sia Giesu Christo per

modo che sia udito e tutti gli altri rispondano senpre e levinsi su ritti in piede perserverando nell oratione per ispatio d una quarta ora. E passata la quarta ora si ponghino ginochioni e stieno tanto che dichino sette Pater Nostri e sette Ave Maria o tanto piu quanto piacera al correttore. E poi si dicha questa oratione *Vicita quesumus Domine abitatione ista* e poi nel nome di Dio si ritornino a sedere istando onestamente in silençio e divotione di quore. E incontanente s aciendano due cierotti per reverençia di Dio e della Vergine Maria e due i quali sara inposto comincino ginochione a chantare l Ave Maria e poi una bella lalda. E gli altri sedendo si riçino e rispondino con divotione di quore e legreçça sprituale. E ditta la lalda quegli a chui sara inposto comincino a dire a dire [sic] adagio i sette salmi penetenciali con *gloria patri e filio.* E stando tutti ginochioni a choro e detti i salmi si dicha l antifana cioe *Ne reminiscaris Domine* colle letanie e versiculi e oratoni seguenti. E detti i salmi tutti si pohghino a sedere chon silentio e posti a sedere due a quali sara inposto chomincino divotamente a chantare quello divoto chanticho cioe crociffisso in carne laudemus e gli altri rispondino Alleluia alleluia alleluia facendo le nvenie chosi richieghono e poi una oratione della croce cioe *Deus qui pro nobis filium tuum crucis patibulum.* E questo si dicha nel tenpo Pasquale della resurresiono [sic] per insino alle pentecosta. E poi si chanti quello nobilissimo cantico il quale fece la gloriosa Vergine Maria cioe *Magnificat anima mea Dominus.*"

[12]Ibid., fol. 5[r]: "faccia porre a sedere i frategli e uno a chui sara inposto leggha uno sermone di sancto Agostino e letto il sermone si dicha sette Pater Nostri e sette Ave Marie a onore e reverencia de sette doni dello Spirito e poi si dicha l oratione dello Spirito Sancto. . . . E poi posto a sedere il correttore faccia corretione de falli de nostri frategli che ssi contenghono ne nostri chapitoli. E poi il chamarlingho si pongha a sedere e richiegha ciascheduno per nome e ciascheduno sia tenuto di portare al charmarlingho uno quatrino per dare aiuto alle spese della conpagnia e chi non vi fosse sia apuntato e paghilo al altra tornata. E facto questo il correttore si levi suso e vada di la all altare chominciando *Miserere mei* e *De Profundis* e frategli il sequitano e ponchinsi ginochioni all altare e dichansi quelle tre oratoni consuete de morti e poi vadino colla gratia di Dio a dormire con silençio." I have translated *quatrino* as "an offering of money"; more specifically it signifies one-sixtieth of a Tuscan lire (i.e., an amount equal to four denari), while figuratively it was used to denote a very small sum.

[13]Ibid., fol. 2[r]: "We ordain that the meetings of the company should

be these, that is, the solemnity of the birth of Our Lord Jesus Christ, and the solemnity of the Epiphany, and the solemnity of the Resurrection of Our Lord Jesus Christ, and the solemnity of the Ascension of Our Lord Jesus Christ, and the solemnity of the coming of the Holy Spirit, and the solemnity of the Holy Trinity, and the solemnity of the body of Our Lord Jesus Christ [Corpus Christi], and the solemnity of all four feasts of the glorious Virgin Mary and all of the apostles of Jesus Christ, and the solemnity of St. John the Baptist, and the solemnity of All Saints and St. Lawrence and St. Nicholas, and the solemnity of St. Zenobio and all the Saturdays of Lent and all the Saturdays of Advent, and other meetings which our *Correttore* should desire. And whoever misses the said meetings without being excused should, in virtue of holy obedience to the service, say Our Father and Hail Mary, and after being excused shall say ten Our Fathers and Hail Marys."

"Ordeniamo che lle nostre tornate alla compagnia sieno queste coie la solenita della nativita del nostro Signore Giesu Cristo e la solenita della Befania e lla solenita della Pasqua della Resurresione del nostro Singnore Giesu Cristo e lla solennita della Asensione del nostro Signore Giesu Cristo e lla solennita della avenimento dello Spirito Sancto e lla solennita della beata Sancta Trinita e lla solennita del Corpo del Nostro Signore Giesu Cristo e lla solennita di tutti e quatro le feste della gloriosa Vergine Maria e tutte le solennita di tutti gl apostoli di Giesu Cristo e lla solennita del glorioso Meser Sancto Giovanni Batista e lla solennita di tutti sancti e di Sancto Lorenço e del glorioso Meser Sancto Nicholo de lla solennita di Messer Sancto Çanobio e tutti i sabati della guaresima e tutti i sabati della avento e qualunque altra tornata parra al nostro correttore e chiunque manchasse le dette tornate e non avendo iscusa vada in virtu di sancta ubidienca a servi dicendo Pater Nostri con Ave Marie e avendo iscusa dicha dieci Pater Nostri con Ave Marie."

[14]See Federico Ghisi, "Un Processionale inedito per la Settimana Santa nell'Opera del Duomo di Firenze," *Rivista musicale italiana*, 21 (1950), 4.

[15]Serafino Razzi, *Libro Primo dell Laude* (Venice: Giunti, 1563), p. 61.

[16]*Quem terra pontus* is the hymn at Matins, Common of the Blessed Virgin.

[17]"And for the Archbishop of Florence" has been added in the margin by a later hand. The city was raised to the status of an archbishopric

in 1411.

[18]Fol. 5ʳ-5ᵛ: "Ordiniamo che 1 nostro correttore e chamarlingho ordini*n*o di chiamare o fare chiamare i frategli a ora debita del matutino e raghunati tutti si cominci il matutino della Vergine Maria a choro divotamente e adagio e chantisi 1 inno cioe *Quem terra pontus* ecetera. E detto il matutino tutti si ponghino a sedere e 1 chamarlingho tolgha la disciprina e vada dandole in prima al correttore e poi agli altri frateli. El chamarlingho incontanente ispengha i lumi e facciasi disciprina con cinque *Pater Nostri* e cinque *Ave Marie*. E poi a uno a chi sara inposto dicha una lalda della passione di cinque stanze e poi a uno a chi sara inposto dicha la racomandigia col *Miserere* e *De Profundis* coll oratione de morti. E fatto questo il correttore faccia priegho per la santta chiesa et per Messere arcivescovo di Firenze e per la nostra cittad e pe morti della nostra conpagnia e per ongni altro priegho che bisogniasse. E fatto questo dicha divotamente salutate la Vergine Maria e ciaschuno si vesti. El camarlingho racienda i cierotti e due a chi sara inposto dichino il *Credo in uno Deo* istando ritti e quando si dicie *ed omo factus est* e ciascheduno s inginochi e stia tanto che si dicha *resurresit terzia die* e alora ciascheduno si levi ritto. E detto il *Credo*, 1 oratione . . . e ll'oratione della prima ora del di cioe *Domine Deus onipotens quia principio huius diei* e dette queste oratione si legha due capitoli e poi si dicha sette *Pater Nostri* e sette *Ave Marie* e poi si dicha 1 oratione dello Spirito Sancto. E se nel detto uficio vi fosse alchuno debile che non potesse istare ginochioni come gli altri domandi la parola e sieglie data e stia come meglio puo a llalde di Dio senpre con divotione a dDio. El correttore sia tenuto di fare dire 1 uficio al modo sopradetto rimettendo senpre nella sua discrezione di provedere di piu e di meno sechondo i tenpi."

[19]This entire nocturn exhibits the widest divergence from its model. Where the readings of the Divine Office are drawn from *2 Cor.*, those of the ufficio are from *John* 13 and a homily of St. Augustine.

[20]Following the Masoretic enumeration, these are: Psalms 120-25 and 148; and the Penitential Psalms 6, 32, 38, 51, 102, 130, and 143.

[21]Fas, CRS 439: "*La sera del mercholedi sancto alle tenebre le prime lectioni che sono le lamentationi di Hyeremia si dichono da due in luogho seperato e i risponsi in loro cambio gli ripiglia il ghovernatore. L'altre sei lectioni si dichono da uno come 1 altre volte e cosi il risponsi cominciando il fratello che dice 1 antifane e ripigliando quello che ha decto*

la lectione. Non si dice ad alcuno salmo i Gloria Patri *ma si finiscie in voce di passione non si suona campanuzza ma si fa cenno colla mano. L antifane si dicono doppie accendendosi quindici lumi de quali a ogni salmo se ne spegne uno excepto l ultimo del Benedictus. E perche i salmi ordinari non sono in uso dichisi in quello lougho e primi sei salmi graduali e gli altre tre penitentiali pe tre nocturni e per le laude gli altri quatro salmi penitentiali con* Laudate Dominum *de celis et* Benedictus. *Et cosi ordinati in coro il ghovernatore inclinato dica* Pater Noster." The portion of this manuscript which contains the Office lacks folio numbers.

[22]Ibid.: *"Spenta la XIIII candela il ghovernatore dicie l antifana del* Benedictus *la quale finita si nasconde il XV lume et si si fa la prima volta le* tenebre. *Poi si canta da dua o tre fratelli il* Benedictus *in mezzo l un verso loro l altro in coro il quale finito si fa la seconda volta le* tenebre. *Et quelle rachete il governatore replica l antifana la quale decta si fa la terza volta le* tenebre."

[23]Ibid.:
Il sermone o divotione altrimenti ferventi che gl usati. Racomandigia nissuna in queste tre sere lagrime. . . . El giovedi sera oltre al predecto ordine si prepara la lavatione de piedi e la colletione. Commettesi
 Chi canti le lamentationi
 Chi rispondi all' antifane co risponsi
 Chi impongha i salmi
 Chi faccia il sermone
 Chi canti el mandato
 Chi canti Ubi caritas
 Chi canti Dulcis Iesu Memoria
 Chi canti le lectioni
 Chi canti il Benedictus

[24]All of the Latin references throughout are taken directly from the Gospel of the Mass for Maundy Thursday: *John* 13.1-15.

[25](See fig. 15.) *"Le laude colle tenebre dopo la lavatione & posti a sedere sia preparato da lavare i piedi & il fratello a chi e commesso cominci il mandato & al* surgit ad cenam *si lievi in pie & al* posuit ves-timenta *si cavi il suo mantello. & quando dice* cum accepisset linteum *lui pigli lo sciughatoio & facci similemente & cominci a lavare & aiutandolo e consiglieri. & quello che dice il mandato si fermi a* postquam ergo *& intanto si canti* Ubi caritas. . . .

"*Non essendo ancora finito di lavare e piedi a tutti efrategli si canti* [see fig. 16]:

"DULCIS YHUS MEMORIA

"*Et facta la lava et rassettato quello s e operato cerimonia simile seguiti el fratello il mandato che lascio al postquam et mentre lo dice si faci la collatione sanza superfluita solo a similitudine come si conviene in ta l di.*

"POSTQUAM ergo lavit ecc.

"*Finito questo mandato & la collitione si faccia il sermone di simile suggietto da governatore o se alcuno altro gli pare piu acto & apresso cominciando il governatore ginochione abbraciando come dio lo spira adomandando perdono & si raconcilii con gli altri frategli seguitandolo ciaschuno l uno coll altro successivamente. Apresso finito simile acto d umile carita riordinati a coro seguitino il mattutino cominciando sotto silentio il ghovernatore il Pater Nostro inclinato & poi l antifane & le laude.*"

[26]"*si canti da due fratelli ripigliando il coro il medesimo principio.*

"STABAT MATER DOLOROSA

"*Finita dicta lalda con ritornello il coro risponda* Amen."

[27]Bca F. O. 83 (35).

[28]Ibid., fol. 2[v].

[29]*Salve Regina* is the Marian antiphon at the end of the Divine Office of Compline during the period between Trinity Sunday and Advent.

[30]"Fratielli carissimi quando se comenca l offitio prima se dica per quello che de dire l offitio uno *pater nostro* in secreto, po dicha *Ave Maria gratia plena dominus tecum. Benedicta tu in mulieribus et benedictus fructus ventris tuy.* Stagando in genochie apresso l altaro e puossa dica la lauda desedate o peccatore. Et finito la lauda lo P O dica la confessione et poy li fratielli la respondano come se fa ala messe cum una oratione drieto. Et de novo comienci quello che dice l offitio lo invitatorio di nostra donna. Fenito questo se comienci li septe psalmi penitentiali se dixeno per li fratielli che sono alli luoghi usati. Fenito i psalmi quello che dixe l offitio se dica una lectione di nostra donna. Poi letanie cum certe orationi come se contene tutto in suxo e libro dal offitio. Et fenito questo offitio lo sagrestano si amorti tutte le lume. Et facasse la desiplina devotamente in suxo le carne nude o altramente segondo che paresse alla soa cunsentia cum licentia del nostro P S cum grande timore di dio dicendo prima lo P O *Fratres*

apprendite disciplinam cum timore de peccato vestro ecc. Poi comienci per quello che dise l offitio Yesu Christe filij dei. . . . *Miserere nobis* respondando i fratielli. Poi se dica el *Miserere mei* cum una oratione per remissione di nostri peccadi. Poi dicassi el *de profundis* cum la soa oratione per li aneme di fratielli muorti. Poi dicasse una laude de passione di Yesu Cristo per uno altro di fratielli che sera ordinato per lo padre ordinario. poi se faça oratione universale per lo beato Papa et signuri cardinali et arceviscovi et viscovi et prelati de la sancta madre ghiesia. Et per lo realle imperadore et per tutti i realli signuri cristiani et per questa nostra citade et per tuti li padre spirituale et per tutti i fradielli de questa cumgregatione e de ciascuna altra et per vedoe pupilli amalati via andanti naveghanti incarcerati et rumei et per ciascuna altra persona che fusse in alcuna afflitione. Poi se recorra a li meriti de la passione de Yesu Cristo et pregharlo che luy ce conceda tute le gratie che nuy i domandemo et tute le altre che ce fano di bisogno et perche piu degnamente ce debia exaudire a soa lauda se dica V *Pater Nostri* cum V *Ave Marie* faciendo la disciplina a reverentia de le cinque piaghe di Yesu Cristo. Et questa recomandasone la dica uno altro di fratielli a chi la sera inposta per lo P O et fenito questo lo P O si faça spetiale oratione per li fradielli dela congregatione li quali veneno fredamente al offitio et poy per lo nostro padre spirituale et per li nostri fratielli che sono pasato de questa vita et altre cose segondo che acade alle volte. Ditto questo se ricorra a la nostra avocata vergene Maria et pregharla che la interceda per nui a impetrare.

. . .

"se dica uno *Pater Noster* e una *Ave Maria* in secreto et *salve regina* cum la soa oratione facendo la disciplina. Poi se faça vestire ciascuno cum la benedictione del signore. Et ciascuna faca oratione in nel so core in secreto infino che l e aprexo le lume al'altaro. Apresso questo se canti el *credo* grande cum la sua oratione et le *magnificat* cum la soa oratione et la *salve regina* cum la soa oratione come se contene tutto in suxo e libro dal offitio. Po sia fine al ditto offitio a lauda de Yesu Cristo. Et facto tute queste cose se faça l offerta all altaro per chi po. . . ."

³¹Ibid., fol. 5ᵛ.

³²Ibid., fol 14ᵛ: "*Siegua lo lectore drieto al passio e liegalo infino che el nostro signore volse lavare i pie ali suoi appostolli fa punto.*
"*Qui comenca el segondo sermone le quale fe el nostro Signore prima che lavasse i pie ali discipuli.*"

. . .

Fol. 16ʳ: "Lieto che ara el ditto sermone lo P O comandi alli fratielli che si descalcino lo pe dritto e alora li serventi seranno ordinati arechino l aqua calda e le altre cose necessarie. Et per lo P O sera per quelo tempo sia quello che per umilita lavi el pie alli fratielli. Et continuamente lo lectore che ligiva el passio siegua la lectione infino che sera conpiuto de lavare li piedi a tuti li fratielli a cio che continuo stagano atienti a la passione del Signore. Conpiuto la lavanda e calçato li fratielli se faça punto a liegere. Et per lo P O se faça segno che ciascuno si pona in genochie a le banche al usato modo per nuy. Et puosti che sono in genochie lo padre ordinario comandi ali sagrestani che apiglino quelle XIII candele che serano poste in suxo quello candiliero sera amanoato in suxo l altaro."

[33]Fol. 16[r]: "Et aprexo le lume in suso l altaro se comienci l ofitio per quello che sera ordinato per lo P O in questo modo cioe vada denanci dal altaro drito in pie e dica questo prima se comienci i psalmi. Versicle *Fratres sobrii estote vigilate quia adversarius vester diabolus tamquam leo rugiens circuit querens quem devoret cui resistite fortes in fide. Tu autem Domine miserere nobis.* Versicle *Deo gratias.*"

[34]*Benedictus, Dominus Deus Israel* is the Canticle of Zachary, *Luke* 1.68, sung in the Ordinary of the Office at Lauds.

[35]Fol. 17[r]: "quili due seranno ordinati per lo padre ordinario vadano denanci al altaro e ponasse in genochie e per lo simele tuti le fratielli commencandosse l offitio se de fare in la oscurita e disiplina cum gram reverentia e timore de Dio. Et li sagrestani si amortino tute le lume. Amortade le lume quilli duy che sonno denanci al altaro comiencino a cantare *Benedictus Dominus Deus Israel quia vifivavit et fecit redemptionem plebis sue.* Et tuti li altri fratielli lo debiano respondere facendo la disciplina per onne verso che se responde e questo se faca in luogo de scandallo. Conpiuto che arano el ditto psalmo se comienci de novo a disciplina cum gram reverentia et timore de Dio subito che començara lo P O a dire *Fratres dillectissimi aprendite disceplinam cum dolore de peccato vestro.*"

[36]Ibid., fols. 17[v], 18[v], 19[r].

[37]See Varanini, *Cantari religiosi senesi del Trecento* (Bari: Laterza, 1965), pp. 537-90.

[38]See Terruggia, "In quale momento," p. 444.

[39]Fol. 3[r].

[40]For example, Ad 76, *Inventario della Fraternita di San Lorenzo* (bound with statutes).

Select Bibliography

Manuscripts

Laudari

Ac 705	Laudario della Compagnia di San Stefano (Codex Illuminati Assisi)
Ad 36/i	Laudario della Compagnia di San Stefano, Pt. I, Assisi
Ad 36/ii	Laudario della Compagnia di San Stefano, Pt. II, Assisi
Ad 36/iii	Laudario della Compagnia di San Stefano, Pt. III, Assisi
Ad 36/iv	Laudario della Compagnia di San Stefano, Pt. IV, Assisi
Ad 36/v	Laudari della Compagnia di San Stefano, Pt. V, Assisi
Ar 180	Laudario della Fraternita dei Laici, Arezzo
Ct 91	Laudario di Cortona
Fn Landau 39	Laudario di Gubbio
Fn Mgl[1]	Laudario della Compagnia dello Spirito Santo, Florence (Banco rari 18)

Fn Mgl[2]   Laudario della Compagnia di San Gilio, Florence
(Banco rari 19)

Pa 8521   Laudario di Pisa

PEc 955   Laudario della Compagnia di Sant'Andrea (formerly
Giustizia 5)

Rn 478   Laudario della Confraternità di San Pietro, Assisi
(formerly Frondini)

Rn 527   Laudario Orvietana

Rv A26   Laudario della Compagnia di San Simone e Firenze
in Perugia

Capitoli, Statuti, Ordinamenti

Ad 74   Capitoli della Compagnia di Sant'Antonio, Assisi

Ad 75   Statuti della Fraternità di San Rufino, Assisi

Ad 76   Ordinamenti della Confraternita di San Lorenzo,
Assisi

Ad 78   Statuti della Compagnia di San Stefano, Assisi

Bca F.O.   Capitoli della Còmpagnia della disciplinati della
83 (35)   Madonna dal Baraccano, Bologna

CRS 345   Capitoli della Compagnia di San Giovanni Battista,
Florence

CRS 439   Santissima Regola della Compagnia delle
disciplinati in Santa Maria del Carmine, Florence

CRS 474   Capitoli della Compagnia della Presentazione di
Maria Vergine, Florence

CRS 476   Capitoli della Compagnia del Sacramento, Florence

CRS 544   Capitoli della Compagnia del Gesù, overo della
                 disciplina di Santa Croce, Florence

CRS A VIII 1   Capitoli della Compagnia di Sant'Agostino,
                 Florence

CRS Z I   Statuti della Compagnia di San Zenobi (1326),
                 Florence

CRS Z 154   Statuti della Compagnia di San Zenobi (1508),
                 Florence

Ct 120   Capitoli della Confraternita di Santa Croce, Cortona

Fn B. R. 336   Capitoli della Compagnia di San Gilio,
(Pal. 1172)   Florence

Fn Pal. 154   Capitoli della Compagnia di San Frediano, Florence

Fr 391   Statuti della Compagnia di Orsanmichele, Florence

Fr 1685   Capitoli della Compagnia di San Bastiano, Florence

Fr 2382   Statuti della Compagnia di San Girolamo, Florence

Fr 2535   Capitoli della Compagnia di San Giovanni dello
                 Scalzo, Florence

Fr 2566   Capitoli della Compagnia dell'Assunta, Florence

Fr 2567   Capitoli della Compagnia dell'Annunziata al
                 Borghetto, Florence

Fr 2577   Capitoli della Compagnia di San Pietro, Florence

Fr 3014   Statuti della Compagnia di San Domenico, Florence

PEc 955   Costituzioni e laudi dei disciplinati di Sant'Andrea,
                 Perugia

Miscellaneous

Ad 20   Ordo della Compagnia di San Stefano, Assisi

Ad 21   Ordo della Compagnia di San Stefano, Assisi

Ad 58   Inventari della Compagnia di San Stefano, Assisi

Ad 76   Inventari della Fraternità di San Lorenzo (bound
                with Ordinamenti), Assisi

CRS 4   Libro di Partiti A, della Compagnia di Sant'Agnese,
                Florence

CRS 98   Entrate e Uscite 1471-1502, Compagnia di Sant'
                Agnese, Florence

CRS 102   Vol. 292, Uscite 1313-94, Santa Maria Novella,
                Florence

CRS 113   Vol. 30, Libro Inventario, 1370, Santa Maria del
                Carmine, Florence

CRS 115   Campione A, Compagnia di Sant'Agnese, Florence

CRS 125   Entrate e Uscite 1471-1502, Compagnia di Sant'
                Agnese, Florence

CRS B707   Notarile Antecosimiano, 1366, Capitani
                Orsanmichele, Florence

Printed Sources

See also the citations of printed works in the notes, above (pp. 151-96), since those items are not repeated in this bibliography.

Alaleone, Domenico. "Le laude nei secoli XVI e XVII," *Rivista musicale italiana*, 16 (1909), 89-102.

Ancona, Alessandro d'. "Due antiche devozione italiane," *Rivista di filologia romanza*, 2 (1875), 5-28.

Angeno, Franca Brambilla. "I Proverbi di Ser Garzo," *Studi Petrarcheschi*, n.s. 1 (1984), 1-37.

Ardu, Emilio. "La data d'inizio del movimento dei disciplinati." In *Il movimento dei disciplinati nel settimo centenario del suo inizio*. Perugia: Deputazione di Storia Patria per l'Umbria, 1960. Pp. 368-70.

Attal, Francesco Salvatore. *Frate Elia, compagno di San Francesco*, 2nd ed. Geneva: Società editrice internazionale, 1953.

Baldelli, Ignazio. "La lauda e i disciplinati," *La rassegna della letteratura italiana*, 64 (1960), 396-418.

Bartholomaeis, Vincenzo de. *Laudi drammatiche e rappresentazione sacre*. Florence: F. Le Monnier, 1943.

_____. *Primordi della lirica d'arte in Italia*. Turin: Società editrice internazionale, 1943.

Becherini, Bianca. "Musica italiana a Firenze nel XV secolo," *Revue Belge de musicologie*, 8 (1954), 109-21.

Becker, Marvin. "Aspects of Lay Piety in Early Renaissance Florence." In *The Pursuit of Holiness in Late Medieval and Renaissance Religion*, ed. C. Trinkhaus and Heiko A. Oberman. Leiden: Brill, 1974. Pp. 177-99.

Belcari, Feo. *Sacre rappresentazioni e laude*. Turin: Unione Tipografico-Editore Torinese, 1926.

Bertoni, Guilio. *I trovatori d'italia*. Modena: U. Orlandini, 1959.

Bettarini, Rosanna. "Notizia di un laudario," *Studi di filologia italiana*, 28 (1970), 55-66.

Bettazzi, Enrico. *Due laudi del codice Aretino 180*. Arezzo: Bellotti, 1890.

Blanshei, Sarah Rubin. *Perugia, 1260-1380: Conflict and Change in Medieval Italian Urban Society*, Transactions of the American Philosophical Society, n.s. 66, Pt. 2. Philadelphia: American Philosophical Society, 1976.

Boileau, Jacques. *Historia Flagellantium*. Paris: J. Anisson, 1700.

Brunacci, Gilberto. "Il codice e l'oratorio dei laudesi," *Polimnia: Bolletino dell'accademia etrusca di Cortona*, 8 (1931), 14-24.

Callebaut, André. "Saint Antoine de Padoue: recherches sur ses trente premières années," *Archivum Franciscanum Historicum*, 24 (1931), 449-94.

Cattin, Giulio. "Contributi alla storia della lauda spirituale," *Quadrivium*, 2 (1958), 45-75.

_____. *Music of the Middle Ages I*, trans. S. Botterill. Cambridge: Cambridge Univ. Press, 1984.

Dent, Edward J. "The laudi spirituali," *Musical Times*, 18 (1917), 213-14.

_____. "The laudi spirituali," *Proceedings of the Musical Association*, 43 (1916), 63-95.

Domenichelli, Teofilo. "La leggenda versificata, o il più antico poema di San Francesco," *Archivum Franciscanum Historicum*, 1 (1908), 209-16.

Dutschke, Dennis, and Shona Kelly. "Un Ritrovato laudario aretino," *Italianistica Revista di letteratura italiana*, 15 (1985), 155-83.

Fabbri, M., E. Garbero-Zorzi, and A. M. Petrioli Tofani, eds. *Il luogo teatrale a Firenze*. Florence: Electa Editrice, 1975.

Fabris, Giovanni. *Il più antico laudario veneto con la bibliografia delle laude*. Vicenza: G. Riemor, 1907.

Faloci-Pulignani, Michele. "Manoscritti francescani della libreria del comune di Cortona," *Miscellanea Francescana*, 2 (1887), 65-75.

Frati, Lodovico, ed. *Lamenti storici dei secoli XIV, XV e XVI*. Bologna: Romagnoli-Dell'Aqua, 1887-90.

Fusi, Daniele. "La compagnia della Vergine Maria e di Madonna Sant'Agato di Bibbiena," *Annali della Facoltà di Lettere e Filosofia dell'Università di Siena*, 2 (1981), 21-33.

Gebhart, Émile. *Mystics and Heretics in Italy at the End of the Middle Ages*, trans. Edward M. Hulme. London: G. Allen and Unwin, 1922.

Ghisi, Federico. "Gli aspetti musicali della lauda fra il XIV e XV secolo." In *Natalicia musicologica Knud Jeppesen*. Copenhagen, 1962. Pp. 51-57.

_____. "Strambotti e laude nel travestimento spirituale della poesia musicale del quattrocento." In *Collectanea Historia Musicae*. Florence: Olschki, 1953. Pp. 45-78.

Guerrini, Paolo. "Statuti di un antica congregazione francescana di Brescia," *Archivum Franciscanum Historicum*, 1 (1908), 544-68.

Hatfield, Rab. "The Compagnia de' Magi," *Journal of the Warburg and Courtauld Institutes*, 33 (1970), 107-61.

Kristeller, Paul Oskar. "Lay Religious Traditions and Florentine Platonism." In *Studies in Renaissance Thought and Letters*. Rome: Edizioni di storia e letteratura, 1956. Pp. 99-122.

Landini, Giuseppe. *Appunti di critica storica per la città della fraternite laicali in Italia*. Perugia: Unione Tipografia, 1915.

_____. *Il codice aretino 180: laudi antiche di Cortona*. Rome: Tipografia Editrice Nazionale, 1912.

Lazzeri, Zefferino. "I capitoli della compagnia dei disciplinati di Cortona (anno 1300) e il laudario dell'accademia etrusca," *Primo Annuario dell'accademia etrusca di Cortona*, 12-13 (1934), 120-39.

Liuzzi, Fernando. "L'espressione musicale nel dramma liturgico," *Studi medievali*, n.s. 2 (1929), 74-109.

_____. "Melodie per un mistero italiano del duecento," *Scenario*, 1, No. 7 (1932), 15-27.

Mandonnet, Pierre. "Les Regles et le gouvernement de l'Ordo de Poenitentia au XIIIe siècle." In *Opuscules de Critique Historique*. Paris: Fischbacher, 1903. Pp. 155-205.

Manselli, Raoul. "L'anno 1260 fu anno Gioachimitico?" In *Il movimento dei disciplinati nel settimo centenario del suo inizio*. Perugia: Deputazione di Storia Patria per l'Umbria, 1960. Pp. 99-108.

Mazzatinti, Giuseppe. *Costituzioni dei disciplinati di Sant'Andrea di Perugia*. Forli: Orlandini, 1893.

Meersseman, Gilles Gérard. *Difensore dei mendicanti*. Rome: Santa Sabina, 1938.

_____. "Études sur les anciennes confreries dominicaines," *Archivum Fratrum Praedicatorum*, 20 (1950), 5-113; 21 (1951), 51-192; 22 (1952), 5-176.

Méhus, Lorenzo. *Dell'origine, progresso, e riforma delle confraternite laicale*. Florence: Cambiagi, 1785.

Mira, Giuseppe. "Primi sondaggi su taluni aspetti economico-finanziari delle confraternite dei disciplinati." In *Risultati e prospettive della ricerca sul movimento dei disciplinati*. Perugia: Deputazione di Storia Patria per l'Umbria, 1972. Pp. 229-60.

Moorman, John. *A History of the Franciscan Order from Its Origins to the Year 1517*. Oxford: Clarendon Press, 1968.

Morghen, Raffaelo. "Le confraterite di disciplinati e gli aspetti della religiosità laica nell'età moderna." In *Risultati e prospettive della ricerca sul movimento dei disciplinati*. Perugia: Deputazione di Storia Patria per l'Umbria, 1972. Pp. 317-26.

_____. "Ranieri Fasani e il movimento dei disciplinati del 1260." In *Il movimento dei disciplinati nel settimo centenario del suo inizio*. Perugia: Deputazione di Storia Patria per l'Umbria, 1960. Pp. 29-42.

Nicolini, Ugolino. "I Frati della penitenza a Perugia alla fine del secolo XIII." In *Il movimento dei disciplinati nel settimo centenario del suo inizio*. Perugia: Deputazione di Storia Patria per l'Umbria, 1960. Pp. 371-94.

Pericoli, Mario. "La Matricolo dei disciplinati della fraternità di S. Maria Maggiore in Todi." In *Il movimento dei disciplinati nel settimo centenario del suo inizio*. Perugia: Deputazione di Storia Patria per l'Umbria, 1960. Pp. 293-304.

Porto, Giuseppe. *Lauda drammatica del Venerdi Santo*. L'Aquila: del Romano, 1974.

Rondini, Giuseppe. "Laude drammatiche dei disciplinati di Siena," *Giornale storico letteratura italiana*, 2 (1883), 273-302.

Rubinstein, Nicolai. *The Government of Florence under the Medici (1434-1494)*. Oxford: Clarendon Press, 1966.

Russo, Francesco. "Gioachimismo e francescanismo," *Miscellanea francescana*, 41 (1941), 50-73.
_____. "San Francesco e i francescani nella letteratura profetica gioachimita," *Miscellanea francescana*, 46 (1946), 232-42.

Sabatier, Paul. *L'Influence de Saint François d'Assise sur la culture italienne*. Paris: Leroux, 1926.
Sticca, Sandro. *Il Planctus Mariae nella tradizione drammatica del medio evo*. Sulmona: Teatro Club, 1984.

Toschi, Paolo. *Del dramma liturgico alla rappresentazione sacra*. Florence: Sansoni, 1940.
_____. *Le origini del teatro italiano*. Turin: Boringhieri, 1955.
_____. *La poesie popolare religiosa in Italia*. Florence: Olschki, 1935.
Trexler, Richard C. *Public Life in Renaissance Florence*. New York: Academic Press, 1980.

Van Dijk, Stephen. "The Breviary of Saint Clare," *Franciscan Studies*, n.s. 8 (1948), 25-46, 351-87.
_____. "The Liturgical Legislation of the Franciscan Rules (Conclusion)," *Franciscan Studies*, 12 (1952), 241-62.
_____. "Some Manuscripts of the Earliest Franciscan Liturgy," *Franciscan Studies*, n.s. 14 (1954), 225-64; n.s. 16(1956), 60-101.

West, Delno C., Jr. "The Reformed Church and the Friars Minor: The Moderate Joachite Position of Fra Salimbene," *Archivum Franciscanum Historicum*, 64 (1971), 273-84.
_____. "The Present State of Salimbene Studies, with a Bibliographic Appendix of the Major Works," *Franciscan Studies*, 32 (1972), 225-41.

Index

207

Qui chomincia vna sanctissima reghola della conpagnia
della disciplina in sancta maria del carmino difirenze comin
cia il promisso

Inome delpadre e delfigliuolo edello
spirito sancto e adonore e reuerenci
a del nostro signore giesu ypo e della
sua sanctissima madre madonna san
cta maria vergine e di tutti ghange
li e archangeli di paradiso e delglori
oso confessore meser sancto nicholao
e dimeser sancto giouanni batista
e di meser sancto giouanni apostolo e
uangelista e di meser sancto elia pro
feta e degloriosi apostoli digiesu ypo meser sancto pi
ero e meser sancto pagolo di meser sancto matteo e di
meser sancto bartolomeo e di tutti sancti apostoli di
giesu ypo e di meser sancto stefano e di sancto lorenço
e di tutti sancti martiri di giesu ypo dimeser sancto
siluestro e sancto gregorio e disancto eusebio e di sco
beznardo e dimeser sancto antonio e di tutti sancti
confessori di giesu ypo di sa. ta anghela vergine.
e di sancta maria magdalena e sancta caterina e di
santa reparata e di tutti glialtri sancti e sancte di dio
adonore e buono stato del sacra sancta vniuersa
le chiesa di roma e del sanctissimo in ypo padre
e signore meser lopapa e perla diuina gratia
e de suoi fratelli chardinali e dereuerendo ixpo
padre e signore meser larciuescouo difirençe
ea mantinimento e conseruatione della sancta
e chatolicha fede cristiana ea salute e pace del
la nostra citta edongni attalmo ea consolati
one ispirituale etemporale dongni viuo emor
to della nostra sanctissima conpagnia eadulti
mo sterminio dongni erelia edongni eretcho
contradicente oneghante lasantissima fede del
nostro vero iddio redentore giesu cristo. ;...
Capitolo primo delnumero defrategli.

1. *Disciplinato* in the Habit. *Regola delle Disciplinati in Sancta Maria del Carmine*, Florence. Archivio di Stato, Compagnie Religiose Soppresse, 439, fol. 1r.

2. The *Mandato*, above, and *Disciplinato* in the Habit, below. Office of the Compagnia della Madonna Santa Maria dal Baraccano, Bologna. Biblioteca Comunale dell'Archiginnasio, Bologna, MS. Fondo Ospedale 83 (35).

3. *Signore scribe*, with marginal stage directions. *Laudario* of the Compagnia di Sant'Andrea, Perugia. Biblioteca Comunale Augusta, Perugia, MS. 955, fol. 34ᵛ.

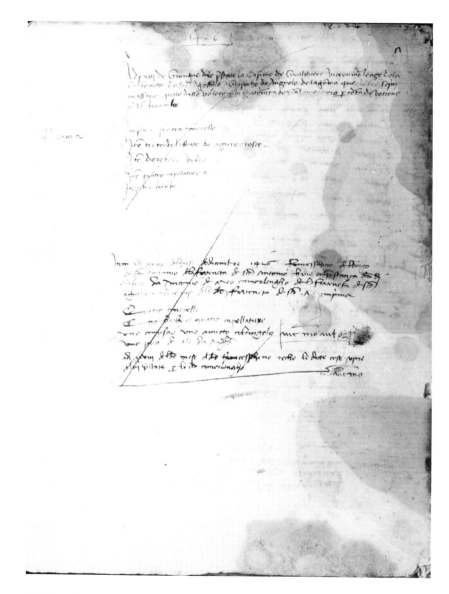

4. List of costumes and properties. *Libro di prestançe* of the Compagnia di Sant'Agostino, Perugia. Archivio del Pio Sodalizio Braccio Fortebracci, Perugia, MS. A 440, fol. 2ᵛ.

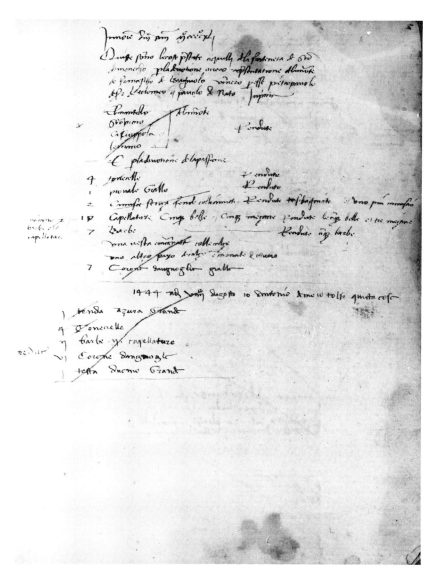

5. List of properties and costumes on loan to the Compagnia di San Domenico. *Libro di prestançe* of the Compagnia di Sant'Agostino, Perugia. Archivio del Pio Sodalizio Braccio Fortebracci, Perugia, MS. A 440, fol. 8[r].

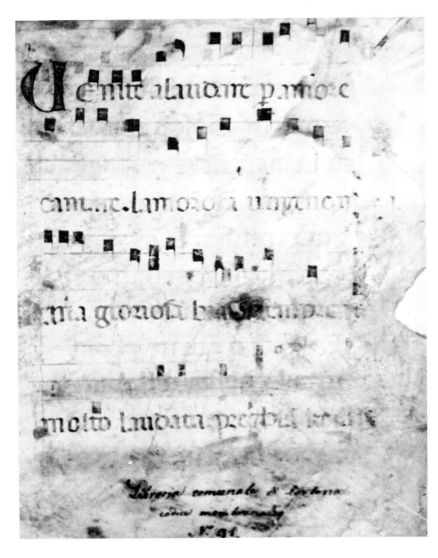

6. Damaged opening page of the *Laudario di Cortona*, MS. 91, fol. 1^r. Biblioteca Comunale e dell'Accademia Etrusca, Cortona.

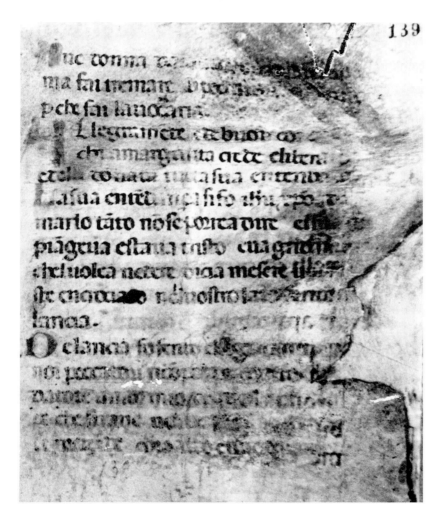

7. *Lauda* No. 51, *Allegramente e de buon core con fede*, to Margaret of Cortona. Part II of the *Laudario di Cortona*, MS. 91, fol. 139^r.

8. Entrance to the Church of San Francesco, Cortona, with the top of the old entry to the Oratory of the *Laudesi* visible above the pavement to the left.

9. Descent of the Holy Spirit upon the Apostles, with SS. Augustine and Benedict. *Laudario* of the Company of Santo Spirito, Florence. Biblioteca Nazionale Centrale, Florence, MS. Magliabechiano II I 122 (B. R. 18), fol. 2ᵛ. Photograph: G. B. Pineider.

10. Illumination showing the Three Living and the Three Dead, above, and opening section of the *Lauda* on Death, *Chi vuol lo mondo dispreçare*. *Laudario* of the Company of Santo Spirito, Florence. Biblioteca Nazionale Centrale, Florence, MS. Magliabechiano II I 122 (B. R. 18), fol. 139ᵛ. Photograph: G. B. Pineider.

11. Christ in Majesty. Single leaf from a fourteenth-century *Laudario*. Pierpont Morgan Library, New York, MS. M742. By permission of the Trustees of the Pierpont Morgan Library.

12. Christ enthroned in mandorla and surrounded by twelve Apostles. Florence, fourteenth-century illumination. The National Gallery of Art, Washington, D.C., Rosenwald Collection, B-20,128. By courtesy of the National Gallery.

13. Christ and the Blessed Virgin Mary enthroned, with forty saints. Florence, fourteenth-century illumination attrributed to Pacino da Buonaguida. The National Gallery of Art, Washington, D.C., Rosenwald Collection, B-22,128. By courtesy of the National Gallery.

14. St. Agnes in Glory. Single leaf of fourteenth-century Florentine *Laudario*. British Library, London, MS. Add. 18196.

§ Si est dolor sicut dolor meus

I nginochiati tutti finire queste lectioni ilgouernatore
impongha il miserere seguendo ogni coro insuo uer
so

6 Miserere mei deus

S anza gloria patri inuoce dipassione finito dica sanza
oremusfo infinem pdinm

R espice quesumus ac finito

L elaude colle tenebre dopo lalauatione e post a sedere
sia preparato dalauare ipiedi e il fratello a chi e co
messo cominci ilmandato e al surgit ad cenam sil
eiu inpre e alposuit uestamenta si caui ilsuo mantel
lo e quando dice cum accepisset linteum lui pigli
loscingatorio e facci simile mente e cominci alaua
re e aiutandolo e consiglieri e quello che dice ilma
dato sesifermi a postq ergo e intanto si canta ubi
caritas

f A nte diem festum e...

P ropterea dixit non estis mundi omes

F acto qui puncto si diferisca elresto per doppo lalauatio
ne depedi e intanto riposto qsto f a sedere due altri
accio diputati almedesimo leggio cantino

ff V bi caritasa amor deus ibi est

c V bi caritasa ef Risponda

15. *Mandato* from the *Disciplinati* Office, Florence. Archivio di Stato, Florence,
Compagnie Religiose Soppressse, 439 (lacks pagination).

Hon essendo ancora finito dilauare epiedi atutti efrate
gli si canti

Dulcis yhu memoria

E t facta lalaua æ rassettato quello seoperato cerimonia
simile seguiti elfratello ilmandato chelasciò alpostq.
æ mentre lodice sifaccia lacollatione sanza superflu
ta solo asimilitudine come siconuiene intaldi

℣ Post q. ergo laui æ c

℣ inito questo mandato æ lacollatione sifaccia ilsermone
disimile suggietto da ⸝ ose alcuno altro gli pare piu
acto æ apresso cominciando il ⸝ ginochione abbracci
ando come dio lospira adomandando perdono æ si
racocili coglialtri frategli seguitandolo ciaschuno lu
no collaltro successiua mente apresso finito simile acto
dumile carita riordinati acoro seguitino ilmattuti
no cominciando sotto silentio ilghouernatore ilpater
nostro inclinato æ poi lanrisane ælelaude

            Laude

℣ Propio filio sùo non pepercit deus sed pronobis omibus
tradidit illum

℣℣ Misere

℣ Ansiatus est in me spiritus meus in me turbatum est cor
meum

℣℣ Domine exaudi orationem meam

℣ At it latro ad latronem nosquidem digna factis percipim'